CAMBRIDGE STUDIES IN SOCIAL ANTHROPOLOGY
GENERAL EDITOR: JACK GOODY

50

KINSHIP AND MARRIAGE

Robin Fox was born in England in 1934. He was educated at the London School of Economics, Harvard, and Stanford and taught at the universities of Exeter and London before being asked to found a department at Rutgers University, where he has been Professor of Anthropology since 1967. Since 1972 he has also served as a director of research for the H. F. Guggenheim Foundation. His first fieldwork was in New Mexico and he later made an extensive study in north-west Ireland, which was published as *The Tory Islanders*. He cooperated with Lionel Tiger on *The Imperial Animal*, a book that helped launch the now well-established "neo-Darwinian" movement in the social sciences. His most recent work is *The Red Lamp of Incest: An Enquiry into the Origins of Mind and Society.* He has taught at the universities of Oxford, Paris, Cambridge, California (San Diego), and Los Andes (Colombia) as a visiting professor. He is currently writing a verse-prose commentary on the human condition and a book on the history of social thought since the Renaissance.

Other books by Robin Fox

The Keresan Bridge: A Problem in Pueblo Ethnology
Encounter with Anthropology
The Imperial Animal (with Lionel Tiger)
Biosocial Anthropology (editor)
The Tory Islanders: A People of the Celtic Fringe
The Red Lamp of Incest: An Enquiry into the Origins of Mind and Society

ROBIN FOX

KINSHIP AND MARRIAGE

An Anthropological Perspective

CAMBRIDGE
UNIVERSITY PRESS

Published by the Press Syndicate of the University of Cambridge
The Pitt Building, Trumpington Street, Cambridge CB2 1RP
40 West 20th Street, New York, NY 10011-4211, USA
10 Stamford Road, Oakleigh, Melborne 3166, Australia

Originally published in a paperbak edition by
Penguin Books, Ltd., 1967
Hardback edition first published by
Cambridge University Press 1983
United States paperback edition reissued (with a new Preface)
by Cambridge University Press 1983
Reprinted 1986, 1987, 1989, 1991, 1992, 1994, 1996

Printed in the United States of America

Library of Congress Cataloging-in-Publication Data is available

ISBN 0-521-277823-6 paperback

TO MY PARENTS

047134

Contents

Preface to the
Cambridge University Press Edition

It is now sixteen years since this book first appeared. The response to it has never ceased to amaze me. I did not expect the wide readership, the many translations (including Japanese, Hindi, and Malay), and the numerous 'adoptions'. When I wrote it, kinship was an exotic concern of a few anthropologists; it has now become part of the common currency of conversation. Some areas remain esoteric – kinship terminology is not yet a popular concern – but debate about 'matriarchy' and the 'nuclear family' is now commonplace, and primatologists and zoologists – to say nothing of evolutionary theorists – are busy analysing kinship systems in areas where, sixteen years ago, the concept was as foreign as it was to the public at large. Of course it never should have been esoteric and only became so because of the myth that kinship was a property of primitive societies and had been replaced by citizenship, or 'universalistic roles', or whatever, in modern ones. There has certainly been change, and opposition between church and state on the one hand and kinship on the other remains strong. But since it has been realized that what we call 'kinship systems' are in essence the assortative mating systems of the species *Homo sapiens sapiens,* and that any and every population of the species must have such a system (as opposed to random mating), then it is easily seen that 'kinship systems' are inescapable. They are always with us as much as the prefrontal cortex or the bipedal walk are with us, no matter what the local circumstances.

It was suggested that I prepare a second edition of this book to elaborate this point. It would have had chapters on kinship in evolution, kinship in nature, the nature of kinship, and so forth. This was tempting, but it would have meant re-writing the whole book, and I was persuaded by my colleagues not to do so for the following reason. As it stands, they said, the book is a good 'neutral' introduction to kinship studies. It contains the basic things that one needs to know to tackle the subject at all. Once learned, these can form the basis for more advanced considerations. Thus a teacher is at liberty to go on to the mathematical analysis of kinship terminology, multidimensional scaling analysis of kinship avoidances, kin-selection theory and inclusive fitness, or whatever. If the book were to be changed and rewritten from a particular point of view (such as that of evolutionary biology), it would be robbed of this neutral quality and become less useful. Also, it was urged, most of what I want to say about kinship as an evolutionary product I have said elsewhere, and people can refer to these other sources.

I am persuaded. It was hard for me to accept easily since I never saw this as a textbook – I do not favor textbooks and have always refused to write them. I actually saw the book, when I wrote it, as a contribution. For one thing it tried to synthesize the two major views of kinship – alliance and descent – that held the field at the time. And it did this from a particular biological, ecological, and logical standpoint: It took the mother-child unit as the basic mammalian and hence human unit, and worked out the logic of kinship systems from there – from the minimum assumptions necessary. I would still stand by both these points. Alliance and descent I no longer regard as competing theoretical views, but as empirical components of all kinship systems. Put simply, whatever else kinship systems do, they divide people into categories of kin and then define marriageability in terms of these categories. They define descent, if you like, and legislate alliance. And they do this because that is what kinship systems do – it is what they are *for*, in nature. In studying human kinship systems we are studying one form of assortative mating which has the interesting component of culturally defined categories. The rest of nature lacks this – but it does not lack kinship and non-random mating. Indeed, if modern evolutionary theory is correct, kinship and differential reproductive success, as summarized under 'inclusive fitness', are at the heart of the evolutionary process. What we study as social anthropologists is an interesting variant of this general process. I only dimly saw, in the 1960s, that the resolution of conflicting ideas on kinship systems would lie in a proper understanding of evolution. But the position I adopted then fits in well with these modern theories. They completely confirm the correctness of the social anthropologist's faith that kinship is the most central of all social processes. I have dealt elsewhere with the peculiarity of the response from many anthropologists that human kinship 'has nothing to do with biology'. I did not accept that in 1967, and I do not do so today. It stems from a narrow notion of 'biology' and boils down to nothing more than the assertion that the cultural categories of kinship and degrees of real genetic relatedness may overlap but are not identical. True but, to my mind, trivial.

In any case, these issues, as we agreed, can be argued after the basics have been learned. Nonetheless, I want to stress that the book had a point of view from the beginning. It was even then making a case. If it is true, as many kind commentators have said, that this is the clearest and most comprehensible account of kinship systems to emerge so far, then that should be attributed as much to the viewpoint as to some contingent skill of exposition.

There are one or two matters of detail that require revision. In most of the chapters, the descriptions of various elements of kinship systems can stand unchanged. There have been later developments, more and better examples, and refined techniques of analysis. But in most cases, the fundamentals have not been altered, and such slight revision as is needed can be supplied by a teacher. This is, after all, an introduction, not a text. I have added a brief bibliography of more recent works which should be consulted. And I never did try to cover everything – this again would have defeated the objective.

In one particular case, however, there is need of revision. My model of the Murngin system in chapter 8, while it works at the analytic level, does not correspond to the total social reality as ethnographers have more recently revealed it. In particular, the work of Warren Shapiro has shown quite clearly that it is the exchange of sisters' daughters' daughters between men of the *same* moiety (but of different patriclans) that is involved. This 'results in' but does not 'result from' the exchange of sisters/daughters between moieties. I corrected the model in a publication in 1972, but this has not been in popular circulation among anthropologists. I mean to spell it out even more clearly in a future publication (in preparation, Cambridge University Press). This is the most important correction.

The most unfortunate omission was probably any discussion of patrilateral parallel cousin marriage (marriage with the father's brother's child). Critics have rightly pointed out that this mars the discussion of cousin marriage and exogamy. It has been dealt with at length by Germaine Tillion and Jack Goody (see bibliography), and readers should refer to these discussions. The 'exogamic continuum' should really start with the endogamic cases – strictly with brother-sister marriage, moving to half-sister marriage, to parallel cousin marriage, then to cross cousins. Even with the latter, the Tylorian theory of 'hostage' exogamy will not really do, since intermarrying lineages or moieties produce, in effect, small endogamic systems. It seems more likely that jockeying for individual (or familial) advantage *within* groups is the starting point for the development of these elementary systems, rather than reduction of intergroup hostility or wider social ties. This should be explored in the light of modern kin selection theory.

That I was right to separate incest and exogamy ('ruthlessly', as Lucy Mair said!) has become more and more obvious, and if anything needs revision it is chapter 2, in order to make the distinction even clearer. However, that chapter has been expanded at length in *The Red Lamp of Incest: An Enquiry into the Origins of Mind and Society* (Notre Dame Press, 1983). Here the latest thinking on the Westermarck effect and primate kinship is examined in the context of brain evolution, and a theory of the basic structure of kinship systems is advanced. Again, rather than make an expensive revision of chapter 2, it is simpler to refer readers to *The Red Lamp,* which is virtually a companion volume.

I have not been much moved by criticism of my failure to include details of the formal analysis of kinship terminology. For a start, most of it is too technical for a book of this kind. However, had it developed to the point where it made a real breakthrough, I would have felt it necessary to give some account. It has not, it seems to me, reached that point, and there would be less than marginal returns in including it. Interested teachers can always deal with it in more advanced courses if they wish. This is not the place to indulge in detailed criticism. Where it has worked best has been in defining with exactitude the differences between different systems of terminology which had previously been lumped together with confusing results (Buchler and Selby 1968, Scheffler 1978).

On one other point I should make a comment. Feminists have complained about the style and substance of some of the earlier chapters. In one or two places I was perhaps less than even-handed in my remarks about women and I regret any offense these now cause. They occasioned no comment at the time, but times change and sensitivities with them. In fact, at the time, this book was regarded by many women as a liberating document, because it attacked the 'tyranny of the nuclear family' and asserted the primacy of the mother-child bond when campaigns for the rights of unwed mothers and concern over 'captive wives' in the suburbs were becoming popular. It is for the sociologist of knowledge to analyse the odd reversal of this attitude in the late 1970s, when many women were denigrating the mother-infant bond as detrimental to their 'self-fulfilment', or whatever, and hence condemning this unfortunate little effort as reactionary. I think the only thing to do is to sit tight. Fashions in indignation change: The facts stay the same.

But on one point of substance I do not follow the objection. I claim as a basic premise that 'the men exercise control'. I should perhaps have written that 'the men *attempt to* exercise control'—but this is a quibble. I do not see the objection, because this is precisely what feminists are objecting to. If men do not exercise control, then what are they complaining about? Also, I was careful to state that this was only with respect to kinship systems, and that while one could see why it was so, in any instances where it was *not,* the argument would not apply. Contraception, high female incomes, productively independent female kin groups, generous welfare systems, child care—all these could affect the premise. I said clearly that *for the systems we would be discussing* it was a necessary premise—it is impossible to understand matrilineal systems without it—but that did not commit us to it for eternity. So I do not feel any need to change it. I have never found any intelligent woman anthropologist who did not fully understand the point, and I am encouraged by the continuing evidence that these are in a majority and that ideology has not totally triumphed over good sense.

On one point I regret not having gone further. The original draft of the manuscript had a proposed final chapter, on what kinship systems are all about. I never wrote it. It was too much perhaps to ask a brash young anthropologist (then not yet 30) to attempt, but I feel no more comfortable with it now. I am further along the way, as the few remarks in this preface suggest and the things I have written elsewhere attest. But the final word on this still eludes us. And so I leave the book as it was: coming to an end rather than a conclusion. This is the only honest thing to do. One can otherwise only alert the reader to the probings and explorations that are going on. There is no final truth. To say that kinship systems are our species' variant of assortative mating systems seems to me to open up new vistas of understanding. But it leaves whole other areas relatively untouched. I hedge here with 'relatively', for in the great untouched area of the 'history of kinship' it may throw some light on the stubborn *persistence* of kinship. (Is it coincidence that in the Weberian world as we know it 'nepotism' is a grave crime, while to kin selection theorists it is a necessary genetic trait?) But that history is not written, and it should be.

The war between kinship and authority is alive in legend. In story and fantasy kinship struggles against bureaucratic authority, whether of church or state. It undermines, it challenges, it disturbs. The Mafia constantly fascinates because 'the family' demands total loyalty and provides total security. When the state fails to protect, people look longingly at the certainty of kinship. And always its language is used for emotional effect: Brothers and sisters take note. A generation of social scientists thought the war against kinship had been won. But I am not so sure. Kinship is resilient and subversive; it is cunning and ruthless. It does not obey the universalistic, meritocratic, and bureaucratic rules. But before the Weberian sociologists read its obituary, let them remember how many obituaries of 'anti-rational' processes they have already recited prematurely — religion and nationalism to name but two. I suspect that kinship will be with us for the forseeable future and may well have a resurgence that will, as usual, have the social scientists coming from behind with explanations. And so it will always be as long as they persist in their delusion that we are simply role-playing morons shaped solely by our cultures. But here I am breaking my own rule and going beyond the self-imposed mandate of the book. So I leave it as I left it originally, with the hope that it will still be 'interesting and useful'.

R. F.

NEW BRUNSWICK, N.J.

March 1983.

Preface

ALTHOUGH the subject of kinship and marriage has long dominated anthropological thinking and teaching, there is no introductory book on it. Radcliffe-Brown's excellent 'introduction' to *African Systems of Kinship and Marriage* (1950) is still the only piece of general work that can be recommended to first-year students and interested laymen, and it is rapidly becoming out of date. There are sections or chapters in some anthropological text-books of course, but these are rather brief. There is a need for a general book that will try to give an outline of some of the methods of analysis used in the anthropological treatment of kinship and marriage; a book that will be useful to the student approaching the subject for the first time, and of interest to the layman who wishes to know more about this central topic of social anthropology.

I did not set out consciously to write such a book. But for a number of years I have been giving a course of lectures on the subject to an audience largely composed of second-year university students in the social sciences. The lectures were, in effect, a substitute for the non-existent general book. They were an attempt to give some kind of overall framework of analysis to the students who could then pursue, with their tutors or on their own initiative, points of detail and more advanced issues. They were deliberately designed to provoke questions rather than to provide answers. It was put to me that it might be a good idea to have the lectures easily available in book form, thus freeing lecture time for a more advanced treatment of special topics. This is how the book came to be written. I have retained the rather chatty style of the lectures because it is not wholly at variance with the aim of the book. The introduction was not part of the lecture series. I dealt with the subject systematically and not historically, but when it came to the book I felt that some

kind of sketch of the historical background, however inadequate, was needed.

The subject has been developing now for almost exactly
a hundred years. McLennan's *Primitive Marriage* was published in 1865, Maine's *Ancient Law* in 1861, and Morgan's
Systems of Consanguinity and Affinity of the Human Family in
1871. Over this period a huge body of literature has accumulated which probably accounts for more than half the
total literature of anthropology. It is almost impossible in
the space of a short book to condense this into something
that will be immediately intelligible to a layman. Any of
the following chapters could be expanded into a book or
even an encyclopedia. What I have tried to do, therefore,
is to go back to certain very naïve 'first principles', and to
follow out the logic of these in order to hang the material
on a connected thread of argument about human behaviour
and human nature. To do this, I have had to sacrifice a good
deal of the subtlety and detail that delights the professional.
Some of my arguments may look more like caricatures than
simplifications. But that cannot be helped. This has been
a subject in which specialists talked only to each other
(and some talked only to God), but there is a growing number of students in the social sciences, both in the universities
and outside, and they deserve something better than to be
told that this is a difficult subject and only for the experts. It
is a difficult subject, but that is no reason for throwing in
the sponge.

I have not, even so, tried to write down to the audience.
On the contrary, I have rather thrown them in at the deep
end. Condensation and simplification have meant that in
many ways the argument has become more abstract and
tighter, with less of the 'sexual life of savages' and more of the
analysis of systems almost as systems of logic. Kinship is to
anthropology what logic is to philosophy or the nude is to
art; it is the basic discipline of the subject. And like both
formal logic and figure drawing it is at the same time simple
and difficult. This, I feel, is part of its attraction.

As the subtitle of the book suggests, this is *an* anthropological perspective. The perspective I have chosen is that of the analysis of kinship *groups*. Thus a great deal of the familiar material on interpersonal kinship relations has been left out completely or only hinted at. I have chosen this approach because I think that it is the best way to put over the peculiar contribution of anthropology to the study of this field of social relations. Also, once the reader has grasped the principles involved in this aspect of kinship analysis he will be well equipped to deal with other aspects. Such an approach may also be more useful to teachers and students of sociology who wish to include the study of kinship groups in the study of social groups generally.

As the subtitle also insists, it is an *anthropological* perspective. I am not concerned therefore with all the fascinating questions that people might raise about kinship and marriage; I have only dealt with those questions that some anthropologists have found, in Radcliffe-Brown's mandarin words, 'useful and interesting'. Even so, anthropological opinion is divided about the *general* aims of the subject. Unlike most of my sociologically inclined British colleagues I am not primarily interested in the question 'what is society?', but in what I take to be the truly anthropological question, 'what is Man?'. Sociological analysis in this perspective becomes a means to an end rather than an end in itself; by analysing variations in social structure we learn something about the species *Homo sapiens*.

Finally I must emphasize what should be already clear: this is not a 'text-book' or a 'manual', but an 'introduction'. My aim is to get people interested and to give them a base from which to work. I have not bothered much with the technical terminology of the subject, nor have I used footnotes, references or other scholarly devices. I have not tried to cover everything.

It is not a definitive statement of known truths, but a series of working papers; attempts to arrive at some limited conclusions that can be tested. If I can persuade some readers that the testing of the conclusions might be a 'useful and interesting' activity, then the book will have served its purpose.

R. F.

KINGSTON-UPON-THAMES
August 1966.

Introduction

I

THERE must be few of us who are not susceptible to the suggestion of famous or notorious ancestry. Most of us are fascinated by 'family trees' and indeed there are firms making a handsome profit from the compilation of genealogies – particularly for Americans. Even if the best we can muster is proven descent from someone hanged for sheep stealing in the seventeenth century, we still derive a sense of pride from the knowledge that our ancestry is known in such depth. In noble families, length of genealogy is a measure of relative prestige; and who has not heard a commoner relate with obvious delight, but without obvious foundation, that he is descended from the illegitimate offspring of an eighteenth-century duke?

There is no practical advantage to be gained from making such claims, so why should there be pride in, and fascination with, ancestry and descent? Psychologically it may be that there is security to be derived from a sureness about one's ancestry. We perhaps feel less contingent and our place in the scheme of things may seem less arbitrary, if we know that we are part of a chain stretching into the past. This knowledge rids us of anonymity: we are not dropped into the world without a history. To use the metaphor most often associated with the search for ancestry, we have *roots*.

These feelings may seem out of place in our modern world simply because nothing of practical importance attaches to them; but over a large part of the globe both at the present time and throughout history, they have been supremely important. In many societies, both primitive and sophisticated, relationships to ancestors and kin have been the key relationships in the social structure; they have been the pivots on which most interaction, most claims and obligations, most loyalties and sentiments, turned. There would have been nothing whimsical or nostalgic about genealogical knowledge for a Chinese scholar, a Roman citizen, a South Sea Islander, a Zulu warrior or a Saxon thane; it would have been essential knowledge because it would have defined many of his most significant rights, duties and sentiments. In a society where kinship is supremely important, loyalties to kin supersede all other loyalties, and for this reason alone kinship must be the enemy of bureaucracy. In our modern technocratic and bureaucratic age, the complexity of our social structure demands that ideally a man should fill a position because he is proved capable of filling it – not simply because he is the son of his father. Furthermore we demand that a man be loyal to his State and his office before his kin. But kinship is tenacious. In the developing countries bureaucratic rationality often loses out to kinship loyalties; an official selects his subordinates not on the criterion of ability to do the job, but on the basis of closeness of relationship. What to us is rank nepotism is to him a high moral duty. And even in our own enlightened and rational society the web of kinship and marriage around our 'great families' – the Cecils, Devonshires, Churchills, etc. – spreads into most corners of political and public life. In some working-class enclaves also, kinship networks seem to be important. It is in the less conservative and more mobile middle-classes that kinship now seems to be of little relevance beyond the level of parent-child relationships, and even these have a looseness about them that would shock many of our primitive contemporaries. That old parents should be left by their children to live and eventually die in loneliness – or be put into homes – would seem to many to be the depths of immorality; but our whole system of architecture and social welfare is geared to the elementary family of parents and dependent children.

We may be a relatively 'kinshipless' society (although sociologists have probably exaggerated this tendency) but the sentiments of kinship still linger. Would we not, if a long-forgotten first cousin turned up having fallen on hard times, feel *some* obligation towards him *simply* because he was a cousin? And if we could find out who our great-great-great grandfather was, would we not be pleased, in some irrational way, at the knowledge? It was Bertie Wooster's opinion that there were few of his acquaintances who were not living on remittances from uncles and aunts. This may be less true than it was, but do we not feel that we have *some* claim on uncles and aunts simply by virtue of their relationship to us? Blood, as the old adage has it, is thicker than water.

But why should it be? When the demands of our industrial civilization drive us towards an impersonal, bureaucratic, rational social-structure, why should these irrational sentiments of kinship still have a hold? I heard of a man who collected old family albums and pored over them, because he was fascinated by what he thought of as the Victorian ideal of the family: a group in which everyone was loyal to everyone else without question, simply because they were 'of the same blood'. The same feeling attaches to aristocratic codes of honour in which a true aristocrat should avenge the death or dishonour of a kinsman without question. In Mediterranean countries this code of honour is still a force to be reckoned with. These unthinking, familistic, kinship-centred loyalties run in opposition to the laws of church and state and the demands of an expanding industrial society. Whence their strength, and if not their strength then at least their fascination? Could it be the hangover of centuries, not to say millenia, of kinship-centred experience? In societies less rationalistic, less governed by impersonal law, less dominated by the state, it was clearly of great importance to have, for example, automatic support in dispute. For the longer period of human development, mankind lived for the most part in societies in which kinship-based groups were the constituent units. A man's health and security, his very life and even his chance of immortality, were in the hands of his kin. A 'kinless' man was at best a man without social position: at worst, he was a dead man. Thus, even our

relatively kinless society cannot throw off this slowly accumulated, almost innate wisdom of the blood. If it is
basic in our natures to trust the familiar and fear the
strange, then those who share our blood share part of ourselves, and so are by definition the most familiar of all.

Be this as it may, the anthropologist is interested in the
comparative study of societies and cultures at all times and
in all places. To him no society is more important than
another; societies that place little emphasis on kinship – and
this is not confined to the advanced industrial ones – have
to be placed alongside those that are obsessed with it. But
whatever the degree of intensity with which kinship ties are
utilized to forge social bonds, no society so far has managed
to dispense with an irreducible minimum of kinship-based
social relationships. And until Huxley's *Brave New World* is
realized and bottles are substituted for mothers, they are
unlikely ever to be dispensed with.

II

The study of kinship as an aspect of social structure began
with the lawyers and students of comparative jurisprudence.
That is why the study of kinship today is replete with legal
terminology and concepts: rights, claims, obligations, *patria
potestas*, contract, agnation, corporate, etc. The reasons for
this are quite simple – inheritance, succession and marriage.
Every society makes some provision for the transfer of
property and social position on death and the transfer is
usually to a kinsman. A son may inherit the property of his
father for example and, if his father was a king, may succeed
him on the throne. A good deal of any legal system, including our own, is concerned with laying down rules about
who may succeed whom – to titles of nobility for example,
and who may inherit what from whom – usually property
of some kind, but also obligations and duties. If 'next of
kin' are to inherit, then nearness of kinship has to be
defined; and among these near kin some order of preference
has to be set up. Are all sons and daughters to inherit, or
only sons? And if sons only, then do all the sons inherit or

only perhaps the eldest? What happens in the case of intestacy and a lack of immediate heirs? If legitimate heirs are the children of a legitimate marriage, how is the latter defined? These and many other questions form the core of problems settled by 'family law' – law pertaining to marriage, parenthood, legitimacy, inheritance and succession. Now even amongst the European nations these codes differ, often quite markedly. Thus lawyers when comparing different systems of family law were often faced with the question why there should be these differences. More importantly they were constantly referring back to Roman law, the source of most of their ideas. Even today the study of Roman law is an essential part of legal training. But there was much about the Roman legal system that was strange and curious to the nineteenth-century jurists who pondered it. It was true that Roman civilization was the most successful in the ancient world, but Rome was in fact founded on a federation of tribes, and there was much in the Roman law of kinship and marriage that was more reminiscent of tribal custom than civilized sophistication.

The nineteenth-century lawyers who puzzled over these facts turned for an explanation to the theory of social evolution prevalent at the time. In this, one explained the existence of an institution by showing how it originated and the series of stages through which it had passed. Thus the Scottish lawyer McLennan felt that the symbolic bride-capture found in ancient Rome was a 'survival' of an earlier tribal stage in which men had indeed forcibly abducted women from other tribes. He went on from this discovery to elaborate a series of stages through which the customs of kinship and marriage of all mankind had passed. In the beginning there was promiscuity, but this gave way to a system in which kinship was traced through females only (which he thought to have been the case in ancient Greece), and this was in turn followed by the tracing of kinship through males only (as in ancient Rome); finally monogamy and the tracing of kinship through both males and females became dominant. Slightly before McLennan's *Primitive*

Marriage, the more cautious English lawyer Sir Henry Maine had published his *Ancient Law*. Maine was chiefly interested in Indo-European institutions, and in particular in the 'patriarchal joint-family' – the family of fathers and sons holding property in common which was the main kinship unit in India, and in Maine's opinion the original form of the Indo-European 'family'. McLennan violently opposed Maine's conclusions as they violated his principle that kinship through females was the original form. This debate between the 'matriarchal' and 'patriarchal' schools of thought proceeded with mounting acrimony for the next fifty years, and is not quite dead even yet, as readers of Robert Graves and Mary Renault will know. The speculations of some of these early evolutionists now appear very naïve. The data they used was poor and their conclusions about the 'history of mankind' quite staggeringly without foundation. What they failed to realize was that kinship systems are not subject to *cumulative* evolution in the way that, say, technology is. Kinship systems, unlike technological inventions, cannot be ranked as better or worse, higher or lower; they simply represent alternative ways of doing things. Also the evolutionists failed to see that the *whole* of mankind need not have gone through the *same* series of stages – that there were alternative possible routes. Because they insisted on universal evolution, they regarded any contemporary tribe that showed 'archaic' traits as somehow retarded – a kind of fossil. They overlooked the fact that this tribe itself was the end product of an evolutionary process. But these mistakes should not blind us to their virtues. They founded the study of kinship, gave it its terminology, and pointed out many connexions between forms of marriage and other institutions that bear examination today. Also they grasped an important principle that we have perhaps lost sight of: that kinship systems *do* change, and that there are regularities in the process. Some anthropologists have now returned to these questions of change with better data and more caution.

It was an American businessman rather than a British

lawyer who gave a further impetus to kinship studies. Lewis Henry Morgan was very interested in the Iroquois tribes of his native New York State and made a life-long study of them. He noticed that their method of *naming* kin was very different from our own. The word for 'father', for example, was applied not only to the direct male parent, but also to other male kinsmen. The word for 'mother' was similarly distributed more widely than ours. In pursuit of an explanation for this seemingly curious phenomenon, Morgan began collecting schedules of 'kinship terminologies' from all over the world and from the societies of classical antiquity. He noted that many nations, far separated in time and space, had similar types of kinship nomenclature, and that there were a few standard 'types' of such nomenclatures. On the assumption that these words referred to biological relationships, he attempted to explain how the seemingly odd distributions came about. If a system designated many men 'father' other than the actual biological father, then could it not be that some custom of 'group marriage' prevailed in which many men might be the putative genitors of the child and hence be addressed as 'father' by it? Again he put his theory into an evolutionary framework and traced a series of stages comparable to, but different in detail from McLennan's. This roused the ire of the belligerent Scot who accused Morgan of putting too much faith in terminology which did not in any case have anything to do with biological relationship but was merely a 'code of courtesies' showing 'degrees of respect'. However, the ship was launched and from then onwards anthropologists have been concerned with kinship terminologies almost to the point of obsession. For a time, indeed, the 'study of kinship' was virtually the study of kinship terms and a debate about the explanation of them. It is now more or less accepted that Morgan was right to point out the importance of terminology, but wrong about the meaning of it. He, of course, shared the other errors of the evolutionary school.

But perhaps we can catch some of Morgan's excitement. He not only studied terminology but the structure of social groups. He found, for example, that the Iroquois were organized into kinship groups based on 'descent in the female line'. These groups were organized into larger groups which he called *phratries*. When he turned to the more sophisticated town-dwelling Aztecs, he found that they were organized into kinship groups based on descent in the *male* line, and again these were organized into larger units which the Spanish had called *barrios*. When he turned to ancient Europe, Morgan found the civilized town-dwelling Greeks and Romans organized into *gentes* – the Latin for groups descended in the male line from a common ancestor. These groups were again organized into larger groups – the *phratry* in Greece (after which he named the Iroquois grouping) and the *curia* in Rome. He had good reason, he thought, to believe that the primitive Greeks had kinship groups based, like the Iroquois, on kinship in the female line. Here, he thought, he had one of the clues to social evolution. It fitted very well with the theory derived from terminological studies. Out of promiscuity came 'kinship through females only' in the more primitive societies, then there was a change to 'kinship through males only' and the development of cities and civilization. With the growth of complexity of civilization the larger kinship groups withered away – as happened in historical times in Rome. It was a very imaginative scheme, but it was based on facts which were wrongly interpreted, and by no means represented a universal process.

The advent of psycho-analysis, and in particular the theory of the Oedipus complex, dropped a bomb into the rather arid discussions of the evolutionary school. At the same time, the work of anthropologists in America like Lowie and Boas was doing much to undermine the more far-fetched evolutionary schemes. But it was the Polish émigré Malinowski, combining an interest in psycho-analysis with an intensive period of fieldwork amongst the Trobriand Islanders of Melanesia, who put fresh life into kinship studies. Terminology interested him not at all, neither did evolutionary speculation. He was interested in trying to explain the customs of the Trobriand Islanders in the context of their own culture. It was thus primarily to the feelings and sentiments amongst kin that he turned, showing how these were moulded by the institutions of the society. The fact that among the matrilineal Trobrianders the father was not an authority figure, led to some rethinking of the 'Oedipus' theory. At the same time an Englishman – Radcliffe-Brown – also turning his back on evolution, but retaining the interest in terminology, produced a new and elegant *comparative* approach to kinship which sought to make generalizations about kinship systems, comparable to the 'laws' of natural science.

Malinowski's psychological interests have not had very much influence, at least on British anthropology, though his method of detailed field studies has become an established institution – some would say a sacred cow – of the profession.

Radcliffe-Brown's insistence on studying a kinship system as a field of rights and obligations (the legal influence again), and of seeing it as part of the social structure, has been much more influential. His comparative method has been less avidly adopted, and his notion that the 'laws' of anthropology are comparable to the laws of natural science has been more or less abandoned.

Another important turning point was the work of Evans-Pritchard, whose book on the Nuer of the Southern Sudan appeared in 1940. It focused attention on kinship *groups*, particularly groups based on descent in the male line from a known ancestor. These were the *gens* which Morgan found so fascinating in Rome and Greece but about which so little was known. Evans-Pritchard showed how they functioned as *political* groups in Nuer society and so turned attention to the recruitment, perpetuation and functioning of such groups, particularly in Africa. That this was a valid and useful way of looking at descent groups was underlined by the work of Meyer Fortes whose *Dynamics of Clanship among the Tallensi* was published in 1945. This book showed in enormous detail how the descent groups of these people in northern Ghana were the framework of their social and political structure. There followed a spate of books by British anthropologists describing the functions of descent groups in many societies, particularly in Africa, and this way of looking at kinship systems came to dominate anthropological thinking. Fortes' second book was called *The Web of Kinship among the Tallensi*, and in it he took a different focus. He looked at kinship from the point of view of the way individuals and groups are tied together in a 'web' of relations of marriage and descent.

Now this is an important distinction. We can always look at what anthropologists have called 'kinship relations' in two ways: on the one hand, we can look at the total society and ask how it forms its kinship *groups* (such as *gens*, *curia*, *phratry* etc.) and how they function, and on the other, we can look at the network of relationships that bind individuals to each other in the 'web' of kinship. Some anthropologists have argued that only the second study should be truly called the study of 'kinship'; the first is the study of politics, and it just happens that the political units are kinship-recruited groups. After all, one could describe the 'political' system of the Nuer, as Evans-Pritchard did, without ever talking about the web of interpersonal relationships, the relations between father and son, the relations between a man and his wife's family, the rights of brothers over their sisters or parents over their children, the laws of inheritance, the rules of marriage and legitimacy etc. However, because the political units are recruited on a kinship basis, one can still discuss this process of recruitment under the heading of 'kinship'. The actual political functions of the groups, it is true, are the province of 'politics'.

In the earlier part of this book I will be largely concerned with the ways in which kinship groups are formed and perpetuated, and with some of the reasons for the variations between types. I will not be very much concerned with their various functions – they can serve almost any function – but with their *mechanics*. Thus the seemingly slight variation between choosing to trace descent in the female line as opposed to the male, has far-reaching consequences when one comes to form kin groups on this basis. There are problems involved in perpetuating the group and recruiting new members, in keeping the group together, in allowing the group to segment into smaller units and yet remain united, etc. It is with problems like this that I am concerned.

In the latter part of the book there is some change in focus. This change of focus reflects a change of interest that came over kinship studies with the publication in 1949 of two books: Murdock's *Social Structure* which revived evolutionary interest, and Lévi-Strauss's *Les Structures Élémentaires de la Parenté* (Elementary Kinship Structures), which focused attention on kinship systems as methods of organizing *marriage* relations between groups. Both books put great stress on kinship terminology, which has been almost totally neglected since the 1930's.

Before Lévi-Strauss, marriage had been discussed largely in the context of recruitment to kinship groups; legitimate marriage was necessary to provide for legitimate offspring to replenish the group. Lévi-Strauss turned this on its head. Kinship groups, he argued, were simply units in a system of 'alliances' made or 'expressed' by marriage. The real differences between kinship systems, then, lay in the different ways in which they moved women around the system in marriage.

The different focus introduced by Lévi-Strauss can perhaps be illustrated if we imagine two historians interested in European dynasties. One historian is primarily interested in the ways in which royal houses perpetuated themselves, arranged their rules of succession, and ensured that the succession did not fail. Marriages were means to this end. The other historian, however, sees the royal houses as units in a series of complex alliances binding together various countries, and these alliances are cemented or 'expressed' by royal marriages. One sees marriage as useful in providing royal heirs: the other sees royal heirs as useful in that they can be used in dynastic marriages.

Now this is a vastly oversimplified view, but it may help

to give a perspective to the reader. Lévi-Strauss's massive
book has its devotees, but it has not penetrated very quickly
or very far into Anglo-American thinking, largely because
it is written in French and is extremely long. It runs counter
to the theoretical tenor of most British and American work.
But as I hope to show, his approach (even though I disagree
with many of his conclusions) has a lot to commend it. It
does enable us to put all kinship systems on one continuum
and discuss them as variations on the 'alliance' theme. The
approach of the British Africanist anthropologists was
excellent for dealing with societies in which descent groups
of a particular kind were the basic units in the social system;
but it broke down when it came to dealing with societies
of other kinds. It had very little to offer us in helping us to
understand kinship and marriage in our own society where
large and politically important kin-groups are *not* the basic
units.

It is fair at this point to say that Dutch anthropologists
had anticipated Lévi-Strauss's approach. But even fewer
people read Dutch than read French, so their influence was
negligible.

III

This absurdly brief sketch sets the scene for the anthropological study of kinship. There is no good history of
the subject, and this is not the place to write one; but such
a history is badly needed. It is almost impossible, as the
evolutionists saw, to explain the present state of things
without saying how they came to be that way. Without
knowing the history of the subject many of its debates and
controversies will seem like so much scholasticism to the
general reader. Hence, while giving this minimal background to show how the subject has arisen and developed, I
will not pursue a historical course in the book that follows.
I will attempt to make the presentation systematic and self-
contained, and the interested reader who wishes to pursue
the issues raised will be able to see how much my approach
improves on, differs from, and falls short of, that of my

predecessors and colleagues. My approach is something of an amalgam, and it differs perhaps from most other work in being more deductive, more concerned with the exploration of possibilities than with the deducing of laws from empirical data. This is partly because I believe that such an approach will genuinely improve kinship studies by cutting through the verbiage and confusion that follows from a too-simple inductive method. But also I feel that it will make more sense to the general reader and the beginner this way. I have tried to show how kinship systems are responses to various recognizable pressures within a framework of biological, psychological, ecological and social limitations. Many anthropologists write as though kinship systems have dropped from the sky onto societies – they're there because they're there because ... In truth they are there because they answer certain needs – do certain jobs. When these change the systems change – but only within certain limits. It is these limits that will be our starting point.

I should perhaps here put in a note of explanation about method: I will frequently talk of 'models' of systems. By this I mean much what an economist means when he speaks of a 'model' of 'perfect competition', for example, or a physicist when he describes the behaviour of an 'ideal' gas. The economist takes a few features – a large number of small firms, perfect knowledge of the market, etc. – and deduces theoretically what would happen if they appeared in combination. This is his 'model' against which he can compare actual markets. Probably very few markets will tally *exactly* with his basic model, but the model serves as the limiting case. Many of the 'systems' of kinship and marriage that I will describe will be models in the sense of limiting cases. Almost all 'real' systems will have some idiosyncratic variations. (Readers familiar with sociological literature will recognize Weber's method of 'ideal types' of social systems and social action here.)

CHAPTER ONE

Kinship, Family, and Descent

I

KINSHIP and marriage are about the basic facts of life. They are about 'birth, and copulation, and death', the eternal round that seemed to depress the poet but which excites, amongst others, the anthropologist. Copulation produces the relation between mates which is the foundation of marriage and parenthood. Birth produces children and the lasting mother-child bond, the most fundamental and basic of all social bonds. Death produces a gap in the social group and demands a replacement. Birth and parenthood provide an answer – provide an heir. The fact of there being two sexes with different functions, however, means that there are alternative means of deciding on who will be the heir. And although Man has these facts of life in common with other mammals, he differs in that he can choose between the alternative courses that they offer him in the way of group-formation, succession, mating arrangements, etc. His choice is often constrained within narrow limits but the fact remains that he can *do* things with the basic bonds arising from the processes of mating, childbearing, and childrearing. The study of kinship is the study of what he does and why he does it, and the consequences of the adoption of one alternative rather than another. This is a basic study in the social sciences because these are the most basic social bonds.

Man is an animal, but he puts the basic facts of life to work for himself in ways that no other animal does or can. Let us explore this point a little further. Man is first a mammal, and then a primate. He is warm-blooded and his young are born alive and suckled, and he belongs to that group of mammals which includes the monkeys and great apes, tarsiers and lemurs. Many of the facts of life – including the all-important gregariousness that produces societies – he shares with the primates and other mammals. But a feature he shares with the higher apes, and yet in which he excels even these, is his large brain.

Exactly what is cause and what effect in human evolution is often difficult to ascertain, but the general sequence of events was probably something like this. The development of predatory tendencies in the earliest of our sub-human ancestors, possibly accentuated by the early discovery of weapons, led to upright stance, bipedal locomotion, the better coordination of hand and eye, group cooperation, and a host of other features favouring the development of a larger brain in this weapon-using ape. The upright stance, however, reduced the size of the human pelvis just at the time when the human head was growing larger to accommodate the large brain. In consequence, the process of giving birth became (and remains) difficult and possibly dangerous. There was no alternative therefore but for selection to favour those mothers who dropped their young early and let the head grow outside the womb rather than inside. Consequently, unlike most other animals, the human infant was born, in a sense, far too early. He should still have been in the womb; instead he was outside – a creature of enormous potential, but for many years of his young life in a precarious, helpless and dependent position. The fact of his large brain, however, and his relatively unspecialized physical make-up, meant that he had an enormous capacity for learning. In the long stretch between his rude and premature awakening from the womb, and his full physical maturity, he could amass skills and knowledge, and so the otherwise unpromising-looking creature prospered and finally conquered, to become the dominant animal on earth.

But to get this precious creature to adulthood required a good deal of care and effort on the part of the mother. For almost a year she bore him, and for several more years she would be his source of food and succour. During this time she would be relatively helpless, preoccupied with bearing and raising the child, and probably getting pregnant again while doing so. For the successful rearing of the young, then, and so for the survival and success of the species, the mother had to be protected.

Again, there is no reason to think that man differs from other social animals in this. All primates developed society as a weapon in the struggle for survival. Sometimes this society is as small as the elementary family of the gibbon, sometimes as large as the baboon hordes of 400 individuals. The nature of caretaking, therefore, will differ according to the composition of the group. In the larger groups, everyone is to some extent everyone else's responsibility. Howler monkeys have a special cry for 'infant fallen from tree', and at its utterance all the troop sweep down to pick up the unfortunate youngster. The males of some primate groups do their share of baby-minding and caretaking. In the monogamous primates, and in those either permanently or sporadically arranged in bands with one male and several females, it is clearly the father of the children who takes care and protects them. (By father here we mean the mother's mate, not necessarily the progenitor of the child – a distinction that will become more significant when we move to the human level – although these will most often correspond.) In the larger hordes, this is not necessarily so. But in most of the hordes there is some kind of order in the mating arrangements. Random promiscuity is rare and usually the result of some kind of social breakdown. The more socially organized the group, the more likely is a 'consort' system to prevail in which definite male-female pairs, or males with several females, are the reproductive units.

Thus, in primate society, we have some kind of ordered mating and a protective function exercised by the males over females and young. But the most successful primate adds to this the large brain and the consequences of this in a prolonged socialization period. This period brings with it many difficulties, and not least the fact that the young become capable of reproductive behaviour before they are fully physically mature and able to take on the responsibilities of parenthood. But the large brain and its most important outcome, the development of language, mean that man can go much further in what he *does* with these basic ties and drives that are part of his primate heritage. Some animals may 'know' their parents, siblings and children. But beyond this there are simply 'others of the species': hostile, friendly; our band, another band; older, younger; more dominant, less dominant; male, female – these are probably the limits of comprehension and classification in the animal world. No primate other than man can remember his ancestors up to the thirteenth and fourteenth generations, nor can he conceptualize 'second cousin once removed', even though he *has*, biologically, such a relative. And certainly he could not attach legal, political or economic significance to such a relationship. He is unlikely to ban mating with such a relative. All these things man can do and does do in many rather complicated ways. His hindsight and intelligence enable him to look back to his ancestry and to calculate degrees of relationship and to utilize these for the forging of social bonds. He is working with the same raw material as exists in the animal world, but he can conceptualize and categorize it to serve social ends.

The study of kinship is the study of what man *does* with these basic facts of life – mating, gestation, parenthood, socialization, siblingship etc. Part of his enormous success in the evolutionary struggle lies in his ability to manipulate these relationships to advantage. And this is important. He does not simply play games with them for sheer intellectual excitement. That is a sport reserved for anthropologists, and perhaps some Australian Aborigines. He utilizes them in order to survive, and beyond survival, to prosper. At some level he is bound by circumstances to adopt one mode of adaptation rather than another; but he is free to vary this within limits and to his advantage. I am not implying that he does this as a result of conscious choice, indeed this can rarely be the case, but that natural selection can, as it were, take advantage of his powers of choice and intelligence to make him exploit possibilities to their fullest range, and probe modes of adaptation and advance that are unknown and unknowable even to the most intelligent of his primate cousins. No Australian Aborigine sat down and worked out a blueprint for the complicated systems of kinship and marriage for which he is justly famous; but his ability to conceptualize and classify was as much a factor in this successful development as the claws of the tiger or the neck of the giraffe were in the survival and success of these species.

II

There is a good deal of the primate heritage that is relevant to any study of human society: dominance and hierarchy, territoriality, group cooperation, consort and mating behaviour, bonding behaviour, ritualization, etc. But the 'facts of life' with which man has had to come to terms in the process of adaptation, and which are immediately relevant to the study of kinship and marriage, can perhaps be reduced to four basic 'principles':

Principle 1   The women have the children.
Principle 2   The men impregnate the women.
Principle 3   The men usually exercise control.
Principle 4   Primary kin do not mate with each other.

Gestation, impregnation, domination and the avoidance of incest, lie at the root of all social organization. The first two are unremarkable but unavoidable. They do raise complications, as we shall see. The third is no doubt contentious, but I feel that objections to it are somehow unreal. By and large it is overwhelmingly true and for very good reasons. One does not need to recapitulate the evolutionary history of man to see why. For the greater part of human history, women were getting on with their highly specialized task of bearing and rearing the children. It was the men who hunted the game, fought the enemies, and made the decisions. This is, I am convinced, rooted in primate nature, and while social conditions in the very recent past of some advanced societies have given women the opportunity to have more say in things, I still think that most women would agree with the contention. This is not to say that from her hearth the woman does not exercise enormous influence – that is why I have qualified it by saying 'usually'; but the sheer physiological facts of existence make her role secondary to that of the male in the decision-making process at any level higher than the purely domestic. Women who disagree with this and try to avoid its consequences have to put the female role behind them, wholly or partially. If a majority of women had not been attending fully to their specialized task, then the consequences might have been disastrous. Now it is possible that a minority will be able to make some impression on the male monopoly of power, and the social circumstances of many very advanced industrial societies make this more likely. As society becomes more technocratic, then the recruitment of suitable people to fill its many roles must mean that the net has to be thrown wider than just over the males, and that women will achieve positions of dominance in some spheres. But this will usually conflict with the basic female function. Where this is not so, then Principle 3 will not hold and we can trace out the consequences of this change. For example, in advanced industrial societies, there is often a tendency to limit the size of families rather than to let the female go on bearing children until she has run her course. Voluntary abstention, and then contraception, have made this possible. Also women now live for many years after the menopause – a relatively new trend. Thus, for a good part of her life a woman may be free to make some impact on the male world. It is curious therefore that this has not been felt more. Even with these increased opportunities the woman's role is still secondary. Whether this is morally justifiable is not our concern. Given a few 'by and large' and 'other things being equal' clauses, I feel that Principle 3 holds good. Certainly for most of the people we will be dealing with here it does.

For many of the issues with which we shall deal, this Principle is not desperately essential, but for others it is crucial to the understanding of the arrangements arrived at.

'Primary kin', in Principle 4, are an individual's mother, father, son, daughter, brother and sister. This proposition, while not contentious, does raise problems. For the moment, we will take it for granted as it is obviously true (given a 'by and large' clause again), but later we will wrangle with the reasons for this seemingly strange limitation on sexual proclivities.

III

Let us leave our Principles for the moment and look at some more abstract problems in the study of kinship. These will give us the opportunity to examine the terminology and symbols used by anthropologists. In its commonest definition, 'kinship' is simply the relations between 'kin', i.e. persons related by real, putative or fictive consanguinity. 'Real' consanguinity is difficult to pin down of course, and our own scientific notions of genetic relationship are not shared by all peoples and cultures. Who does, and who does not, count as 'blood' kin, varies considerably. Each of us, for example, has many many thousands of 'blood' kin whom we do not recognize, for we tend to stop short in our reckoning very quickly. Most of us perhaps know the descendants of our two pairs of grandparents (our uncles and our cousins and our aunts), but how many of us know the descendants of our four pairs of great grandparents – eight pairs of great-great grandparents – sixteen pairs of . . . and so on? Yet all these are, by our definition, 'blood' kin – genetically related to us. This is because we know – and before we knew we assumed – that both parents contribute to the creation of the child. Thus a child is equally kin to father's and mother's kin. This is not a universal notion. Either the father and mother are reckoned to contribute differentially to the child (one the body, one the soul; one the blood, one the bones etc.), or only one or other of them is supposed to have a direct hand in the actual creation. Either the mother is thought of as a kind of incubator, in which the father plants the seed which becomes the child; or the child is seen as having been wholly created by the mother, with the father's duty being merely to 'open up the passage' from the womb or something such. These seemingly bizarre notions of ethnophysiology will make sense when we come to see the kinds of kinship system in which they occur. But they do make the idea of 'real' consanguinity somewhat useless for anthropological analysis. A consanguine is someone who is defined *by the society* as a consanguine, and 'blood' relationship in a genetic sense has not necessarily anything to do with it, although on the whole these tend to coincide in most societies of the world. Thus anthropologists tend to distinguish, for example, the 'pater' or legal father from the 'genitor' or actual biological father. (Logically of course they should distinguish the 'mater' from the 'genetrix' as well.) But as has been recently pointed out, in many societies the 'genitor' is also a socially defined character and his identity depends on canons of evidence. Thus, although the deed may be pinned on some unfortunate fellow, he need not in fact be the progenitor of the child in question. The best we can say on this is that, quibbles aside, actual or putative genetic connexion, according to the local definition of 'genetic' or 'consanguineous', is usually the basis of kinship relations. And even when it is not, genetic kinship is the 'model' for fictive kinship relations. The most obvious case here is that of adoption. Although the adopted child is not related by blood to his parents and siblings etc., he can be fitted into the niche of 'child', and assume this role as though he were in fact the offspring of his legal parents. In many societies, large-scale adoption or 'fosterage' is practised, and most people do not in fact rear their actual children, but there is nothing to stop the system working 'as if' they did. No society treats this in an arbitrary fashion. It does assume some theory of consanguinity, and it does give weight to presumed consanguineous relationships. That these may not, in our scientific view of the matter, be 'true' genetic relationships, is irrelevant. Once we accept that 'consanguinity' is a socially defined quality, the definition of kinship holds. What we must avoid doing is foisting our own particular view of consanguinity onto the rest of mankind, however 'true' we may think it. In fact, it is shared by most peoples, but there are enough dissenters to command respect, and a failure to take their view of the matter often leads to confusion.

For example, this book is called *Kinship and Marriage*, and we tend to think we know the difference. Consanguinity has long been distinguished from affinity – relatives by blood from relatives by marriage. *Affines*, then, are people married to our *consanguines*. But, as we have seen, this all depends on the local definition of consanguinity. To us, with our genetic outlook, a father is genetically connected to his children in the same way as a mother: he is a consanguine. But if we took the view that the father had no part in the creation of the child, then he would not be a 'consanguine'; he would simply be the mother's husband – like a step-father in our own society – and of the same order of relationship to us as, say, a brother-in-law. He would be a man married to a consanguine woman, that is all. Our 'social' relationship with him may be all that sentiment demands of a relationship between child and 'father', but our presumed genetic relationship would be nil. He would be an 'affine': a relative by marriage to our mother, as our sister's husband is a relative by marriage to our sister. If we took the reverse view, then the mother would be as a sister-in-law: our father's wife, but of no blood relationship to us. Now, I quote these extreme cases to show that the definition of 'consanguinity and affinity' cannot be taken for granted, and that we must treat each case on its merits. And, above all, we must always remember that it is what people *do* with their definitions – the social use to which they are put – that matters.

The above considerations, and others that we will come across later, have led some anthropologists to deny that 'the facts of physiology' have anything to do with 'kinship'. Well, the facts of the physiology of parturition, for example, may not have. These are of no concern to the anthropologist.

But, as we will see when we look at the workings of kinship systems, those two rock bottom facts of physiology – that women have the children (which no one disputes) and that men generate them (which may be disputed but which is none the less true) – provide basic limitations which all such systems have to take into account. We will see how, when groups try to adapt to various ecological and environmental pressures, within the limits set by our four principles, 'systems of consanguinity and affinity' come into being. To these, ideological notions are grafted concerning 'true' relationship and the like, and these make sense in the framework of the system as it works. What is more, they tend to react back on the system, and the ideology becomes one of the facts which the processes of adaptation must take into account.

IV

To get a preliminary idea of the complexities that can arise, let us take an abstract problem in social recruitment. One of the commonest uses of 'kinship' ties is in recruitment. Thus, social groups are recruited on the bases of blood ties (assumed, putative or fictive) or affinal ties. Now the group with which we are most familiar is the nuclear or elementary or conjugal family. (There are a host of other words for it and no agreement, but 'conjugal' seems to be the best as it begs the least questions about what is in fact the 'nucleus' or 'elementary' unit of social organization.) This is the family consisting of a man and a woman and their dependent offspring. We symbolize it thus:

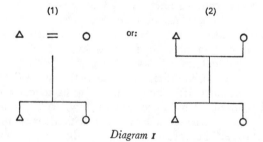

Diagram 1

Here the phallic triangle is the male and the female is naturally a circle. Either the = sign or a bracket under the two symbolizes marriage. A bracket *over* the two symbolizes siblingship: in this case they are the children of a male-female pair, but if the father or mother was unknown or irrelevant we could symbolize the 'parent-child' tie by a vertical line thus:

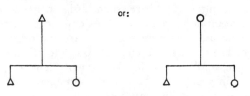

Diagram 2

The vertical line, then, represents *descent*. If the sex of the person concerned is irrelevant, then a neutral square is used. (Sometimes a diamond.) Decease is indicated by crossing out the dead person thus: ⌀ ⌀ ⌀

These are about all the symbols we shall need. Modifications can be dealt with as they arise. Here we should note that the triangles and circles can either stand for single individuals or for a collection of individuals, and this should always be indicated. Thus, in the diagrams above, the 'sibling' symbols can either refer to two actual individuals – a brother and sister, or to all the male and female offspring of the pair – all the sons and all the daughters.

To return to our conjugal family – the one formed by the marriage of the two parents. This is often stated by anthropologists to be the 'basic' and 'universal' unit of human society, and certainly of kinship systems. This is, however, an assertion of dubious truth and utility, and facts have to be forced unnaturally in order to fit it. The irreducible and elementary social grouping is surely the mother and her children. Whatever else happens, this unit has to survive for the species to survive. It is not *strictly* necessary for any adult males to be in constant association with the mother-child unit. Providing it can manage to feed itself and defend itself, and bring its young to maturity, then it can survive. In many advanced societies this is possible and occurs. Even in cases where the unit needs male care and protection, it need not be the genitor of the children who provides this. If the higher unit is some kind of horde, then the males as a whole could care for the women and children as a whole without specific assignment. Where such assignment occurs in primate groups it has to do with the dominance pattern and male sex-needs, rather than with the care and protection of children. The males sort themselves out into a hierarchy of dominance, and the females then assign themselves either singly, or in groups, to the males of the hierarchy. (Some males – young or inadequate – are often extra-hierarchical, and without mates for some portion of their lives.) Circumstances can arise, however, which make a nuclear family the best survival unit. The bird-like gibbon, living in his tree-top nest-building security, lives in such a unit. But the ground-dwelling primates, especially, have made the horde and not the family the basic unit of survival, and within the horde it is, on the one hand, the hierarchy of males and, on the other, the mother-child units which are the operative groups. Similarly, with that remarkable terrestrial primate, Man, some circumstances make for the development of family units, others do not. (Some writers have maintained that the lack of 'oestrus' [rut or heat] in human females, leads to the setting up of nuclear families. The human female is sexually receptive at all times, the argument goes, unlike her primate counterpart who has an oestrus cycle. Primate males are only interested in a female during her receptive period and hence there is no permanent sexual bond. With human females this is not so and hence a permanent bond is possible. There is something to the argument, I think, but it probably both overestimates the human male and under-estimates primate bonding tendencies. It is too complex an issue to pursue at length here.) Because the family seems to be the predominant unit, we must not be bemused into thinking it is the 'natural' or basic one. Take, for example, the well-known case of *polygyny*, in which a man has several wives often housed in different huts, and sometimes in different parts of the country. This has been described as a 'series of linked nuclear families with a "father" in common'. What sense does such an assertion make? The 'facts' here are that several mother-child units exist, and that one male is responsible for them – circulating among them as it were. In other cases, there is no institution of marriage at all, and the mother-child unit is *not* supported by the mother's mate or mates. There is a good deal of confusion here, and we should always be careful to discover what a writer means by 'nuclear family'. In all societies there is some form of more or less regularized mating. Often a female has only one mate. Very often circumstances are such that the female and her mate form a domestic unit – living under one roof and raising their children together. But this is a highly variable arrangement. Sometimes the males spend all their time together, associating only briefly with the females. Sometimes the female has more than one mate, but none of these associates with her domestically. Sometimes sexual access to a female is limited to one male, but even so, he does not form a domestic unit with the female – and so on. Sometimes, even though the 'one male, one female' pattern is regularized, and the male is the 'recognized father' of the female's children, this unit is lost in a larger unit from which it can only be separated artificially. Thus, there may be a 'unit' of several 'mothers' and their children, to which males are attached. But this is not necessarily *constituted* of 'linked' nuclear families. The 'universality' of the nuclear family can only be sustained by the loosest and broadest of definitions and the ignoring of 'exceptions'.

In any case, the nuclear family is bound to be derivative and not 'basic', which is why I have preferred 'conjugal' as a description. The basic unit is the mother and her child, however the mother came to be impregnated. Whether or not a mate becomes attached to the mother on some more or less permanent basis is a variable matter. This attachment varies from non-existent, through highly doubtful to fairly stable. The mother-child tie is inevitable and given. The 'conjugal' tie is variable. There are other ways of dealing with the problem of survival than by the institutionalization of the conjugal tie, and when we see it firmly institutionalized we should ask why this is so rather than take it for granted. In the animal world generally, there are sufficient variations in this patterning to make us ask what selection pressures have led to what kinds of familial arrangements. We should only take for granted what is obviously 'given' – such that women bear and rear children. Whether or not father can be persuaded to stay at home is another matter. If all the proponents of the nuclear family theory want to say is that there is usually in human society some pattern of regular *mating* such that a child tends to have a recognized father as well as an obvious mother – then I would, granted some exceptions, go along. But to proclaim the husband-wife-plus-wife's-children *unit* the nucleus of all human society, the most basic of all human institutions, is to force categories onto the facts. What we must do is to look at exactly what arrangements are made, and not prejudge the issue. It is difficult to see why anthropologists should want to make this assertion unless some moral ethnocentricism drives them to it. (Historically the nuclear family argument stems from the 'patriarchal origins' theory. Why this should be may become clear when we discuss patrilineal systems.)

This may seem a quibble, but it really is fundamental. If we start on the study of kinship with preconceived notions about the basicness of the nuclear family then we shall be lost before we begin. Where a true nuclear family occurs, there are usually very good reasons for it, and the fact of its prevalence has to be examined. But even this prevalence can only be explained if we start with the more basic unit – mother and child. It is, as we have seen, by *adding* to this unit the 'conjugal' tie of husband-wife, that 'fathers' and nuclear (or I would prefer 'conjugal') families are created.

V

The recruitment of the 'father' to the mother-child group is then one form of recruitment and it is affinal. Now let us explore the logic of some forms of 'consanguineal' recruitment that take us beyond the simple limits of the family and into the realm of extended kinship groups like the *gens, clan,* and *phratry* that fascinated Morgan. These would be classified by anthropologists as 'descent groups', that is, groups whose members claim to be descended from a common ancestor. At some time either a real person or a mythical hero or animal is supposed to have founded the group, and its members are all descendants of the founder. As we saw, with the Iroquois this descent was traced in the 'female line', while with the Romans it was in the 'male line'. Let us look further into this in the light of our four principles.

Take our basic group again – mother and children – and assume, say, that it has a territory or some other property (real or incorporeal). This property can be exploited by a limited number of people and our group wishes to recruit these. It wishes to be self-recruiting and self-perpetuating; that is, to recruit and perpetuate itself on a kinship basis. How can it do this? Once the mother herself is past childbearing and can introduce no new members we are left with the brothers and sisters as the basic unit to be perpetuated.

Perhaps the most obvious solution is for the group to take advantage of our Principle 1 and let the women of the group have children who will become the heirs to the property. Thus, the brothers and sisters can perpetuate themselves and recruit as new members the children of the sisters. However, we have to take into account Principle 2 (men beget the children). The most convenient men for the job are the brothers, but this runs up against Principle 4 (the incest prohibition). Thus, if the sisters are to be impregnated it has to be by men other than the brothers. Some kind of mating arrangement has to be arrived at with men of other groups, but this may or may not lead to permanent liaisons. As long as the sisters are regularly impregnated, then all will be well. The 'brothers' of our group, of course, will be performing the same service for the 'sisters' of other groups – or rather for their brothers, for we have to remember Principle 3 (male control).

Thus the sisters would produce new male and female members:

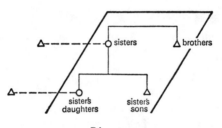

Diagram 3

The daughters of the sisters would produce further new members in their turn, with the aid of men of other groups, and the group would build up over time.

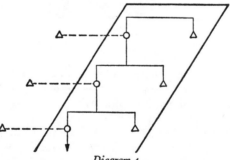

Diagram 4

This diagram shows the development schematically with the triangles standing simply for 'men of the group' and the circles for 'women of the group'. The actual development of such a group over time, with the symbols standing for actual individuals, might look like this: (Taken from the actual genealogy of a group of American Indians in New Mexico.)

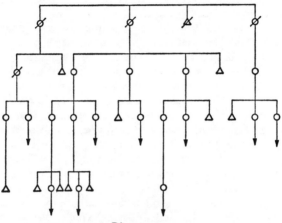

Diagram 5

This is simplified, but it illustrates the point. The arrows indicate the women and girls who will continue the line.

Thus our original group will restrict the inheritance of its territorial rights, property, title or whatever, to the children of its female members. This could be viewed in various ways: as a series of successive mother-child units, or a series of successive brother-sister units with the children of the sisters forming the succeeding generations, or as all the descendants of the original 'mother' through females; her sons and daughters, the sons and daughters of her daughters and so on.

It follows that the members of our group will all be related to each other *through females only*. Anthropologists refer to such a method of tracing relationship as *matrilineal*, or in the female (mother's) line. (Sometimes *uterine* is used as a synonym for matrilineal.) Thus, for whatever purposes this group of people exists, membership in it is gained by being the child of one's mother. If relationships between members are traced out, they then will be consistently traced through females. Thus, my mother's sister's children will be members with me, but not the children of my mother's brother, for they are related to me through a male, and will be members of *their* mother's group.

We must also take Principle 3 into account (male control). If the men are to own and control the property then a situation curious by our standards arises: a man's own sons will not be his heirs, but his property will pass to the sons of his sisters or to his nearest male matrilineal relatives.

Let us try another solution. Let us say that the children of the *brothers* should be members, but not the children of the sisters. This fits nicely with Principle 2, and accommodates Principle 4, but comes up with a bump against Principle 1. Men do not bear children, and hence, if they wish to perpetuate the group, they must gather unto themselves wives. They cannot really do this on a casual basis. They have to get a woman and keep her until she is impregnated, has delivered the child, and in all probability has reared it. By and large, then, something above a casual 'mating' arrangement has to be arrived at. We can symbolize the result as follows:

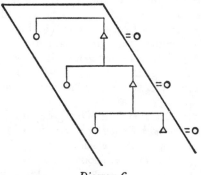

Diagram 6

Thus the group will restrict inheritance to the children of its men. Again this can be viewed as a series of father-child units, or as a series of successive brother-sister units with the children of the 'brothers' forming the next generation, or as all the descendants of the original 'brothers' through males – their sons and daughters, the sons and daughters of these sons, and so on.

The way in which an actual group of this kind might develop is shown on diagram 7. (This again is taken from the actual genealogy of a group of American Indians.)

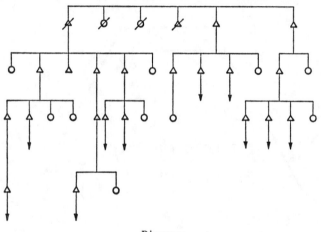

Diagram 7

As opposed to the case in our first example, the members of this group will be related only through males. This mode of relationship is called *patrilineal*, or in the male (father's) line, with the term *agnatic* (borrowed from Roman law) as a synonym. I gain membership through my father, and if I trace out my relationship to the other members (my 'agnates'), I trace it through males only. Thus my father's brother's children are members, but not my father's sister's, for they are related to me through a female and are members of *their* father's group.

In this case Principle 3 raises no problems; property and control will be passed from fathers to sons, or to near agnates. The problem here is where the sisters fit in.

There is one other obvious solution. Let both the brothers and the sisters have the children and get the best of both worlds. Thus the brothers must find wives and the sisters husbands. It follows that these must be 'husbands' rather than just casual mates, because they will be 'brothers' from other groups looking for 'wives'. We can visualize it as follows:

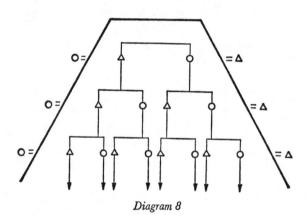

Diagram 8

(It is impossible to show all the 'husbands' and 'wives', so those shown can be taken as indicating 'men and women marrying into the group'.) While this arrangement may seem to be getting the best of all possible worlds it does create difficulties. [In fact it runs up against all our four Principles.] For a start the groups formed on this basis are bound to overlap; for to say that both brother and sister should reproduce the group is to say that I am a member of both mother's and father's group. The overlapping of groups can be visualized as follows:

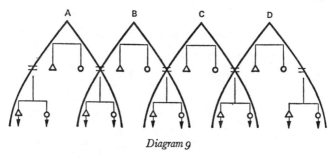

Diagram 9

This arrangement raises problems that are not found with the other two systems. With either of those I am a member of one group only – father's or mother's. With the present system I am a member of at least two groups, however, – father's and mother's. Clearly, then, we cannot have the same kind of organization with this system as with the others. These could scarcely be groups of permanent territorial residents, because I could not be permanently resident in two groups at once. If they are territorial groups, then either I will have to choose one or the other, or divide my time, or something such. Also, on marriage, either husband or wife will have to leave the 'natal' group.

Diagram 10 (overleaf) shows two such overlapping groups, taken from the actual genealogies (simplified) of some Gaelic-speaking islanders in W. Ireland. We can see how in both groups *all* the descendants of the founders are included. The overlapping is illustrated by the fact that the shaded individuals belong to A *and* B: A through a female link and B through a male link.

It is clear that in this system the members of my descent group will be related to me through *both* male *and* female links. We usually call such a system *cognatic,* 'cognates' in Roman law being kin through any sex link (as opposed to agnates, for example, who are kin through male links only). The matrilineal/patrilineal type of system is usually called *unilineal,* using only one 'line' (male or female) in tracing

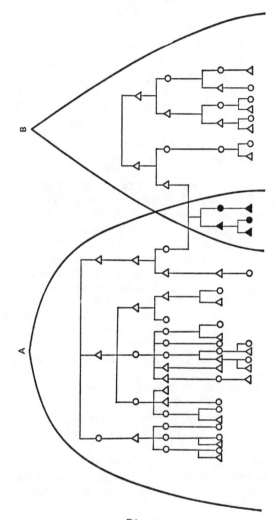

Diagram 10

kinship for some purposes. It really means, I suppose, uni-sexual linkage, and this is perhaps less confusing as a general description. But unilineal is hallowed by use and so we will stick to it. The cognatic principle of tracing kinship can perhaps be best described as *ignoring sex* in tracing kinship links.

The unilineal principle has some obvious advantages. For a start it assigns an individual to one group only, thus avoiding the problems of overlapping groups. If the society is divided into groups based on unilineal recruitment, these will be discrete groups. From the point of view of neatness of organization this is a great convenience. Also, the unilineal principle restricts the numbers of a man's heirs; it prevents the indefinite proliferation of inheritors that the cognatic principle demands. The question therefore arises: why do some societies adopt one principle and some another?

We have been looking at the formation of kinship groups from a certain vantage point. We have taken a starting point in time and asked, in effect, how our basic sibling group might perpetuate itself over time. Whatever groups are formed by one or other process of perpetuation the members of a group will be related to each other by *common descent*; they will be descended from a common ancestor or ancestress in either the male line (patrilineally) or the female line (matrilineally) or through links of both sexes (cognatically). Such a group, which has perhaps a name, property or ritual, or some activity in common, will be a *descent group*; a group formed on the basis of descent from a common ancestor. Where the actual relationship between members in such a group can be demonstrated (as in Diagrams 5, 7, and 10), and is not simply assumed, the group is called a *lineage*. Thus, we have matrilineal lineages (*matri-lineages*), patrilineal lineages (*patri-lineages*), and cognatic lineages (no compound term yet invented). Higher order units often consisting of several lineages in which common descent is assumed but cannot necessarily be demonstrated, are most often referred to as *clans* (after the Gaelic *clann*, meaning offspring or descendants). There are other

usages which cause considerable confusion. Morgan established *gens* for patri-clan and *clan* for matri-clan, with no generic term. American writers often use *sib* as the generic term
with *patri-sib* and *matri-sib* as the sub varieties. This is quite
wrong. As we shall see, the Anglo-Saxon *sib* (German *Sippe*)
was not a descent group at all. But then *clan* is not accurate
either. The Gaelic *clann* were the cognatic descendants of an
eponymous ancestor. Thus *Clann Domhnaill* were the des-
cendents of Donal or Donald (the MacDonalds or O'Don-
nels). This term has now been appropriated to mean only
unilineal descent groups.

Anthropologists are never happier than when coining
natty Latinisms for things. It is a kind of magical belief in
the power of names: if you discover its name then you have
it in your power. This Rumpelstiltskin philosophy (name
it and nail it) means that anthropologists can always substitute word-coinage for thought, and the making of con-
ceptual distinctions for the making of discoveries. When it
gets to the point where an anthropologist can seriously
propose that *kith* should be used to describe a group of kin,
where clans become subdivisions of septs, and where such
monsters as 'sub-sub-sibs' are being spawned, it is time to
stop and ask if we really know what we are at. Much
modern kinship analysis is not analysis at all but an exercise
in bad etymology. This fools even other social scientists into
thinking that the subject is 'very mature and complex' with
a 'highly developed technical vocabulary' (I quote an
eminent sociologist who shall be nameless). What in fact
happens is that anyone trying to understand the subject
has to fight his way through half a dozen conflicting taxon-
omies each with its patchy, *ad hoc* terminology.

There is not much we can do about such confusions except
to note them and warn the reader. Here I will use *clan* and
lineage as the terms for higher and lower order descent-
groups of whatever variety.

VI

In accordance with the brief I set myself – to analyse kinship *groups* – I have concentrated here on ways of forming groups by using kinship ties. These groups based on descent from a common ancestor are not the only kind of kinship groups, but they are the ones that anthropologists have concentrated on. Since their structure will be initially unfamiliar to the newcomer, I have started with them, and for the moment we will stick with them.

It is worth noting, however, at this point, that the principles of descent which emerge from taking each of the three possible decisions about continuity can be used for other purposes than group formation. Thus, in ancient Rome, membership in the gens was patrilineal. But for purposes of individual inheritance a man's kin were divided into his *cognati* – kin through any link, and his *agnati* – kin through male links only. When a man died, his property went to his *primus agnatus*: his nearest living agnatic relative (son, brother, father's brother's son, etc.). If he had no near agnates, then his nearest cognates could inherit, and Roman law laid down 'degrees' of nearness of cognation for this purpose. Thus, membership in the gens was patrilineally determined, but both agnatic and cognatic reckoning were involved in determining inheritance.

Similarly in our own society which lacks descent groups of any kind, we recognize all cognates as 'kin' (up to a certain limit) but surnames are inherited patrilineally as are most titles of nobility.

In yet other societies, which have cognatic descent groups for some purposes, Principle 3 ensures that succession to office, for example, is patrilineally determined.

In many societies which have unilineal descent groups (patrilineal or matrilineal) as the basic political units, individuals recognize their cognates as kin and have obligations to them and expectations of them – in the payment of bride price, for example, or homicide payments.

Thus, kinship ties can be used to define many kinds of social relationships – particularly relationships between owners and heirs, incumbents and successors. Often the principle on which these are determined will coincide with the principle which determines group membership – but not necessarily, as we have seen.

The distinction to bear in mind here is that between *person-to-person relations* of succession, inheritance, etc., and *rights to group membership*. Thus, a society in which most rights and duties – including rights of inheritance and succession – passed in the male line, could be called 'patrilineal', but it need not have patrilineal descent groups. These latter usually emerge, like all descent groups, when there is some form of *group property or obligation*, like the ownership in common of impartible land, or the duty to avenge death, or the obligation to worship ancestors.

The total analysis of any kinship system will involve a description of all the uses to which kinship (and marriage) ties are put. We however are limited to looking at their function in the *recruitment of groups* and in the *relation between groups*.

What we have seen so far is that our four Principles impose certain limits on group recruitment; they limit the possible choices a society can make in the manner in which (speaking anthropomorphically) it decides to recruit its kinship groups. Whatever choice is made – and the decision must often have been a close one – certain complications follow which we have glanced at in a preliminary way. In subsequent chapters, we will explore the reasons for these decisions and the further implications of their consequences. For the moment, the reader should try to fix in his mind the differences betwen the forms of recruitment we have looked at – unilineal and cognatic. We will return to them later.

Perhaps he can try to imagine societies in which descent-groups are the basic political, religious, economic and possibly territorial units: not firms, or associations, or parties, or industries, or classes, or sects and denominations, but groups of people related to each other through common descent, groups like those on Diagrams 5, 7, and 10. So far removed is such a state of society from our own experience that a leap of the imagination is needed in order even to begin to understand it. (This remark is of course addressed to urbanized Europeans and Americans whom I take to be the bulk of my audience. I exempt those Scots with a sound knowledge of, and feeling for, their own traditions. To many Africans and Asians, such an exercise is of course superfluous, and I can only beg their indulgence at what must often seem a laborious statement of the obvious.)

VII

The keen-eyed reader may already have spotted one loophole in the foregoing argument. It may be true that siblings, for example, don't mate, but what is to stop *cousins* from mating? If cousins were to have children, then our descent groups could become – after the first generation – self-sufficient as far as reproduction was concerned. This is quite true, but for some reason such groups tend to prohibit, or at least avoid, marriage within the group. They behave as if they were all indeed *real* brothers and sisters; this is often how they express the prohibition. Not all societies follow this practice, however, and some do indeed encourage the marriage of cousins thus turning the group in on itself. Others have no fixed rule but leave it as a matter of choice whether to marry into or out of the group. The prohibition on marriage within the group (however the group is defined) we call *exogamy*. This can possibly be better stated as a positive injunction – to marry out of the group. When there is a rule that we must marry within the group it is called the rule of *endogamy*. Where it is a matter of choice, the term *agamy* is sometimes used, but this is unfortunate as it suggests that there is no marriage at all.

The group for which the rule of *exogamy* always seems to operate is the nuclear or conjugal family. With a few notable exceptions, societies forbid people to marry their primary kin. They also, as our Principle 4 states, usually forbid them to have sexual relations with these kin. As so much turns on this curious fact of the non-mating of primary kin, we must examine it before we go on to look deeper into the intricacies of descent groups.

CHAPTER TWO

The Incest Problem

I

IF primary kin were allowed to mate, then many of the elaborate arrangements we are going to explore in this book would be unnecessary. Or so it would appear. Given the absence of Principle 4, our mother-children group could settle down to a cosy little inbreeding arrangement and be totally self-sufficient for purposes of reproduction. Almost nowhere, however, is such incestuous mating encouraged, and very often it is banned utterly and offenders against the ban ruthlessly punished. It is this almost universal tendency to ban (or at least to avoid) intra-familial sexual relationships, that we must now consider.

As usual we have to note a number of cavils. For a start, there is a hidden assumption in most discussions of incest that if the ban on such relationships were not present, then people would indulge in them out of choice. After all, if people did not want to commit incest there would be no point in banning it. Secondly, we must underline the distinction between incest and exogamy that we touched on in the last paragraph of Chapter One. This is really only the difference between sex and marriage, and while every teenager knows these are different, many anthropologists get them confused. No society (I believe) is bloody-minded enough to ban sex from marriage, and there is an obvious convenience in combining the two; but sex without marriage one can have and one does. This is important because many theories which purport to explain the outlawing of sex from the family are really explanations of why *marriage* between family members is not allowed. Thus, rules relating to family exogamy do not necessarily explain why sex is banned in the family. There is no logical reason why there should not be a sexual free-for-all within the family and still a ban on marriage between its members – although there may be good psychological reasons. Indeed, when one looks at sexual prohibitions on other than family members one finds that sexual relations are often at a *premium* with precisely those people whom one may *not* marry. Therefore we must distinguish sharply between:

  a. Incest – which pertains to sexual relations
  b. Exogamy – which pertains to conjugal relations

Of course, if one forbids two people to have sexual relations this rather puts an end to chances of marriage between them, but one can forbid them to marry without necessarily forbidding them to have intercourse. Thus, all explanations which purport to cover the banning of sexuality in the family by advancing reasons for family exogamy miss the point – unless they include a clause covering the banning of sex.

This is doubly important because many writers write 'incest taboo/exogamy' as though these were one and the same phenomenon. In trying to explain why many societies forbid marriage between related persons outside the range of the conjugal family, they talk about the 'extension of incest taboos' to these persons. What they often really mean is the extension of exogamic restrictions. It is true that these two often coincide – those who are forbidden in marriage are forbidden as sexual partners also – but it cannot just be assumed that they do; this has to be demonstrated. Clearly, there can be a relationship between incest prohibitions and exogamic rules, but unless we distinguish them and are careful to say which it is we are talking about, then we will only get confused. Our primary concern in this chapter is to explain the ban on intra-familial sex – the incest taboo, or incest avoidance – and we will leave the theme of exogamy to the chapters on marriage proper.

This at least gets clear what it is we wish to explain. We want to know why it is that in most places and at most times there has been a ban on, or if not a positive ban on, at least, an avoidance of, sexual relations between primary kin. So unthinking is our acceptance of this situation that it is often difficult to drive home to people that there is anything to explain. In fact, in the eyes of many thinkers, there is *everything* to explain. If, the argument goes, man had not at some time or other instituted the ban on intra-familial sex, then there would have been no culture, no society; man would have remained in an incestuous animal-like state. Thus, they put the incest taboo at the heart of our humanity. This, as I have already said, assumes that if not forbidden man would be avidly incestuous. We will return to this point.

The placing of incest at the heart of human development raises another point about what we wish to explain. Do we wish to say why the taboo was first instituted – to explain its origins – or do we wish to say why, whatever its origins, it persists. This is important because the reasons for its genesis may not be the same as the reasons for its persistence.

II

Let us look then at the reasons for its persistence that have been mooted. Here there have been three main focal-points of explanation:

a. Why would it be disadvantageous or disastrous to the family, in particular, or society, in general, for sexual relations to take place in the family?

b. Why are people motivated to practise or to avoid such relations?

c. Why do most societies forbid them and punish breaches of the rule?

Now point (c) – which concerns the incest taboo proper – may or may not follow from (a) and (b). Societies do not always do what is to their advantage; the fact that people do not want to have incestuous relationships does not necessarily mean that the society will forbid them; and so on. The answers to these questions may be the reasons why incest is forbidden but it has to be demonstrated that they are, not just assumed.

Explanations of these various points may conflict, or at least not coincide. Let us consider them in turn.

a. *Reasons why intra-familial sex would be disastrous.* Incest is sometimes stated to be disadvantageous to society because it prevents the growth of wide networks of social relationships. This explanation confuses incest taboo and exogamy, of course, and those who see this realize that if the explanation is to be in terms of sexual relations alone, then some other hypothesis is necessary which says that if people have incestuous sexual relationships then they will not want others. There is no evidence that this is so. In some societies fathers are allowed sexual intercourse with their daughters, and the daughters subsequently marry other men without, seemingly, any problems arising. There are many known cases of father-daughter incest (ask any social worker) which do not seem to result in unbreakable bonds. There may be something in the argument but again it has to be proved, not just assumed. If, then, it is possible to have incestuous relationships and still marry out, the advantages of marrying out do not explain the prohibition on sex. They may have a lot to do with the rules of exogamy, as we shall see.

Another disadvantage of incest is said to be the confusion of relationships that would follow if incestuous unions were allowed. As with the man in the song 'I'm my own grandpa', people in incestuous families would be confused as to who they were. This argument is as old as Philo the Alexandrine and as recent as Kingsley Davis. Thus, it says, if a man had a child by his own daughter, then the child would be a brother to its own mother and wouldn't that be confusing. You can run through the catastrophic combinations for yourself if you wish to waste that much time. The theory is really too silly to dwell on, but as some people take it seriously we may as well spell out the objections. Again it confuses incest with exogamy, but more importantly it confuses role with biology. It doesn't take into account that a person can only be one person at a time. If, in the case of a simple incestuous act, the said daughter has a son, he would be her offspring, and it would make no difference if the genitor were her own father or the milkman or an anonymous donor. Even if the mating of father and daughter were formalized and she became his wife, what would follow? She simply exchanges the role of daughter for that of wife.

Her children are still her children and are socially the children of their father. That the latter is genetically their mother's begetter is neither here nor there. After all, in Tibet and other parts of the world, a man may marry a mother *and* her daughter, which is not far removed from what we are contemplating. In many cases of consummated incest the daughter 'steps into the shoes of', that is – takes over the role of – her mother.

Another argument says that incest (or do we mean marriage?) across the generations is 'impossible' because it upsets the authority relations in the family. If this is put in the form that mothers will not share their husbands with their daughters it looks a bit thin. I doubt if mothers have much of a say in it when it occurs. But consider the popular African form of marriage with the wife's sister's daughters. Here a wife shares a husband with her nieces and nothing untoward seems to occur. Add this to the Tibetan example and the argument looks implausible. On the other hand, one can perhaps admit that it is unlikely that a father will want to share his wife or wives with his sons. But if we turn again to Tibet, we find the system of *fraternal polyandry* with several brothers sharing a wife. The age range of these brothers is often large, and the eldest is thought to be in control much as a father is. Here there has developed a system of regulated sexual access within the 'family' which shows that such a method is not impossible.

The prime objection to incest however – the trump card for those who claim that it is disadvantageous to society and hence could not be universally practised – is the inbreeding argument. This is quite simple: incest would be disastrous because the genetic results of persistent close inbreeding would be disastrous. The evidence on the latter point seems to me to be confused and as a layman in genetics I find it hard to follow the twists and turns of the argument. Some authorities seem to think that there is evidence that persistent inbreeding would produce deleterious results, others think it may or may not do so, while yet others seem to think that positive benefits might accrue from it. The weight of opinion *seems* to be that it would do more harm than good, but this is not certain. It certainly seems to be a fixed idea in local folk-genetics that inbreeding produces monsters and idiots. But this is not a universal notion and does not follow with experience in animal breeding. However, even if it were true, how would it help to explain the incest taboo/avoidance? Either we would have to posit a natural selection argument and say that the groups that did not practise familial outbreeding perished for their errors, leaving only those groups who bred-out to survive; or we would have to put it down to conscious insight and say that mankind came to notice the bad results and so came down hard on incest. In either of these cases, we are moving from a mere statement of possible disasters to a statement of reasons for the inception of the taboo.

This latter point brings out the problem with all the 'dire consequences' argument that we have been examining. To say that incest has dire consequences does not *necessarily* explain why it is tabooed or avoided. If it is put the other way round, that is, if the 'functions' of incest taboos are stressed, we are not much better off. Thus it is sometimes put in the form that 'the function of the incest taboo is to ...'. You can fill in the blank with any of the previous theories – widen social relations, prevent confusion, stop conflict in the family, prevent inbreeding, and many others. It may be true that it has these happy consequences, but they do not necessarily explain why it was instituted or why it persists. As we saw with the last example, we have either to look for an argument such as natural selection, or to posit conscious insight, in order to bridge this explanatory gap. This leads us on to the next problem.

b. *Reasons why people are motivated to avoid incest.* There have been many reasons put forward why people either do not want to commit incest, or shy away from it, or are horrified at it. These, as we have seen, are often linked to the 'dire consequences' arguments. Thus, people are said to see, for example, that there are terrible genetic consequences or that the family would get confused, or something such. The trouble with this is that people put forward a bewildering variety of reasons for avoiding incest. Many have the air of rationalizations. Even if it were proved beyond doubt that incest had no bad genetic consequences, would people who had previously given this as a reason against incest then feel relieved and start practising it? I doubt it.

Another reason that has been canvassed is that there is an instinctive aversion to incest. This has been ridiculed, but at least it has the merits of stating the *mechanism* by which incest aversion is said to operate. The argument raised against it is simple: if there were such an instinct then why should there be prohibitions? Why prohibit what nobody wants to do anyway? I feel that this rejection is too facile and will take up the point later. The same objection is advanced against Westermarck's argument that familiarity breeds contempt. This says that people brought up in close familiarity from childhood will be blunted in their sexual appetites for each other. Again the objection is raised, why prohibitions in this case? And again I think this is too facile an objection.

Another argument is that we all *do* want to commit incest. Anthropologists who object strenuously to the instinct and familiarity theses don't always seem to realize that they must of necessity embrace this argument.

The strongest proponents of the 'natural desire' theory are of course the followers of Freud. In this theory, we are all consumed with incestuous desires which we repress. It is not clear how this works. Freudian fundamentalists still accept his view that this repression is inherited. Thus, in the primeval situation (time unspecified), the young males of the horde killed off the old male in order to get at the

females he monopolized. But because they had been conditioned to obey him, they felt remorse and guilt about this
and so renounced the females. We have been guilty about
it ever since, and so although we still have incestuous desires,
we repress them through the mechanism of our inherited
guilt. This theory has been ridiculed in its turn, but Freud
was stressing what most anthropologists have stressed – that
we had to become non-incestuous to become human. What
he is saying is that the business of becoming so may have
been painful, bloody and traumatic, and have left its mark.
Again, although we might be dubious about the theory, it
has the merit of stating the mechanisms involved, and as we
discover more about primate society and early man, we will
be able to construct, perhaps, a more plausible theory about
the transition to humanity. I would not be as prepared
as most of my colleagues to ridicule Freud. He was probably wrong about the details, but he asked the right questions.

And this leaves us with the problem of conscious and unconscious motivations in determining why it is that people
do not commit incest and why they punish those who do.
They may say they do not do it because the crops will fail
if they do, or God may strike them dead, or that they don't
like their sisters anyway. There is a large variety of such
conscious motivations. But it may be that they don't in
fact know why they have these reactions, which may have
been the results of early conditioning or have been inherited.
This raises a crucial point. Type a. explanations say that
societies do not practise incest because incest has dire consequences and so 'cannot' happen unless the society is to die
out. But as we have seen, this does not explain why people
do not commit incest, or why they come down on it, unless
one posits that they see the possible dire consequences, or
that they have somehow inherited the appropriate attitude.
Thus, one has to be careful not to jump from explanations of
the *consequences* of the avoidance of incest (social survival e.g.),
to explanations of the *motivations* for incest avoidance
(conscious or unconscious).

c. *Reasons why society forbids incest and punishes offenders.*
Clearly this is connected with the other two questions, but
again there may well be no connexion between the happy
consequences of the taboo, the reasons people have for
observing it (conscious or unconscious), and the reasons
why societies have laws prohibiting incest – where they do.
People themselves may be horrified of incest because they
think it produces madness or monsters, but the law may
prohibit it because it is an offence to God for some reason
better known to Him. Laws and feelings and the happy
consequences of action do not always march hand in hand
and we may well be faced with a different explanation on
this level than was needed for the other two questions. In
small-scale homogeneous societies, all these things may well
be bound up: survival, feelings and sanctions may well be
closely related. But this is not universally so.

III

To recapitulate, then, we are faced with explanations of

1. Incest taboo (sexual restrictions) and exogamy rules
(conjugal restrictions).

2. Origins and persistence of 1.

3. Consequences (survival, good breeding, etc.), motivations (fear, indifference etc.), and sanctions.

These may all be related, but unless we keep the distinctions clear we will never discover the relations.

One problem with all these theories – other than the way
some of them jump from consequences to causes – is their
claim to universality. The result of this claim is that they
run up against each other and seem irreconcilable. Take
the following two:

a. There cannot be sex in the family because of its authority structure. If incest were allowed then there would be
fights over the women which would be disastrous, etc. etc.

b. There cannot be sex in the family because this would
dam up libidinous energy in this unit and people would
have no desire to leave it. First love-choices are always in-

cestuous and people have to be knocked out of them; without an incest taboo this would not occur and hence there would be no exogamy and hence . . .

Now these are clearly at odds. The first one says that the more we lie together the more we will tear each other apart: the second that the more we lie together the merrier we will be and nothing will ever tear us apart. If these are supposed to be universally true, then at least one of them must be false. Or take these two which we have encountered before:

a. People have repressed desires for incestuous relations which are very strong and hence they institute stern penalties for incest to keep them repressed.

b. People reared in close familiarity from childhood do not develop sexual feelings for each other and are therefore averse to incest.

These two cannot both be right if claimed to be universally true. But in any of these four cases, need the truth seen by these very intelligent observers necessarily be universal? Must all people in all societies at all times have had repressed incest wishes? Must all cases of intra-familial sex lead to conflict for women? The very rigidity of the theories makes them difficult to use and is in stark contrast to the malleability of human beings.

There is not in fact a universal horror of incest, and many societies do not have severe penalties for it; others practise it, and in yet others there does seem to be a genuine indifference to it. When one begins to look at these differentials then the question becomes not one of finding some good knock-down universal answer, but of asking about the *range of variation*. By and large incest does not occur or is forbidden or both (although this is less universal than is commonly imagined), but it does not follow that in all times and in all places it is outlawed for the same reasons and for the same motives. Societies, cultures and typical personalities differ quite markedly and so do the reasons for action.

IV

While I think that this range of variation is capable of explanation (and I will later try to explain it) it would be curious indeed if a whole range of different causes had led independently to the same result in nearly all the societies of the world. To explain the near universality of some kind of incest avoidance, I think we must take up the question of origins. This is why I was chary of dismissing Freud and made a respectful bow in the direction of the natural selection theory. Let us first of all look at the latter.

The best version of it I have come across argues something like this. Man is one of those late evolutionary products which includes the larger, longer-lived, slower-maturing and more intelligent animals. Together with these he is subject to the deleterious effects of persistent close inbreeding. The theory regards this point as established. Most of the animals in the category mentioned have some mechanism for preventing persistent close inbreeding. Asexual imprinting (which need not concern us), intergenerational competition and promiscuity are the most common. With competition we get the phenomenon of the mature individuals driving out the maturing young. This reduces inbreeding as the young have to look elsewhere than their natal family for mates. Promiscuity also reduces inbreeding as it increases greatly the number of extra-familial matings. But if early man, or even his sub-human ancestors, lived – as some animals do – in relatively stable family groups (the theory assumes this too), then either expulsion or promiscuity would not be suitable as mechanisms for reducing inbreeding. As we saw in Chapter 1, one of the problems of the slow maturity of the human infant was the fact that he became sexually mature before he was fully equipped to take an independent role. And in a band society, for example, the band must stick together. Thus, the driving out of the maturing young would be disastrous and could not be a solution. Nor could promiscuity work if one assumed that relatively stable family groupings were involved. Thus we have the problem of a creature unable to expel the maturing young who are subject to an increasing sex drive. This raises the problem of conflict. The only way for the young to satisfy the sex drive, would be within the family. In many animals of the kind we have mentioned, strife amongst family members is of this nature – with the young usually being driven off.

Thus, the human animal had two problems: the problem of the effects of inbreeding, and the problem of competition in the family group. The latter could be solved as we have seen by some kind of regularized mating in the family – but this would not solve the problem of close inbreeding. The only mechanism by which *both* these problems could be met and solved was the development of a taboo on intercourse between family members. Natural selection worked, therefore, to promote the survival of those groups that bred out, and failure of those that did not.

Now this theory assumes a lot that is questionable about genetics, and about the early existence of specifically *familial* groupings. The kind of animal group to which we belong, however, does tend to form this type of group – probably a result of its long life-span and greater intelligence. What is certain is that until man developed stable familial groupings, then random promiscuity within the horde would probably have served just as well to limit the bad effects of inbreeding. It would not, however, have been quite so genetically efficient as the method proposed, and thereby may hang a tale.

If, however, we accept for the sake of argument that something like this development may have occurred (and I have done less than justice to the ingenuity of the argument), then it follows that the incest taboo is a mechanism that originated because of its superior selective advantages. But this still leaves open the question of why it cropped up in the first place. The theory of natural selection does not require this question to be answered. It does not matter why it cropped up – it can be considered a kind of mutation – it only matters that it had a superior selective advantage. Thus, those groups which refused to allow primary relatives to mate with each other survived and succeeded. The theory suggests that it was intergenerational competition that did it. The father (as in Freud's theory) would not let the sons get at the women of the family – particularly the mother. Since in many animals this is what happens, it is plausible that at least some human populations followed the same course and so survived to become our ancestors. It does not explain why the taboo should hold for fathers and daughters, but one should add that this seems to be the relationship least affected by the taboo.

Another theory is in many respects neater than this one as it does not even need to assume that natural selection was at work. This theory states, quite simply, that the demographic features of early human populations made inbreeding relatively difficult. Thus, man bred out because he had no alternative, not because of a taboo on inbreeding. Consider the demographic facts that must have been true of early human populations. Life would have been short (a maximum expectation of say 35 years), and puberty late – say 15 or later. The infant mortality rate would have been high – at least 50 per cent. Man tends to produce infants singly rather than in litters, and hence there is spacing of births. This spacing can be increased by the death of a child, and by such population-control measures as infanticide, abortion and abstinence, all of which are known to have been practised in very primitive conditions. There is also a possibility that long suckling in relatively undernourished mothers inhibits ovulation. As most children under primitive conditions suckle for a number of years, this too would limit births and increase spacing. All these factors would place severe limits on the possibilities of inbreeding. By the time a young boy reached puberty, his mother would probably be past breeding age or dead. Similarly with siblings, although the chances would be better for brothers and sisters, they would still be slender, especially if, as the theory assumes, a sexual division of labour was necessary for survival and men wanted mates for this purpose as well as simply for sex. A boy's elder sister would in all probability be 'taken' by the time he reached puberty, and he himself would be mated by the time his younger sister came of age. A run of same-sex children in the family would of course increase the chances of out-breeding.

Thus, the theory claims, the earliest hominids were per-haps unable to commit incest very often even if they wanted to. In the simplest ecologies (and similar ones exist today) most of the people most of the time mate out, not because of the problem of inbreeding and competition, but in order to mate at all.

Now again the theory assumes a good deal – usually with justification – about the social and biological conditions of the earliest humans. Some of these assumptions – like the need for a sexual division of labour and the effect of lacta-tion on pregnancy – may not be justified, but the theory has a certain attractiveness in its very simplicity. There are some facts about early hominid life that neither theory takes into account. For example, we saw in Chapter 1 that all primates living in hordes have a dominance hierarchy and that the males of this hierarchy monopolize the females. Most of the young and inadequate males are driven to the edge of the horde and shut out from the mating process. This, in itself, must have served to prevent inbreeding, but the units in-volved were hierarchical males versus non-hierarchical males, rather than 'fathers' versus 'sons' within a nuclear family. Females tended to move up and down the hierarchy, high-ranking females becoming the consorts of dominant males but also falling from grace. This too must have randomized mating, and none of these processes involves an incest taboo. It is only at a stage of cultural development when stable family groups have crystallized, that a full scale incest taboo is needed (i.e. one covering all members of the family).

What about contemporary conditions then? The demo-graphic theory and the natural selection theory both as-sume that the *consequences* of the avoidance of incest had adaptational advantages, over and above the prevention of inbreeding. These were the social advantages of the forging of wider networks of alliances for defence and economic cooperation. Thus, in kinship-based societies, the natural selection argument says, the taboo was maintained because of these advantages. The demographic argument puts it this way: because since earliest times men have bred out, they have erected a whole lot of institutions at the kinship level that assume outbreeding – that are predicated on it. Now, as technological sophistication increased, life lengthened and infant mortality and all the other barriers to incest progressively disappeared. In many societies today, therefore, it would be quite possible for most people to commit incest if they wished, i.e. there would be a partner available. But it is in a sense too late. We have already built up our societies on the premise that people will breed out of the family, and we cannot easily reverse this. The improvements we have mentioned are, in evolutionary terms, very recent. So the taboo persists. Both theories admit the possibility that it need not persist forever.

Of course, there are many examples of societies in which incest is either allowed or even enjoined for some sections of the population. (This perhaps gives the lie to the idea that people 'see' the deleterious effects and therefore ban incest.) On the demographic theory, when the possibility of incest became more common, most societies nevertheless persisted in their established pattern of outbreeding, but in some cases where the advantages were not all that obvious, and where there might have been positive advantages to inbreeding, then inbreeding was allowed or even encouraged. (For example, royal families or religious cults wishing to preserve exclusiveness of blood might practise brother-sister marriage.) The demographic theory thus neatly ties up the origins and persistence of the incest taboo.

The natural selection theory moves in this direction also. The taboo originated because of its selective advantages but had important social consequences which led to its persistence. But there is another conclusion which the theory shies away from and that is that a long process of natural selection may have produced a creature with something like an outbreeding *instinct*. I think the difficulty here is that what was produced was not necessarily a *specific* instinct. It is the idea that there may be a *specific* instinct that has been ridiculed, and perhaps rightly, but it does seem to me that a possible period of say a million and a half years of selection process should have left its mark. The mark it left is not necessarily an instinct of aversion to *incest*, because the cues are obviously difficult to establish. If a child is separated from its parents at birth, for example, how would it know who to avoid later on? But what has been produced is a syndrome of biological characteristics surrounding the sex drive, and that most important of evolutionary mechanisms – conscience.

One of man's most important features is his relatively unspecialized nature – his freedom from the domination of particular instincts. Now while this gives him great advantages it robs him of the sureness that comes from being directed by instincts. To replace this instinctive sureness, man developed the self-inhibitory mechanism of conscience. The group – the society – is the unit of human survival, and for the group to survive it must ensure that its members obey those customs and rules that time has shown to be advantageous to survival. In animals, this is ensured by the development of suitable instincts: in man it is the capacity to inhibit personal desires in favour of group rules that operates to the same ends. This capacity is lodged in the central nervous system and enables men to inhibit their own drives and to be conditioned to accept learned rules. Guilt (however mild) is the means of reminding them that they are breaking the rules. How does this tie up with incest? Well, if the natural selection theory is correct, over many thousands – even hundreds of thousands – of years, only those groups survived that instituted the incest taboo. Thus, they must have been groups in which the members were susceptible to conditioning in the sphere of sexual and aggressive behaviour to a quite remarkable degree. Sex is a human drive of high intensity and yet – and this is the rub – of high malleability. It is capable of being worked on extensively by the self-inhibitory mechanisms of conscience, perhaps because it is so strong that the nervous system goes into an inhibitory reaction against it. Aggression is a similar human propensity. Now, the groups which survived must have been groups of individuals with high aggressive-sexual drives if they were to survive and propagate. These drives were nevertheless checkable by strong inhibitory mechanisms and the internal sanctions of guilt and remorse. Only thus could the sexual drive towards the other family members, and the aggressiveness of the young males towards the older have been contained. (That this seems to work least well with fathers and daughters would fit our ideas about proto-human society and the nature of the conjugal family.) I have not any direct evidence here, except to say that it seems easier to induce guilt over sex than over any other drive (hunger isn't in the picture), with aggression not far behind. And it is a physiological fact that cortical control of sexual activity distinguishes the higher apes and Man from other animals.

Thus, on this, probably unwarranted, extension of the natural selection theory we could argue that there was a syndrome of genetically-determined behaviours which made the pubescent human in particular, susceptible to guilt and other forms of conditioning surrounding the sexual-aggressive drives. While this is not a specific anti-incest instinct, it is a set of instinctual responses which would have made the development of inhibitions over familial sexuality an easy matter, and thus led to the survival of the populations displaying these features. To the argument of 'why should we need a taboo if there is an instinct against the practice of incest' – I think the above serves as a partial reply. And in any case, the more we learn about instincts the more we realize that 'instincts' are really potentials for behaviour and they need 'releasers' – cues in the environment – for their full realization. Many circumstances in so malleable a creature as Man might act to prevent the proper realization of these inhibitory mechanisms and so render incest a possibility. Hence, the rest of the population might well feel it necessary to have some kind of sanctions to prevent the occurrence of something they know they feel 'guilty' about and hence must be wrong.

V

This point about the malleability of human beings needs pushing a little further, as I think it helps to explain the range of variation in the reactions to incest that we noted earlier. If we accept, on one or the other of the origin theories, that Man somehow became 'stuck' with the incest taboo even though he perhaps didn't realize why he had originated it, we still have to explain why there seems to be a wide range of variation in the enthusiasm with which he pursues offenders against it, and in the horror with which he regards it, and even in the laxity he allows to creep in at many points over the practice of it.

Let us note first that it is no good to lump all incest under one heading as many writers do. This is to ignore the crucial fact that the three possibilities – father-daughter, brother-sister, and mother-son – are in many ways quite different. The clearest difference lies between intergenerational incest and sibling incest. In the intergenerational cases we have the interaction of mature organisms with maturing organisms over a long period; in the sibling case we have the interaction of two maturing organisms. The next most important difference is in the mother-child versus father-child situations. This harks back to our discussion of the conjugal family and the very different places that the father and mother have vis-à-vis their children. These differences are reflected in known rates of occurrence. These are hard to come by for obvious reasons, but my reading of the situation is that father-daughter is easily the most common, brother-sister variable but not so common, and mother-son rare or non-existent. This latter seems reasonable perhaps in that by the time a man reaches maturity he will probably not want to have much to do with a relatively aged woman. This of course will be less true in

advanced societies where puberty is earlier and women
well-preserved longer, but here as elsewhere father is likely
to come down hard on this one. The brother-sister relationship is peculiarly open to variations in socialization experience. Father and daughter, however, are clearly most open
to incestuous possibilities. Neither relative age nor authority
are likely to interfere here, and this is brought out in the
rates of occurrence. But all these are malleable relationships
and the sexual content of them can be heightened or lessened
by a host of socio-cultural conditions. Sexual behaviour, as
we have seen, is based on so strong a drive that it is peculiarly
subject to conditioning. I would suspect, for example, that
those societies that make a great song and dance about incest –
burning offenders at the stake and the like – make a hefty
fuss about other things sexual as well. On the other hand,
societies which are relatively indifferent to incest probably
have pretty low-keyed sex lives all round. The price we
pay for the malleability and conditionability of our sex
drives is what Freud called the 'vicissitudes of the *id*' – the
fact that our sexuality is capable of a high degree of variation and perversion.

A point I have been making throughout this chapter is
that incest is not so much *prevented* as avoided. It rarely needs
fierce sanctions and superstitious horrors to prevent people
from committing incest – they just seem to avoid it anyway.
They reject it because they don't want it. The sanctions
have to be explained but, as we have seen, they may not
be related to the way people feel about incest. There seems
to have grown up an anthropological folk-belief that all
incest sanctions are fierce – but this is not so. Some are
extremely mild, and in some societies the whole matter is
left to the workings of conscience and self-punishment. In
many societies, there is simply an indifference – a feeling
that only half-wits would want to sleep with their sisters
anyway. It is 'disgusting' and such people would be thought
disreputable and perhaps mildly rebuked; but no one gets
into a sweat about it.

Now, if incest is generally avoided how do we get round

the problem posed for both the 'instinct' theory and the 'familiarity breeds contempt' theory: if it is avoided why do we need sanctions? The answer to this is that for one thing there are not always sanctions and for another that avoidance is never complete. The fact that most men are heterosexual does not preclude the existence of homosexuals. The same is the case with incest. There will always be a minority that will want to do it even if the majority don't – and the minority has to be pulled into line. Very few murders are committed each year, but this does not stop us from having fierce sanctions against murder. The fact is that most people do not murder other people and our institutions are predicated on the fact that this is so. So most people do not commit incest and our institutions (and particularly those of primitive societies) assume this to be the case. Therefore sanctions have to be instituted, however mild, to keep the deviants in line. The ferocity of these sanctions is probably related to the general ferocity of the society concerned, and as we have said to the relaxed or anxiety-riddled nature of its sexual life. The focusing of explanation on sanctions has been perhaps the worst red herring in this tortuous debate.

I would assert then that incest is generally avoided rather than actively prevented, and I would add another premise – that sexual relationships between primary relatives are not in any way different from those between non-relatives. Thus I would not subscribe, as I have said, to the notion of a specific instinct regarding intra-familial sex. This rules out both the notions of 'natural' avoidance and 'natural' incest-desire. What is different about family members is their close association with each other. It is the turns that this takes that will determine whether or not there will be indifference to incest or excruciating horror over it.

We can perhaps set up two extreme types. In the first type the socialization process is 'easy'. Siblings are allowed a great deal of familiarity with each other, and parents with their children. As a result of this, their sexual attraction for each other is muted – reduced to a low key – and as long as there are plenty of sex objects other than family members, the children of the family will choose voluntarily to mate-out at puberty. Why this muting of sexual attraction might occur (and it does seem to very often) is difficult to say. I have previously suggested either that sheer physical interaction might produce it (there is animal evidence for this), or that boredom may be involved. The first condition depends on physiological arguments that may be incorrect, but the second is the true 'familiarity breeds contempt' argument. It says that the male is usually the initiator of sexual inter-action, and that the male primate at least (although pri-mates are not alone in this) thrives on *variety* of stimuli. The same sexual stimulus repeatedly presented leads to 'stimulus saturation' – or as we might say, boredom. The animal is simply not roused after a certain point. Breeders find this with cattle and zoo animals, and men who insist that their wives change hairstyles frequently are probably uncon-sciously reacting to the same problem. Whichever of these views or combination of them is correct – and I cannot spell out the details here – then a spontaneous avoidance of the opposite-sex family member at puberty would result. Father and daughter are probably the least intimate of all members and hence the syndrome may not operate as well for them as it does for the others.

Now at the other extreme we have a type in which the sexual life of the family is not easy. For whatever reason, there may be considerable prudery and modesty in the family with the result that the members remain 'strangers' to each other. Under these circumstances they will be as sexually arousing to each other at puberty as strangers will. No process has intervened to produce a natural aversion. It may be that they can easily turn to other sexual partners at puberty thus easing the strain, but it is probable that in such a society there will be restrictions (on premarital sexuality, for example) that may prevent this. If these people are then in any way cooped-up together, then they will have an acute problem. It may solve itself in that the very strength of the drive may be such as to produce its own inhibition. People are so scared of strong sexual feelings towards their family members that they withdraw into fantasy, producing weird incest myths, or they project their feelings onto witches who commit incest with impunity, or they work the whole thing out of their systems, when anyone does give way and commit the super-crime, by killing them with revolting tortures etc.

Now these are two extremes, and societies probably fall along a continuum from one to the other with many other factors intervening to heighten or lessen the sexual feelings between family members. But this would account for the range of variation. It would also solve the problem of the seemingly intractable opposition of Freud's and Westermarck's theories – the 'natural desire' versus 'natural aversion' argument. If neither of these is taken as universal then they can be fitted neatly into the picture.

VI

The point we have arrived at is as follows: the incest taboo – that is the notion that incestuous matings should be avoided – is part of our cultural heritage. It originated either because it was of selective advantage in preventing the disastrous results of inbreeding, or because it was the inevitable outcome of demographic limitations on inbreeding. In either case, it became woven into the fabric of our institutions, and was taken as a kind of 'given' by all societies that developed. However, once the period of early natural selection and demographic limitations was over, there was not always quite such a good reason for the taboo. In this case it was either relaxed or preserved according to a number of factors. On the whole, however, it was preserved. This might be because there are biological factors which make for the rapid learning of feelings of guilt and inhibition over early sex experiences – factors which may have developed through natural selection to cope with the problem of perpetuating the taboo; or because of equally biologically based factors of inhibition which work to produce aversion; or because, even in the absence of these, other inhibitory responses are generated. In any of these cases the results will not be perfect. Incest does sometimes occur. But usually for one reason or another it does not. And if all laws against it were dropped tomorrow it still would not.

The reader will no doubt be dismayed to hear, having ploughed through this chapter, that this is not even the half of it. I have only been able to skim the surface of the complexities involved. But let no one now say that there is nothing to explain.

CHAPTER THREE

Local Groups and Descent Groups

I

IN this chapter I want to take up the themes touched on in Chapter 1 regarding the various modes of recruitment to kinship groups. We saw that there were a limited number of possibilities, and that the limits were set by our four Principles. (See p. 31.) I want to discuss here the ways in which such possibilities might become probabilities; in other words, *why* some societies have chosen to institutionalize one or other of these modes of kinship organization. Now here I make an assumption that no society does this in an arbitrary way. People do not sit down as we did in Chapter 1 and say – 'Now look, there are three possible ways of deciding who shall be members of kinship groups, which shall we choose?' This 'choice' is in fact developed out of real situations in which groups of men try to master, or at least not succumb to, their environments and other groups. To meet these situations they form kinship groups, or evolve methods of transferring property rights from generation to generation through kinship links. At some point in human development, choices may be more or less forced onto groups; at other points, they may be in a position to determine these things with more freedom. Thus societies *do* legislate about kinship; but even so, they do so as a result of changed circumstances and fresh exigencies.

The angle from which I will approach this topic is, as I have said, that of group formation. The forming of groups is, as we have seen, only one of the tasks of kinship. Thus, a society in which property passed exclusively through males could in some sense be called 'patrilineal' even though there were no patrilineal descent groups present; the patrilineal principle would be restricted to the regulation of inheritance.

But the principles and problems of kinship systems stand out more starkly if we consider group formation. And it is my hunch that, in an evolutionary sense, the formation of groups came before more abstract principles of kinship ideology. This distinction and its importance should emerge as we pursue the issue of the change from kinship systems composed of simple residential groups, to more elaborate systems. Let us look then at some simple 'ideal type' situations and see what kinds of groupings of kinsfolk they might produce.

We might as well start with our 'basic' group of mother and children. As a result of several acts of sexual congress the mother has produced a number of boys and girls. Thus, there exists the basic unit and the male or males who produced it. What thereafter happens to the group depends largely on factors external to it. If these permit the group to subsist without the help of a specifically attached adult male, then the group could survive and the young reach maturity. It may be, for example, that the adult males of the horde as a whole look after the women and children as a whole. Even if a specific male has to be attached, it need not be father. If the bond of mother and child is indeed strong, then there is no need why it should ever be broken. Father will go back to his mother, and the children stay with theirs. The logical conclusion of such a system, once it has received its initial push, would be a series of groups composed thus:

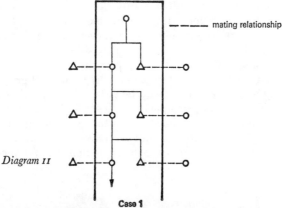

Diagram 11

Case 1

i.e. mothers and their children in successive generations. Alternatively we could phrase it as 'brothers' and 'sisters' and the children of the sisters. As such a group proliferated over time, of course, the actual biological relationship between the members would get to be remote, and we might expect that it would split up into smaller units.

The basic unit here is as much the pair of siblings as the mother and children. The brother and sister make up the unit, with the children of the sister, and then the children of her daughters, grand-daughters, great grand-daughters etc. until such time as the unit splits up. The brothers remain attached to their sisters and have loose mating relationships with women of other such units without ever being really 'detached' from their natal group. The sisters on the other hand will have loose mating arrangements with men of other such units without ever joining them. Here the consanguine unit and residential unit are coincident.

Clearly this is a feasible and logical arrangement. To some evolutionary writers it was the only really logical arrangement. The only biological necessity is that the women become impregnated from time to time. The male care and protection can come from the mother's brothers – father is redundant except in his role as impregnator. The ties between siblings are basic, as is the tie between mother and child from which the sibling tie is derived. Ties between mates are not basic and have to be enforced. Why bother to enforce them when this arrangement can be instituted?

This is not a contingency existing only in the cunning brains of anthropologists. There are societies that follow this pattern of grouping with various modifications today, as we shall see in later chapters. At the moment, I only want to establish the possibility.

Of course, the environment may not favour such a method of grouping. If, for example, one is not living in a cosy horde, then things are different. The area may not be able to support a large horde. Thus a smaller group becomes a necessity for survival. The above method would not really work if these groups were scattered because the sexual and reproductive needs of the group members could not easily be met. (Remember the year-round fertility and constant sexual appetite of the human.) The 'sisters' have to be impregnated for survival, and the brothers (and the sisters too of course) have to have their sexual drives satisfied. They could, of course, satisfy each other's and solve the problem, but *Homo sapiens* was never for an easy way out and this runs up against Principle 4.

Hence, once the young have reached maturity they may be forced into leaving the family and setting up for themselves. If the groups are isolated, then the only feasible way this can be done is to link male and female in a fairly permanent sexual union. This produces the nuclear family. It is not of course the only thing that produces the nuclear family. In our own society this unit has emerged from the breakdown of a more extensive grouping, for example, but it illustrates the kind of pressures which can produce the essential link between mates and offspring.

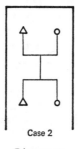

Case 2

Diagram 12

A much more likely and much more prevalent arrangement is one which is forced onto a population of an area by the exigencies of hunting, herding or farming. If these require a fairly large labour-force of males, and if these males need to be carefully trained up from birth, then an arrangement like the one we discussed first is scarcely feasible. It is much more likely that fathers will really stick around and try to raise suitable male offspring. They will need women for this purpose, and so will have to obtain wives. The resultant group will be as follows, with 'sisters' being exported to other groups and wives brought in:

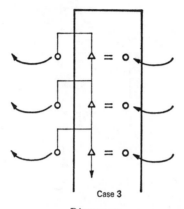

Case 3

Diagram 13

This differs radically from the first possibility in that here the 'marriage' tie is firmly established and necessary to the continuity of the group. Also, it differs from the second in that the tie between a man and his offspring is firmly established – at least his male offspring. Thus, father has really come home to stay; and as we might expect, out of rank self-interest.

We might get him home on a shaky but relatively permanent basis in another set of circumstances. If, for example, there was a situation which allowed mothers and daughters to form a viable unit, but in which they needed male help, it may be that, instead of relying on brothers they would import husbands. Again, problems of relative isolation may be involved. Thus, the women may be the agriculturalists and the men the hunters, with the women living together in a series of scattered settlements. The only really feasible arrangement here would be the following in which 'brothers' were exported and 'husbands' brought in from other groups:

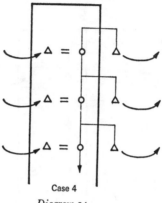

Case 4

Diagram 14

This has similar features to the first arrangement, but again, it involves an institutionalization of marriage and co-residence that the first does not. It could, however, work on a high turnover of husbands while Case 3 could not really work on a high turnover of wives. The point of getting the wives in after all was to hang onto them for purposes of producing and rearing offspring. This is a prolonged business and requires that the wife stick around until the child is mature enough to leave her. By then, of course, she is pregnant again so she can't win. In our latest arrangement, however, the husband can leave anytime without much damage being done, and in actual empirical examples of this type of grouping he usually does, although not inevitably.

The number of possibilities of grouping, given some environmental pressures of the kind envisaged above, is not

large. It is limited by the possibilities inherent in the biological situation of human breeding. Of those groupings
that are possible, not all have been tried – or rather if they
have they haven't all survived. One other possibility with a
little more flexibility than the above might arise from the
fact that while males need to cooperate, it might not matter
too much if they had not all been associated from early
childhood. In an economic system such as farming often
presents, where skills are readily transferable from one farm
to another, then any adult male is as good as any other.
Thus, we might get a situation which was indifferent as to
whether the males were 'sons and brothers' or 'sons-in-
law and brothers-in-law', or a mixture. Schematically we
could envisage it roughly as follows:

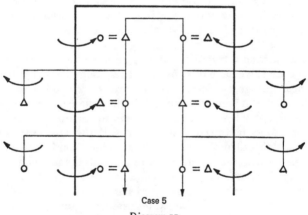

Case 5

Diagram 15

In this case, either daughters stay and bring in husbands or
sons stay and bring in wives. All that matters is that there
shall be enough males and females in the unit – but not too
many. The flexibility of this system makes for mobility and
easy distribution of population among farming units.

II

The reader who has been referring back to Chapter One will have seen that Cases 1 and 4 look very 'matrilineal'; Case 3 has all the features of our 'patrilineal' example; and Cases 2 and 5 involve cognatic principles. But here we should pause and note that this is not because any of these peoples have institutionalized rules and regulations concerning modes of tracing kinship. They are *de facto* matrilineal or patrilineal or cognatic, not *de jure*. And in fact they may not be thorough-going in their approximation to one or other of these principles except in Case 1. What happens, for example, to the 'brothers' in Case 4, or to the 'sisters' in Case 3? They are lost to the core of the residential group. On either of our unilineal principles they remain 'related' to the core members – they are members of the same consanguine group; but do any such consanguine groups exist here? Obviously not, at this stage, but there are the germs of them. It is clear that it will only take a small push, in some of these cases, to produce groups of people claiming descent from a common ancestor on one of our Principles. In Case 1, we have this anyway. The group here is a matrilineal lineage by default, as it were. It does not have to decide that it will 'trace kinship in the female line only' – it has no option. As 'fathers' are not in the picture, then kinship cannot be traced through males. But what about Case 4? If the exiled brothers could somehow continue to associate with the sisters who remain at home, then we would have our matrilineal consanguine group. What we have at the moment are groups based on some principle of common residence. Case 4, for example, would be known in anthropological parlance as *matrilocal* residence, because the couple on marriage live with the wife's mother. The term *uxorilocal* has been suggested – meaning living in the wife's group – and is perhaps better. Sometimes the compound *matri-uxorilocal* is used. For Case 3 the opposites, *patrilocal, virilocal,* or *patri-virilocal* are employed. All these are somewhat tortuous, but they provide a convenient shorthand. For Case 1 there is no agreed term but perhaps *natolocal* is best, implying as it does that the spouses stay in their natal homes on marriage – if indeed marriage is involved in this case. We can complete the list by adding *neolocal* for Case 2; the couple form a *new* residential group on marriage. Case 5 has no agreed term to describe it as it is characterized by a lack of a firm rule. Perhaps *ambilocal* will do, implying, as it does, that there is a choice involved. I give these terms because some of them crop up so often in the literature that it is well to be armed with them. They all refer to the mode of residence at marriage – who moves where.

There is one point that also harks back to Chapter 1 and that has to be dealt with. Our groups will obviously grow and proliferate, and after one generation will in all probability come to contain people who are not siblings but cousins. The matrilocal group (Case 4) will contain people who are the children of sisters, and the grandchildren of sisters – matrilineally related cousins. If these were to marry, then there would be no need for the group to look outside itself for spouses. The same would apply to the other cases. However, as we saw, the rule of exogamy – 'out-marriage' – tends to apply to these groups; not always, but in a majority of cases. Again, we will deal with this when marriage is discussed in more detail; for the time being we will have to take it for granted. It is important because it means that our groups will have to look elsewhere than among their own members for spouses – matrilocal groups for husbands and patrilocal for wives. Case 1 is perhaps rather special here as 'husbands' are more or less unnecessary to it.

III

It might help, at this juncture, if we looked at some examples from actual societies which showed these factors at work – particularly if we could find examples of moves from simple residential groups to descent-group structures. Luckily there are examples of the latter.

I am a little wary of introducing examples at all into this book. This is perhaps unusual as anthropologists are, of all social scientists, the most unhappy sufferers of 'amongitis' – the disease characterized by starting almost every utterance with 'among the so-and-so'. This ethnographic detail tends, in my aberrant opinion, to fog more issues than it illuminates. This does not mean that the details are unimportant, but that we have to get the issues and questions straight before we can argue about the nuances. No tribe is obliging enough to produce a system that corresponds point for point with an ideal type, any more than any economic system corresponds exactly with the model of 'perfect competition'. But without the models and the types, we would find it impossible to make sense of economic or kinship systems.

We might take as our starting point the Shoshone Indians who lived primarily in Utah and Nevada but spilled over into western Colorado, eastern Oregon, and northern California. They were divided into various loosely defined groups, the Ute, the Paiute and the Shoshone, who were themselves subdivided into smaller loosely organized bands. Now, the territory of the Shoshone was a high desert plateau, a truly inhospitable and harsh environment. High population centres were impossible, as the country could not support them. There was scattered small game and few root crops, and it took an enormous area to supply even a few people with their needs. Thus, a situation such as we described for Case 2 existed, in which the most adaptive unit for exploiting this type of country was the nuclear family. Once the young of the family reached maturity, they sought marriage partners from other families and set off on their wandering in search of food. They did not, however, lose contact with their families of origin. There were periods when the cooperation of several families was needed for the collective hunting of small game – rabbits in particular – and also for religious ceremonies. On these occasions, the families living in closest proximity to each other and related in some way to each other, would gather and camp together. Marriages would in all likelihood be arranged on these occasions.

The individual family, then, was largely self-sufficient. It gathered its own food and made its own weapons. But these families were scattered over such large distances that the only feasible form of marriage arrangement was one involving the young of nearby families. It was these families that cooperated when cooperation was needed – when Shoshone bands were attacked by other Indians, for example – and thus the unit of the society over and above the nuclear family was a group of interrelated families. The ideal form of marriage was 'sister exchange'. In this, the sons and daughters of one family would marry the daughters and sons of another. This linked the two families and the families of the children in a convenient way. Demographic pressures, of course, made it impossible always to have the right number of children of each sex to exchange, so both forms of plural marriage were practised. A son of one family would sometimes marry two or more daughters of an adjacent family (*polygyny*). Alternatively, if a family had only one daughter it could give her in marriage to two or more sons of another (*polyandry*). These were usually temporary arrangements as the nuclear family was the ideal unit for survival.

This is, however, a pretty simple system. But it has the germs of much more complex arrangements in it. Already we see that some kind of systematic exchange of women between families was favoured for the setting up of links, and that plural marriage of both kinds was practised as an expedient. Also, wherever possible, brothers tried to remain in the same territory, even when they split up, so that the larger group which met for hunting, war, or ceremony, would perhaps have a patrilocal tinge to it. This would be strong or weak according to the demands of the terrain and the scattering of families etc.

More interesting for our purposes – although the patrilocal tendency should be kept in mind for future reference – was the fate of some Shoshone who wandered to the southern boundary of their territory. Here they found an area which, while still desert-like, was suitable for some small-scale agriculture. There was water from the rivers for minor irrigation, and stone from the mountains for building houses. Their area was probably already occupied by some agriculturalists whom the Shoshone assimilated. The amount of agriculture – the cultivation of maize largely – was still limited, and so the men had to supplement this with hunting. A sexual division of labour was established, with the women tending the crops and the men doing the hunting. The ideal set-up, then, as we have seen, was the matrilocal residential group. A small group consisting of perhaps an old grandmother, her daughters, and their daughters, lived in a house or group of connected houses and looked after the plots of corn. To these houses came husbands who spent most of their time away in hunting or warfare or religious activity with other males of the band. This latter would be a group of related households holding a common territory.

We do not know the exact form of social organization that must have prevailed, but it must have been something like this: relatively isolated houses with their women, and the men – somewhat peripheral to these residential units – perhaps loosely attached to them. The ecological and military conditions were such that large population centres were impossible or, even if marginally possible, not necessary. Now, these reformed Shoshone for some reason moved further south. They may have been forced south by marauding bands of Apaches from the north. But, in any case, they moved into larger agglomerations and either began to build for themselves, or take over from previous inhabitants, large compact villages or groups of related villages. At first, these were built in the valleys, but finally they came to rest on the tops of the great *mesas* – high flat-topped spurs of rock in the Arizona desert, not far from the Grand Canyon. They became the Hopi Indians, one of the best known tribes in anthropological literature.

When they moved into their larger villages, the matrilocal household remained (and remains to this day) the basic unit of their social organization. But an important consequence followed from the crowding together of the previously scattered households. The men born into the

household – the natal members – had previously been lost
to it on marriage. They had gone perhaps many miles away
and become totally absorbed in another unit. They may
have returned home from time to time – on divorce or
estrangement, for example – but they cannot have been able
to keep up any constant contact with their natal households. Once in the villages, however, such contact became
easy and natural. The loose nature of marital arrangements,
for example, might have sent the men frequently back to
their natal homes. Indeed, a situation approaching our
Case 1 might well have developed in which men never left
their natal homes at all except for the brief mating expedi-
tions; but things never went quite that far, staying at a high
turnover of husbands. The pattern of landholding was
maintained in the villages. Patches of land went with the
houses and were owned by the women. The men of the
household helped to work the land, as by now agriculture
had become more important, but the produce stayed with
the women to be used by them for the household members.

Out of this situation an organization of genuine descent
groups emerged. *De facto* matrilineages of course existed
as long as all the household members all associated together, but things went further than this. The religious
ceremonies of the Hopi centre on certain fetishes and religious paraphernalia, and these, in the early days of this
group's development had been kept in their only structures –
the houses. Thus, each house would have a fetish attached
to it. Now the care and protection of these fetishes was in
the hands of the women of the house, but the conduct of
the religious ceremonies was in the hands of men – remember Principle 3. Thus, there was a firm religious basis to the
growth of descent groups: the ritual property of the house.
It is likely that each of the houses was named after some
natural phenomenon: rabbit, sun, corn, antelope, snake etc.
These named houses became the basis for the growth of
clans.

Each household, as we have seen, has two lots of males
attached to it: the husbands who are relatively peripheral,

and the natal males – the 'brothers' – who are permanently attached, even if not permanently resident. This group of resident women and natal males is a matrilineal group – a lineage. But households grow and get too large; some daughters move off and form new households. However, when they do so, they retain the name of the original house – they are 'rabbits' or 'snakes' or whatever. Thus there grows up a body of households all bearing the same name – and more importantly, all attached to the same fetish and its rituals. It may be that over time the original house will be forgotten, and people will forget exactly how they are related to each other – but they will still know that they are rabbits or snakes, and hence that they are related through the female line to all other rabbits and snakes. Another contingency that might arise is the dying out of one household completely. What then happens to its lands? The answer is that they pass to another of the related households – to another snake or rabbit.

Such groups as we have described, which claim common descent from a common ancestor, even if they cannot demonstrate exactly how this descent came about, are known as *clans*. They differ from lineages as the word is usually used in that members may not be able to state their exact links to each other. But, in effect, they can be thought of as long-lived lineages. Sometimes, they have a legend that they are all in fact descended in some miraculous way from the animal whose name they bear: that the snake or rabbit is their ultimate ancestor. It is common to call such an ancestor the '*totem*' of the clan. The Hopi have no such belief, but usage is loose enough to allow their eponyms to be called totems.

Clans then are descent groups whose members claim to be descended – on one principle or another – from a common ancestor. We have seen here how, in one society, a clan system may have originated as an extension of the matrilocal system. I must stress that this is only one way in which matrilineal clans and lineages can originate. There are other ways, and we may be able to consider these. But it is important to know, if the knowledge is obtainable, how the system originated, because much of its present organization will rest on this historic factor. Simply to say of two societies that they have matrilineal descent groups in fact tells us very little about them, because as we shall see, there are many different types of such groupings which have grown up in different ways.

For the moment, the reader should try to picture an ideal type of matrilineal descent group. It will have an ultimate (real or mythical) ancestor, and all the members will be descended from this ancestor in the female line. They may all be living together, or they may be scattered. From the point of view of the individual, his closest matrilineal relatives will be his siblings, and his mother and her siblings. His senior male relative will be the brother (probably the eldest) of his mother. Thus amongst the Hopi, priesthoods are held by the matriclans and in particular by lineages within the clans. If a priest dies, then it should be one of his sister's sons who succeeds him in the office.

It is perhaps more common for matriclans to grow up out of a concern for property or defence. Thus, those marauding Apaches that we mentioned earlier as having driven the Shoshone southwards present an interesting picture. They came in in several waves from the north and settled all around the Hopi and other indigenous dwellers of the southwest U.S.A. Some of their number in the east – the Mescalero and Chiricahua of television fame for example – developed a system of matrilocal groupings. They remained primarily hunters and warriors and their organization never got beyond this simple residential base. In the west, however, the Western Apache and the even more famous Navaho took up limited farming and developed matriclans out of their matrilocal material. They may have been influenced by the Hopi in this – but their process of development was similar. Here, however, it was not agglomeration into larger settlements that did it. For the Western Apache, it worked something like this: farm sites came to have names, and the group of related matrilocal units who worked these sites came to be known by these names. As the population increased, these local units split up and moved away, but retained the names and perhaps even rights to the lands. They also came to cooperate with their 'clan' relatives for mutual aid. Thus, here, as amongst the Hopi, a system of clans grew up. It was sometimes the case that a breakaway group became known by another name, but it remained in a sense a part of the original; this happened with the Hopi too. Thus, there may be two or three clans which recognized relationship to each other. It is common to call such groupings of related clans *phratries*.

It may not have been larger settlements, but it was probably population growth and the coming of the horse (from the Spaniards), that helped to develop clans in the west. Agriculture, matrilocal residence, dense population and easy travel must have been all instrumental in this development.

The most important thing about the clans in each of these societies, however, was that they were exogamic groups. It was absolutely forbidden to marry a member of one's clan, i.e. someone descended in the female line from a common ancestor. We have agreed to take this for granted for a while, but it is easy to see its effects. From the point of view of the individual again, in the unit in which he is born, all the members (except for the married-in husbands) will be related to him matrilineally. He will therefore not be able to marry them, and will have to look elsewhere.

IV

I have dwelt on some matrilineal examples here, as they will be the least familiar to the reader. And, again, I raise the warning that they are not altogether typical of all matrilineal arrangements. But bearing this in mind, we can return to the primitive Shoshone situation, and see what kind of push can send it in the other direction. We saw that brothers liked to stay in the same territory but that the environment did not allow them to band together except on a few occasions each year. But say that it did; say the environment was such that it could just about support a band of some 30 to 100 individuals? Steward has worked out the ecological bases of the 'patrilocal band' with some exactness, and I can do no better than summarize them here:

1. A population density of one person or less per square mile in a hunting and gathering technology in areas of scarce food.

2. Principal food is game, non-migratory and scattered, which makes it advantageous for men to remain in and exploit the territory in which they were born and which they know intimately.

3. Transportation limited to human carriers.

4. Extension of incest taboos from biological to extended family. (He means extension of exogamic restrictions of course. Whether the incest taboo is 'extended' remains a moot point. What matters is that the members of the band must find spouses outside it.)

The general trend, here, is for the men to stick together in order to exploit a hunting territory. In circumstances such as Steward describes and which occur in many parts of the world, the most advantageous group for survival – indeed possibly the only group – is the patrilocal band. In some ways, too, the patrilocal band – our Case 3 – is perhaps the most primeval of truly human groups and was probably the social unit of our palaeolithic hunting and foraging ancestors. Thus, it is not only brought into being by those conditions that Steward outlines, although it is true that such conditions could produce nothing else – but persists in even very different conditions. However, in conditions which will allow a greater population density, one can see that, with the advent of settlement and agriculture or even before, patrilineal clans and lineages will easily develop out of patrilocal organization.

We should remember the point we made earlier about the *de facto* nature of the 'lineality' of these groups. In the patrilocal situation, there is no 'rule' of patrilineal descent determining membership in the band. All there is is a

combination of circumstances which produce bands of
males. These males – because of exogamic restrictions –
cannot marry the females that they breed, so they have to
look elsewhere for mates. They have to import wives and
export sisters and daughters as we saw in Case 3. The result
is an approximation to a patrilineal situation except that the
'sisters' are missing. It is the parallel of the situation with
the matrilocal unit where the women stayed put but the
'brothers' left and were lost to the group. At the level of
simple residential units these are the exact opposite of each
other. But once a fully fledged matrilineal and patrilineal
system is working they are not simple opposites as we shall see.

The process of development from a population composed
of wandering patrilocal bands to a tribe composed of
patriclans divided into patrilineages must of course be on
much the same lines as in the matrilineal case, and I feel
relieved of the burden of introducing actual examples.
Indeed, as far as I know, such a history is not available in
the patrilineal case, but that may be just my ignorance.
We can see that any of the conditions we mentioned
earlier will do the trick. As population increases, and technology becomes more sophisticated so that larger groupings
are possible, then farming may become more common. The
band will settle certain farmlands and give them a name.
This name may be the name of an animal or an ancestor
or just a place name. With the splitting up of groups, the
migrants will leave the area but retain the name and possibly
contact with the homeland – and, of course, will be bound
not to marry the females of the home group or any group
descended from it. They may keep up contact for mutual
aid in defence, or for ritual reasons (worshipping of ancestors maybe) or because of a possible claim on the land
of other groups of the clan. Whatever the reasons, instead
of bands just breaking up and the breakaway units becoming autonomous and unrelated entities, these units retain
their identification with the original band through the idea
of common descent. The members of all the bands bearing
the same name are descended from the original through

male links – they are a patrilineal descent group. Insofar as they are settled in large towns or other large population aggregates, then the men of the group can keep up contact with the exiled 'sisters'. But the reader may already have seen that they will have less motive to do this than the women of the matrilocal group had to keep up contact with their brothers.

V

I want to leave on one side for a moment the other possibility that we canvassed in Case 5. Clearly there may be circumstances that render this alternative more likely than those we have discussed, but it might be better for the moment to concentrate our energies on asking about the implications for the societies concerned of adopting one or other of the unilineal solutions. And again we should note that there are other routes to the same solution. In a male-dominated society, where property and office pass through males to males, if groups are formed they will probably be formed on a patrilineal basis – although this is not inevitable. Similarly, if for some reason the matrilineal principle came to be adopted then matrilineal groups might follow. But, personally, I find it hard to imagine, in the matrilineal case, any route other than the residential leading to the principle being adopted.

However, once the principle of unilineal descent is adopted as a rule to be followed (whatever its origins) then certain complications arise: certain consequences follow. This is usually the point at which anthropologists take up the story. They take the principle of descent as given, and ask about its implications. But often this leads them to put the cart before the horse and impute causality to the *principle* – which we take as derivative. Thus, for example, it is often thought that in patrilineal societies the rule of patrilocal residence at marriage is derived from the principle of descent. In fact, the reverse is probably true. In matrilineal societies, anthropologists have wasted a good deal of ingenuity in trying to show how various household arrangements *result from* the matrilineal principle, when, in fact, the household arrangement may be the basis on which the matrilineal principle was arrived at. Thus, we have to keep the question of origins in mind here to avoid making unwarranted deductions. Anthropologists might reply that we more often than not don't know the history of the tribes concerned so we can't ask about origins. Maybe, but we can at least be wary of turning effects into causes and always be ready to ask ourselves if what looks like an effect of a descent system may not in fact be its cause.

Of course it is true that once the principle comes to be adopted and descent groups formed, then, however it came to be adopted, the fact that there is now a *rule* of unilineal descent is of enormous importance and will 'feedback' onto behaviour and action and lead to various complications and developments. This is quite true; and very often the rule has to fight with changes that it never envisaged. Thus, a system of matrilocal residence may have given rise to a matrilineal system with quite strong clans etc., but a change in circumstances may have led to a change in the system of residence. Thus, a changed system of residence will have to come to terms with the matrilineal clan system – and often this may be very difficult.

In the next chapter, then, we will go on to explore some of the problems and complexities of matrilineal and patri-lineal descent-group organization.

CHAPTER FOUR

Unilineal Descent Groups

I

WE have seen how the matrilocal and patrilocal systems are the opposite of each other. In the matrilocal system, the women stay put and the men move: in the patrilocal, the men stay put and the women move. Once a fully-fledged unilineal system comes into being, however, the situation is not quite the same, and patrilineal and matrilineal descent-groups are not simply the mirror opposites of each other. The reason for this lies partly in Principle 3 (Male Control), and in following out the logic of matrilineal organization, we shall see the necessity for this principle. The essence of this problem lies in the fact we have already noted: that while in order to produce a matrilineal situation the men of the consanguine group have to associate with the women of it, it is not necessary for the women of the patrilineal group to be in constant association with the men.

First, then, let us look at the matrilineal situation. We have reached a point where matrilineages and the wider associations of clans – collections of related matrilineages – have become established. Each of the lineages may be property-owning bodies, while the clan may be an organization for mutual aid, defence, ceremony, or vengeance; or the clan as a whole may control the property, with a council of lineage heads running its affairs. It may even be that one lineage within the clan will have become dominant and be senior to the others, thus providing a chief or leader for the clan; and maybe even one clan of the tribe may have come to lord it over the others thus providing a 'royal' clan from which the chief is chosen. All these are further elaborations of the clan system, well known in the literature.

Let us work from the lineage level – the group of kin

descended in the female line from a common ancestress through known links. Given that this unit has come into existence and that it is exogamous, owns property or ceremony, or is geared to mutual aid and assistance amongst its members, what are the possible ways it can organize itself and what problems does it have to overcome? Perhaps we can approach this deductively by the same method as we used in Chapter 1. There seem to be four possible ways of arranging the members of the lineage 'on the ground'. We will call these 'solutions'.

A. Keep all the members of the lineage together.

B. Keep the female members together but disperse the males.

C. Keep the male members together and disperse the females.

D. Disperse all the members.

We can assume that it would be advantageous to have the members in contact with each other – otherwise they would have difficulty in reaching decisions and controlling their joint property – so obviously Solution A. would be the best. This is of course our Case 1 (p. 79) in which the consanguineous matrilineal group and the residential group are one and the same thing:

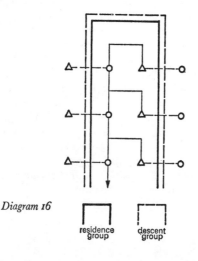

Diagram 16

residence group   descent group

All the features that we noticed for that case would be true of this arrangement. It keeps the matrilineal unit intact, and reduces the role of 'husband' to sexual companion. The husbands, in fact, merely impregnate the women on behalf of the men of the matrilineage. They do not live with the women or acquire any of their domestic services; the reproductive services of the women are still under the control of the matrilineage men – the 'brothers' and 'uncles'. These men of course will have sexual relations with women of other like groups, but they will remain attached to their own group. Paternity is unimportant here, and it really does not matter how many 'husbands' a woman has. Only problems of sexual jealousy, or notions of propriety, might limit and order the mating relationships. This arrangement solves what is the basic problem of the matrilineage – how to keep its members together and in contact. This contact is always threatened because of Principles 1, 2, and 4. As we have seen, the brothers cannot impregnate their own sisters, so men have to be imported to do this. But this importation represents a challenge to the brothers – the 'husbands' may intrude too much. Principle 3 means that the men of the lineage will want to keep control over its women and property. They can do this best by living on the land (if that is the property) and by keeping the women with them. The women, after all, provide them with heirs and successors, and it is convenient to have these around from the start. The natolocal solution neatly ties up all these ends: it is the classical way of solving the problems posed by the four Principles in the context of matrilineal descent.

But here we must heed our own warning and not put the unilineal cart before the residential horse. Let us look at some examples of this form of grouping and see what they suggest. We should note, in passing, that the nuclear family is nowhere to be seen: there just isn't one. It is all very well to call this an 'exception', but it is not all that unlike other arrangements in which the nuclear family is a derivative and secondary unit.

Examples are very rare. The most notorious is the system of the Nayar of Malabar in southwest India. The Nayar were a warrior caste whose men were, when of military age, engaged as full time soldiers. They spent most of this time in barracks or away on wars. The young women often went as house servants in Brahmin households and were often taken as concubines by the Brahmin men. This was considered a great privilege. The men, after their military service was over, returned 'home'; i.e. to the house in which they were born. The girls born there also treated it as a permanent base and finally lived there full-time. Thus, a consanguineal household grew up which fits our example perfectly. Stable marital relationships were difficult to maintain under these conditions, and the natolocal residence pattern was the outcome. The mound on which the house was built was known as the *taravad*, and the unit living there came to be known by this name also. The taravad represented a lineage which was itself part of a clan, as the Nayar had not unnaturally developed a matrilineal system of groupings. The clan was primarily a religious unit, and all the members of the clan worshipped a clan goddess.

The eldest of the warrior brothers of a *taravad* – the one who finished his war service first – would be the head of the group. The *taravad* owned land and livestock and the brothers worked this under the direction of the head. Meanwhile the women of the *taravad* were having children who would eventually take up their places as working males of the unit after their period as warriors.

The impregnation of the women was not a random affair. As we have seen, the girls might well have children by the Brahmin overlords, but also, before they reached puberty, they were 'married' to a man of a lineage with which their natal lineage had a special relationship. This 'marriage' was then dissolved and the woman was free to take as many as twelve 'lovers' or temporary husbands. This has been described as a system of polyandry, but as these were relatively impermanent and non-residential unions, it seems rather too much to call them a form of 'plural marriage'. The number of lovers may seem rather large, but as many of them at any one time might be away on military duties, the large number gave some reserve strength to the task force. These men had visiting rights with their 'wives', and if one of the men on visiting found another's spear or shield outside the house, then he would go away and try again the next night.

Here then is the classic case of the coming together of a system of residence and property, and matrilineal institutions. The lineage, for example, might split and grow. Sometimes a *taravad* would become too large and some members of it would move off and start another. They would keep up relations however, and meet for worship. Also they had some kind of collective responsibilities for their members' behaviour. We do not know if the Nayar in fact developed their matrilineal institutions out of the residential base (itself an outcome of their specialized military role), but if they were going to develop a system of descent groups, then they would have had little option but to make it matrilineal.

The nearest example outside the Nayar of this form of grouping is found amongst the Menangkabau of Malaya who are similarly matrilineal. The well-known Ashanti of Ghana approached this method, but their case is complicated and seems to be an amalgam of several solutions. The Ashanti have been made famous in anthropology for what has been called the 'visiting husband' solution. This is virtually the same as the Nayar method. Any evening in an Ashanti town, we are told, one will see children running between the houses carrying dishes and bowls of food. They are taking it from the mother's house to the father's house. The father will be at home with his mother, and his sisters and their children. Already we can see some differences from the Nayar situation. The children here have an accepted father and their mother has at least to cook for him. The Ashanti live in towns, and so the houses will be quite near and this arrangement feasible. Already then the husband-wife bond appears here to be stronger than in Malabar. There has been more 'intrusion' by the husband: he can make more demands. What is more, in many cases amongst the Ashanti he is able to bring his wife home to live with him. But here is the rub: his children are not his – they belong to his wife's lineage – so that at some point they must return to the lineage house where the mother's brothers live. This problem makes the nuclear family of the Ashanti a tenuous thing, and it is often short lived, with the wife going home to mother.

Both the Ashanti and the Nayar (and the Menangkabau) are relatively sophisticated and advanced peoples, and it may be that this form of solution is commoner at this level than at the hunting, gathering and small-farming stage. At the latter stage, the matrilocal solution is more common, with perhaps loosely-structured descent groups. The 'property' of the women is not of much value, and hence the men are less likely to want to bother controlling it. If it becomes scarce and valuable (or plentiful and valuable for that matter) then some form of control may be necessary and a Nayar-like solution may emerge out of this. Thus, the brothers will be less inclined to leave home and will find some way of staying on the lineage lands. Larger settlements or easy transportation will be necessary to make this work. But it is possible to imagine situations in which the consanguineal household develops without an intervening matrilocal stage. In a Celtic island that I have known for a number of years, it was the custom for men and women to go through the Catholic marriage ceremony but not to set up house together. The man stayed in his natal home and the woman in hers. Many reasons might be found for this, but one was certainly sibling loyalty – a feeling that the tie between siblings was stronger than that between spouses – and an unwillingness to upset household arrangements when people married late. As this was a crowded community the 'visiting husband' situation was quite feasible. No matrilineal institutions had developed, but the roots of them were there. This example shows that if we can find the consanguineal household without matriliny, then it might be too facile to suggest that such a household must be the outcome of matriliny.

II

The second Solution on our list – keeping the women together and dispersing the men – is of course our matrilocal solution out of which, we suggest, most matrilineal systems have grown. Whether or not it represents an adequate form of residential organization, once a fully-fledged system of matrilineal descent-groups is operating, will depend on the functions of the groups. It can operate quite well if, as amongst the Navaho for example, the clans have not very many functions over and above exogamy and the men are equipped with horses so that they can travel to visit their maternal nephews. Also, the development of compact settlements (such as with the Hopi) will mean that contact between members of the lineage is easily maintained. The Hopi system shares features common to both a simple matrilocal system and the Nayar (natolocal) solution. The men are part-time residents in both their natal homes and the houses they marry into. But if the settlements of women are at all dispersed, then the matrilocal solution is at best a partial answer to the problem. It works best in systems where the matrilineal organization is 'weak', i.e. has few functions, and the property is owned by the women with the men engaged in hunting or warfare or both. The problems of Principle 3 do not loom large here as there is not much to control. A man's senior relatives will be his maternal uncles, and it may be that he will wish to associate with them for some purposes, but otherwise the system can get along. If the property of the women becomes important, however, and the men of the lineage wish to control it, then the problems posed by scattered settlements might become acute. It is not only the property that might be a problem, but politics. It is quite usual as we have seen, for the clans or lineages to become political units. They may be *the* political units, with the society little more than a federation of matrilineages/clans. The group of 'political' males, then, will be the men of the matrilineage. But these will not be together, they will be scattered over the country in the homes of their various wives. The scattered nature of settlement makes it difficult for them to achieve a Nayar solution, so they have to work at a number of compromise solutions.

Here the problems of the matrilineage loom very large. The essential bond is that between brothers and sisters, because the children of the sisters are the men's heirs and successors. This sibling bond in the matrilocal situation, however, loses out somewhat to the marital bond. The husbands move in and have the sexual and domestic services of their wives, even if they do not gain control over their children.

Many matrilineal societies in central Africa show up this dilemma. Basically, they have arisen from the matrilocal situation, but they developed in different ecological circumstances and this has affected the manner of their development and the ease with which they work. For a start, some of them are in areas of plentiful land, so that the inheritance of land is not a problem. Others are in areas of scarce land, where the agricultural plots are very valuable; hence the inheritance of these is of desperate importance. In some, there is a good deal of personal wealth to be amassed and the inheritance of this is obviously a matter of concern. This latter point is very important. Under a matrilineal-matrilocal system in which there is not much wealth other than land and this is owned by the groups of women, then the problem of inheritance is not acute. A man will not necessarily need to have very much contact with his mother's brother. But if he is to be his mother's brother's heir, then his relationship with him is quite different. The mother's brother's power over his maternal nephews is likely to be quite strong in such a case. If this is combined with a political situation in which a man succeeds to his mother's brother's office, then this power will be doubled. The rights and duties the maternal uncle has towards his sister's sons, and his power over them, is termed the *avunculate*. In the Nayar solution there is no problem over this as we have seen, but with the matrilocal situation there is because the maternal uncle will be elsewhere. He may find, and indeed he does, that his authority is undermined and challenged by the nephew's father who is in constant contact.

The central African tribes have tackled this in various ways. Take the Yao of Malawi. They are agriculturalists and cattle herders living in relatively permanent settlements. They are divided into matrilineal clans, but these seem to have few functions. Each clan is divided into exogamous matrilineages known as 'breasts' (*mawele*). The effective group is a small matrilineage – the descendants of a common great-grandmother. This usually consists of a group of sisters and their children under the leadership of their eldest brother, forming a small village. But how does the brother come to be there? This is the Yao partial answer to the problem. One of the brothers – the eldest – is exempted from the rule of matrilocal residence. He becomes the headman of the village with the right to rule over his sisters and their children. On his death, he is succeeded by his eldest sister's eldest son. This privileged brother pays bridewealth for his wife and takes her to live with him in his village. His younger brothers and nephews have to go to live matrilocally in their wives' villages under the authority of the eldest male of the wife's lineage. But marriage is brittle. Men are often away from home visiting their natal villages, and marriages easily break up. Men will try to get their wives to come to live with them in the lineage village, but this is rarely possible as the wife's lineage naturally wants to hang on to her. A man will inherit cattle and money from his maternal uncles, and of course, if he is the eldest sister's son, he will someday inherit the headship of the lineage village, pay his bridewealth, and take his wife there.

This is not a complete solution. One brother is exempt

from the matrilocal rule so that there will be someone to keep control of the lineage women and children, while the other men of the lineage fluctuate between their marital and natal homes. Here, the sibling tie and the conjugal tie pull against each other with the sibling tie perhaps having the edge. But even though the 'manager brother' gains permanent control over his wife, he does not gain control over the destinies of his children. Rights over them stay with their mother's lineage. This solution is used by other tribes in this area and is, of course, a compromise between the Nayar solution and the matrilocal in a situation that demands some control by the men of the lineage over its lands and cattle. Other central African matrilineal peoples show different versions of this solution, varying with ecology, the nature of inheritable wealth, the political strength of the matrilineages, etc. Where, for example, land is scarce, then maternal nephews will be keen to be under the authority of their mother's brothers as they wish to inherit the land from them. Under these conditions, we would expect a strong avunculate. Where land is not scarce, then this would not hold and the avunculate would be weak. Here, as amongst the Bemba of Zambia, the authority of the mother's brother is weak, and indeed the father can establish some authority over his children and, after some years of service for his wife's matrilineage, he can often remove her to his own village. Amongst the Kongo of Kasai, he can remove her immediately on payment of bridewealth. If the manager-brother solution is the thin end of the wedge, in this latest development we have the whole 'husband' wedge well and truly inserted into the unity of the matrilineage.

III

This takes us on to Solution C. How is it possible to keep the men of the matrilineage together with the women dispersed? It would not be a bad solution if it could be worked, as it stands by Principle 3, and leaves the controlling males intact. It assumes, however, a Kongo situation in which the husband gains control over his wife – but re-member that her matrilineage keeps the rights over her children. Thus, they can claim the right to reclaim the children, once these are old enough to leave their moth-ers. Hence, a maternal uncle can ask for his nephews back when they reach puberty, say, even though he has let their mother go. The resulting local group will con-sist of a series of matrilineally related men with their wives and dependent children, but without their adult chil-dren:

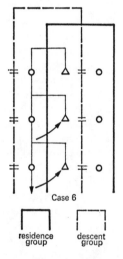

Case 6

residence
group

descent
group

Diagram 17

The rule of residence whereby a boy has to return to his mother's brother's village (his mother's natal home) either at puberty or on marriage, is known as *avunculocal*. This arises out of a prior rule of virilocal marriage. (We can-not call it *patrilocal* in this case because the couple do not live with the groom's father.) Thus, if a man may remove his bride from her natal home to his home (virilocal residence) then he must surrender her children back to her brothers – her male children at least. In the words of

Audrey Richards, this represents the 'lending away of the sister', in the same way that the matrilocal solution represents the 'borrowing of a husband'. Thus the lineage either has its women stay put and their husbands come to them (either on a residential or non-residential – Nayar – basis), or it lends them out to other men for sexual and domestic purposes, but reclaims their sons, at puberty or later. This is a cumbersome but not altogether impossible solution. It perhaps represents a situation in which the lineage is powerful enough to assert its rights over the children of the 'sisters', but not powerful enough to keep them under its wing permanently. There is always this tug in matrilineal systems between the needs of the lineage to keep its autonomy, and the desire of a man to have control over his wife and children – to have his wife around in his own home and not to be on an impermanent or visiting basis with her. He is of course caught in a dilemma, for on the one hand he is a husband and father and wants to have his wife around, while on the other hand he is a maternal uncle with lineage responsibilities to his maternal nephews and hence needs to keep some control over them and their mother, his sister.

It was this aspect of the Trobriand matrilineal system which combines virilocal marriage with avunculocal residence, that was most graphically described by Malinowski. It was, he said, the struggle between 'mother-right and father-love'. Perhaps another feature of this struggle is the notorious 'ignorance of physiological paternity' with which the Trobrianders are credited. This is not so much ignorance as denial; the father is *not*, in Trobriand ideology, the creator of the child, but merely the 'opener of the way' for it. The child is conceived 'spiritually' by the mother (no theological problems in explaining virgin births here). This ideology can be seen as an expression of the matrilineal principle; the Nayar simply eliminate the father role, but the Trobrianders, stuck with fathers, eliminate their procreative role. Where the rule of residence is that a man on marriage should take his bride to live with his mother's brother (or rather to live on the lineage lands or in the lineage village), then the convenient form *viri-avunculocal* is sometimes used.

IV

This brings us to the last and least satisfactory Solution (D) which can scarcely be called a solution at all except in the sense that it is one of the logical alternatives. If we disperse *all* the members of the matrilineage then what is left of it? It is robbed of any residential base at all. This may not matter too much in a densely packed village. In the village of Cochiti, New Mexico, (a neighbour of the Hopi), there were matrilineal lineages and clans which were thus dispersed. This did not prevent them from functioning, as everyone was only a few minutes' walk from everyone else. It would matter very much, however, if the settlements were not compact and travel not very easy. This dispersion of the members can occur in various ways. Thus, we saw that with the Kongo there was no attempt to keep the lineage intact, and men could take away their brides. Now, amongst other central African tribes this has got to the point where patrilocal residence has become the rule. Fathers, sons, and brothers stay together and herd cattle and farm, bringing their wives in to live with them. Cattle are passed from father to son as is the land. What is left for the lineage and clan? Well, it can still be the exogamic unit, and it can still have a good many ritual func-tions – the worship of ancestors for example, or it can have political functions in that offices or priesthoods can descend in the matrilineage. It can be a vengeance unit, or unit for the payment of homicide compensation etc. It *can*: but its functions are bound to be weakened by the dispersion. Once we have patrilocal groups, then the interests of these groups and the patrilineal inheritance pattern that follows from them is bound to take a prominent place in the minds of the men concerned. They may still respect their duties to their maternal nephews, but these will be balanced by duties and obligations to *sons*. Previous examples have not had much time for the role of son, but here he becomes a fixture. We could illustrate it thus:

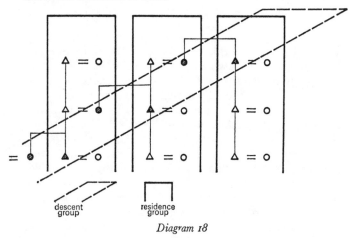

descent
group   residence
                         group

Diagram 18

If the patrilineal descent groups that logically follow from the patrilocal residence pattern get names and functions, then we will have a system that anthropologists call *double descent*, that is, it recognizes both principles of unilineal grouping. But we must be careful not to imagine that double descent always arises from the weakening of a matrilineal system in the direction discussed above. It often does, but it need not.

It may be that over a period of time the matrilineal elements of such a system drop out altogether, being too cumbersome to keep up in the face of changed circumstances; or maybe they will remain in some vestigial form such as the inheritance of names matrilineally with nothing much following from this. As long as the matrilineal group remains *exogamous* however, then it will be a force to be reckoned with.

This changeover can come about as a result of a change of residence patterns from matrilocal to patrilocal – a process that is known to take place, and Murdock has argued that this is the basic reason. But it may also be a result of polygyny. Plural marriage of a polyandrous type, as we have seen, would fit the Nayar case if we define marriage loosely enough. Also, as with the Navaho for example, sororal polygyny – in which a man marries several sisters – would be compatible with matrilocal residence. (Remember this pattern amongst the Shoshone?) But *general polygyny* would not work with matrilocal residence. This is the system in which a man has several wives who are not sisters – so they would be drawn from several groups. Now he could manage to go around and 'visit' them in their matrilocal homes, but it is obviously more convenient for him to have them all around him. Once circumstances permit or encourage general polygyny, then the doom of matriliny is spelt. Only virilocal residence can accommodate such a system.

This is just a guess as to how the changeover might occur, and of course there may be other ways; but however it occurs, some of the Central Bantu tribes illustrate stages in this transition.

v

Let us sum up the problem with matrilineal organization. However it arises, once established it has to come to grips with the problem of combining with the exogamic rule, a system of rights, duties, and even power, based on descent through females. The rule prevents the matrilineage (or clan – whichever is the operative group) from forming its own breeding unit. It has somehow to get its females impregnated and to keep control over these children. To this end, it needs the cooperation of males from other lineages. Therefore, there are various ways that it can achieve this without losing its unity and autonomy. The men of the lineage are in control of it, and it is the all-important relationship between a man and his sisters' sons that we have to consider. We have seen the various solutions, some of which were of course 'built in' at the origins of the system. The Nayar solution is the most complete; the matrilocal solution preserves the unity of the females of the lineage but leaves the problem of the controlling males. It works well if either the lineage is a relatively weak institution, or if the matrilocal groups are close together. The avunculocal solution solves the problem of keeping the controlling males together, but at the expense of losing the sisters to the husbands. In this system, the husband-wife bond is already challenging the brother-sister tie, and there is often friction – so graphically described by Malinowski – between a man and his brother-in-law over the discipline and destiny of the children. Finally, the sibling tie may prove too weak, and the 'father' role – previously unstressed and even almost non-existent – may assert itself at the expense of the 'brother' role. Matrilineal societies seem very vulnerable because of these problems and they are very much rarer than patrilineal. But they are very much more interesting, and when they find an equilibrium and flourish, they represent a pleasing and viable form of social organization that has obvious adaptational advantages in some circumstances.

Without wishing to put facts into too much of a straight-jacket, we might say that there are three basic types of matrilineal organization:

1. That based on the mother-daughter-sister roles and matrilocal residence. Here the burden of control and continuity is to some extent shifted onto the women, and in societies with this basis it is usually the case that women have higher prestige and influence than in the others.

2. That based on the brother-sister-nephew roles, with avunculocal residence preferred, or, failing this, some means whereby the mother's brother can control his nephews. In this type the status of women is usually lower, as control and continuity are monopolized by the men.

3. That based on the full constellation of consanguine matrilineal roles: mother-daughter, brother-sister, mother's brother-sister's son. Here control and continuity are primarily in the hands of the men, but the status of the women

need not be low – it will perhaps be intermediate between that in 1 and 2. Graphically we can visualize the three types thus:

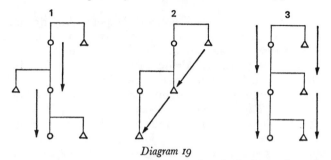

Diagram 19

Early writers called any system that looked to them as though 'kinship was through females only' either *matriarchal* or a system of *mother-right* (to contrast with the patrilineal, *patriarchal* or *father-right*). This implied that power and authority were in the hands of women in such a system. This is, of course, just not true. The whole problem with matrilineal systems arises from the fact that Principle 3 governs the situation: how to combine continuity and recruitment through females with control by the *men* of the lineage. If Principle 3 did not hold, then the problem would not arise, and an Amazonian solution would serve. In this the women would hold the property and the power, men would be of no account and would be used for breeding purposes only. Such a sinister practice exists only in the imagination, although most people have at some time or another accused their neighbours of it, or at least of being in some way 'matriarchal'. Thus Athens accused Sparta, France accused England, and now we are accusing the Americans. It probably arises from a deep-rooted fear on the part of men that they will lose their position, and the fear is projected onto disliked nations. Be this as it may, the true Amazonian solution is unknown. Women don't ever seem to have got quite such a grip on things.

We might call Type 1 in some of its manifestations a form of modified 'mother-right' in that the property is usually

the women's; but in the other types 'brother-right' would
be more accurate.

VI

What then of patrilineal systems? Happily they do not
present us with anything like the problems of the matrilineal,
because they manage to combine residence, descent and
authority very neatly. Almost inevitably the residential
group is a patrilocal unit. Thus, the males of the patrilineage
are intact and together to control and, equally inevitably,
to quarrel. The problem for the patrilineal groups lies not
with Principles 3 and 4, but with Principles 1 and 4. They
can beget their own children, but they cannot do this by
their sisters any more than their matrilineal opposites. So,
if they want descent through males – which we assume to
have been now established – then they must get wives.

Unlike the matrilineage, the patrilineage need not be too
interested in its consanguine women. After all, what use are
they? The patrilineal tribes of Arnhem Land in Australia
refer to 'sisters' as 'rubbish' because they cannot reproduce
the group. So why hang onto them? *Logically*, the patrilineage could do this and produce a kind of opposite of the
avunculocal situation. The patrilineal consanguine group
could stick together – males and females – and the men
could contract marriages with women of other groups,
impregnate them, and then claim their children at puberty
or at the child's marriage. For the sake of completeness
I give this below as Case 7:

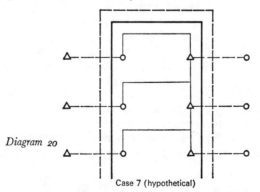

Diagram 20

Case 7 (hypothetical)

But this is never found. And indeed it would be a cumbersome and improbable and, above all, unnecessary device. If the object of the patrilineal group is to keep the fathers, sons and brothers together as an exploitative unit, then this advantage would be lost. If the groups were scattered or nomadic the situation would be impossible at worst, and, at best, pretty frustrating.

It may not seem worth making this odd point, but I think it illustrates something very important: whereas matrilineal systems run through all the possible alternatives open to them in terms of residential grouping, patrilineal systems do not. Either patrilocal or neo-local residence characterize these systems, and usually the former. I will not elaborate this point but will leave the reader to ponder its significance for an understanding of the differences between these forms of organization.

Problems of paternity need not trouble matrilineal societies. It matters little who the father is – a man is his mother's child and this fixes his status. In a patrilineal society however, the problem of paternity is vital. It is not so much a matter of legitimacy, as of the father making sure that the children – particularly males – that are born to his wife are definitely under his control – that they are legally his children. In the charming early-English proverb that Radcliffe-Brown quotes, the sentiment is expressed as, 'Whoso boleth my kyne, ewere calf is mine', or as the anthropologist might more delicately put it: whoever is the genitor, the pater is the legal father of the children. Thus, we might expect in patrilineal societies to find a lot more fuss being made over marriage and the rights over wife and children than in matrilineal. Logically, marriage is only a marginal institution in matrilineal societies. This does not mean that it may not have its importance, but compared with the central place it has in patrilineal societies it is as nothing. In a patrilineal system, a man wants sons. So he must get hold of a woman, or preferably women – the more chances the better – and hang on to her until she produces him some. His sister in the meanwhile has gone off to play the wifely role in some other lineage. (We must never forget the exogamic rule.)

Perhaps we can illustrate this by taking an extreme patrilineal example – for like the matrilineal side of the coin, patrilineal systems vary in the intensity with which they pursue their internal logic. We will not take a really primitive people, but some of the middle range. Of these, three stand out as examples of the patrilineal principle at work – Rome, China and the Muslim world generally. We will have an all-too-brief look at the Chinese lineage.

In south-eastern China the exogamous patrilineage (*tsu*) was usually a descent group of great depth. Sometimes as many as twenty-five generations were known to have elapsed since the founding of the lineage. Each lineage was divided into sub-lineages, and these were sometimes spread over several villages: sometimes a lineage occupied only one village, and sometimes it shared a village with another lineage. Clearly lineages that had lasted for as long as this must have been very large, and indeed some of them were, having a thousand or more members. Each lineage worshipped its ancestors, and 'ancestral halls' contained memorial tablets to the ancestors. Rich and powerful lineages kept accurate genealogies stretching back to the foundation of the lineage. They were often powerful and autonomous units living in walled villages and towns, and were often at war with each other and with the bureaucratic Empire which never really brought them fully under its control. Unlike the lineages of more primitive peoples, the Chinese lineage might well be highly socially differentiated, with some of its members scholars and officials, others rich traders, and the mass of members rice-growing peasants. China probably produced the most elaborate and spectacular of lineage organizations.

As we might expect, residence was patrilocal, but in such a complex society there was room for flexibility, and a man might, if say he were very poor, go to live with his wife's lineage; but this was somewhat humiliating and not approved. A woman on marriage transferred from the lineage village (really a small town) of her birth, and this transfer was for good. As far as her own lineage was concerned, she was lost to it completely and she came under the absolute jurisdiction of her husband's lineage. If her husband died, and she was past childbearing, then chaste widowhood was her approved lot – much as she may have disliked the idea. When she died, her memorial tablet went into the ancestral hall of her husband's lineage, and not that of her natal lineage. Similarly, if she was widowed young, then her remarriage was a matter for her husband's agnates to settle. She did not return 'home'; after marriage her home was where her husband was, and her 'kin' were his kin. It is interesting that the exogamic ban in China extended to the widow of an agnate. Thus, if a man died his lineage had to marry his widow off to another lineage (if she was allowed to re-marry). Usually, in patrilineal societies the opposite has been the case: once the lineage has obtained a woman it hangs onto her. Very often, for example, she is married to her dead husband's brother; a custom known as the *levirate*. China however was an exception to this, and I do not know why this should be.

The important fact is, however, that the lineage unloaded its consanguine women, and once they were gone they were gone. It obtained brides from other lineages to bear up sons to its name. Thus, the Chinese illustrate with harsh clarity the point about the lineage not having any use for its 'non-reproductive' members (its 'rubbish'). A woman has no role as sister and daughter, but only as wife and mother – and particularly as mother-in-law, for she rules over the wives of her sons when they come into the household.

To soften the blow slightly, we might glance at another quite sternly patrilineal society that does not cut off the women from their lineage so severely. The Tallensi are a densely packed people living in northern Ghana. They live in patrilocal settlements, keep cattle and cultivate fields. They are divided into patrilineal clans which are internally divided into lineages. The rule of exogamy applies to the clan, and so as in China a woman on marriage must leave her natal homestead and the territory of her lineage and go to the lineage of her husband. However, the very density of settlement is effective here, as we have seen it to be in previous cases. The women in fact never move more than a short journey from their natal lineage areas, and it is quite easy for them to keep up relations with their brothers and fathers. The Tallensi have a belief that women should not be deprived of lineage membership just because an accident of birth has made them the wrong sex and so deprived them of the power to contribute to the continuity of the lineage. They are therefore given quite a prominent role in the affairs of the lineage and clan of their birth. A striking difference with the Chinese case occurs on a woman's death. When this happens, she is returned to her own lineage with all the various lineages of her clan attending the funeral procession that bears her body home. In various clan rituals, the clanswomen have specific roles to play which are quite important. The Tallensi carry this even further, and because of the belief that a woman is wholly and importantly a member of her clan, they allow that her children have some claim on the clan also. Thus, most strikingly, if a man dies, his sister's son can claim the right of the levirate along with his brothers. Similarly the sons of sisters (clanswomen) are also given roles to play in ancestor worship. There is an almost cognatic element here; all the descendants of a man through both his sons and daughters combine to worship him.

Thus the Tallensi illustrate an extreme that is virtually the opposite of the Chinese. They recognize that for purposes of continuity and the reproduction of the lineage the 'sisters' are useless, but they react to this by saying that they should not be penalized for this biological limitation, but rather compensated for it by being given a privileged role in clan and lineage affairs. What is more, they say, the bridewealth obtained for the women is important, because it enables the men of the lineage to obtain wives in their turn. Thus, in an indirect way the women of the lineage contribute to its continuity.

In these two examples, we have seen how certain customs cluster round the logical working-out of the patrilineal principle of recruitment. The aim is to unload sisters and gain wives, and to control the reproductive powers of the wife. Thus, for example, bridewealth – the payment of goods to the lineage of the bride – establishes a man's rights over the woman and particularly her children. Any children the woman may bear belong to the man who paid the bridewealth for her. 'Cattle', as the Bantu proverb has it, 'beget children'. Sometimes the rather weak anthropological joke is made that the term should be 'childprice' or 'child-wealth', as it is essentially rights over the children – especially sons – of the woman that are involved. The details of bridewealth customs differ, but as a general statement the above will serve. The levirate clearly has a function here in that rights over a woman pass in perpetuity to her husband's lineage. Its companion custom the *sororate* (which again we met among the Shoshone) has a similar function here. If a woman dies, then her lineage should re-place her with another; usually a younger sister, at a re-duced 'price'. Clearly divorce should not be easy in such a situation; in the Chinese case it is impossible. A barren woman, however, can usually be sent back and a replace-ment demanded: it is the products of the woman rather than her person that are wanted – although this point can be exaggerated.

At the ideological level, the opposite of the Trobriand doctrine can be found for example amongst the Kachin of Burma where a woman is said not to be the creator of her child. This is carried to the point of classifying intercourse with the mother as adultery rather than incest – it is an interference with the sexual rights of the father vis-à-vis his wife. Many peoples with a strong patrilineal bent have favoured some version of this ideology. To the Tikopia the mother is simply the 'shelter-house of the child', she does not create it; Albanian hill tribes, ancient Greeks and some West Indians all subscribe(d) to the same doctrine. But not all patrilineal societies are so ruthlessly logical. Why some adopt this kind of ideology of procreation and not others is a matter that has not been fully investigated.

Thus in patrilineal societies the men of the lineage are together anyway, and women of the lineage are not useful to it as far as reproduction is concerned, so they are replaced by wives. The women, as we have seen can remain members of their natal lineages in varying degrees, but this is a kind of optional extra; the vehicle will run without it. But it does show the difference – the radical difference – between patrilineal and matrilineal organization, and particularly the place of marriage in each system.

VII

At this point, we can conveniently sum up the differences between the two systems – or rather between the principles on which they rest. We can return to our point at the beginning of the chapter: that the two systems are not the simple mirror opposite of each other. This can be shown by a statement of the opposite characteristics of the two types. Both types are subject to Principle 3 and hence the men of either the patrilineage or the matrilineage must be in control of it. In the patrilineage, this is easily arranged as the men are together, but the matrilineage has the problem of trying to get the males and females of the lineage into some kind of relationship. The patrilineage does not have this problem; its women are useless to it and there is no point in keeping them. For the matrilineage, control over its women is crucial as they reproduce the group.

In patrilineal systems, it is the *wives* of male members who reproduce the lineage: in matrilineal systems it is the *sisters* of the men who do it. So the essence of matrilineal organization is 'hanging onto the sister', that of patrilineal is 'gaining control over the wife'.

In a patrilineal system, a man gains rights over the sexual, domestic and reproductive services of his wife: in a matrilineal system he may gain rights over the first two, but he never gains rights over the last. Rights in the woman's reproductive services remain with her lineage.

In a patrilineal system, a man gains complete rights over the possession of his own children: in a matrilineal system he has no rights over them.

If we look at it in terms of the roles involved, we see that in the patrilineal system it is the father-son-brother constellation that dominates, with the woman's only real role being that of wife/mother. (Again I stress that this is speaking of the logic of the thing – she *can* be given a role as sister/daughter, but she need not be.) In the matrilineal system, the crucial roles are mother-daughter-brother-sister; the conjugal roles are reduced in importance, and strictly speaking the system does not need the role of husband-father, although again, a matrilineal society *can* create this role and give it some weight. It needs its women impregnated of course, and if it knew of artificial insemination, it could solve its problems easily enough. As it is, it has to 'borrow' husbands to do the job, and this intrusion of the husband role is, as we have seen, often a Trojan horse.

Thus the implications of taking any one of the courses that the biology of procreation offers is very far-reaching. Yet, as we saw in Chapter 1, it is a very simple difference at first blush. If a society could start from scratch with this decision, then no doubt it could work out the implications and reach the best solution. In the matrilineal case, where property was important, the Nayar method could be seen to produce the best results. But this is not how it happens, and societies have to build on the residential and ecological foundations that they inherit. It is the curse of matriliny, in a sense, that it almost always grows out of the matrilocal situation. From this situation, a matrilineal system is the logical step, and yet the situation has built-in difficulties that matrilineal systems find hard to handle.

CHAPTER FIVE

Segmentation and Double Descent

I

I N the last chapter, we diagnosed the problems facing both patrilineal and matrilineal descent-groups as complications arising from the rule of exogamy and the need for male control. Matrilineal groups took advantage of the fertility of their own women to achieve continuity, but to do this they had to acquire the services of alien males: patrilineal descent-groups could not take this same route, but had to acquire the services of women from other groups in order to recruit new members. The consequences of these patterns are far-reaching and influence other features of descent-grou formation. Here we must look at some of these other features.

We saw how large lineages or clans would grow up over time as the descendants of the original ancestor/ancestress accumulated. If the death rate in the clan exceeds its birth rate, then of course the opposite might happen and the clan eventually die out. It is a problem of all societies based on unilineal descent groups that these groups are subject to such fluctuations – some expanding and growing abnormally large, while others decline and become extinct. With this form of descent the problem is particularly acute, because it only takes the members of the relevant sex to die out to seal the fate of the clan. If a lineage in a matrilineal society fails in one generation to throw up any 'daughters', then it is finished. A lot of detailed discussion in anthropological work on kinship surrounds this problem of the vulnerability of unilineal groups to demographic vagaries. Societies resort to all kinds of subterfuges to overcome this problem, but intriguing as these are, we can do no more here than note the problem and press on.

Assuming the lineage is going to grow, it is clearly going

to get quite large as the generations pass. If a man has two sons, and they each have two sons who have two sons and so on, then at the tenth generation there will be 512 male descendants of the original ancestor. If we assume that generations eight, nine and ten are all alive together there will be 896. The more sons there are who live and themselves have sons, the larger the lineage will be, and if we include the female members, even at the two-and-two rate of progress there will be over a thousand descendants. Now it may be that as in China all these can live together and stay as a solidary residentially-united unit. But even in China, as we have seen, the lineage gets too large and has to split up at various times with members hiving-off and setting up sub-lineages. This process whereby sub-lineages are formed is known as lineage *segmentation*. The most usual metaphor to describe it is that of a tree and its 'branches'. The tree is the super-lineage or clan (the distinction is a technical one) and the 'branches' and 'twigs' and even 'leaves' are the sub-lineages. The 'twigs' result from the further splitting up of sub-lineages. This splitting up can occur for various reasons, the most common being simply pressure on land.

It does not always occur in the same way. We saw, for example, how the Hopi households would occasionally split up if they got too large, and some women would set up house elsewhere. They retained their identity with the house of origin for a time, but sooner or later their descendants would forget this and all that would remain to link the households would be common clan membership (snakes, rabbits etc.). Similarly with the Nayar; observers report that sometimes a few of the brothers 'with their favourite sisters' would leave the original *taravad* and set up one of their own. The Chinese, too, seem to work on this 'drift' method; some lineages split up fairly easily and frequently, while others remain unified over many generations. If, like the Chinese, one keeps fairly exact genealogies (even written ones), then the relationship of the lineages to each other can be easily traced. If, like the Hopi, one does not, then it is only common clanship that can unite the lineages rather than a knowledge of exact genealogical relationship.

One type of 'drift' method of segmentation is illustrated in Diagram 21. The original lineage is A. Soon after its

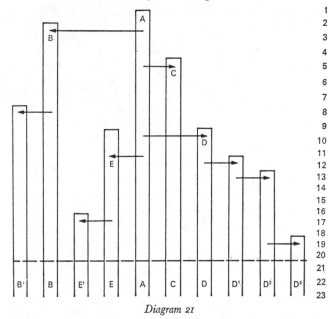

Diagram 21

foundation, some of its members drift off to found B. At a later date, the members of C move off, then D, then E. These lineages that spring direct from the parent stem are themselves subject to the same tendency, producing sub-lineages of their own. On the right is shown the number of generations since the foundation of the lineage, and we will assume that at present generations 21, 22, and 23 are alive (those below the dotted line). The Nayar would remember the order of segmentation in terms of which *taravad* begat which others, and they would all worship the same goddess. But with the Hopi for example, after a few generations, this knowledge would be lost. Thus D³ may just about remember that it came from D², and maybe E¹ that it came from E, but the rest would be lost in the mists of history. It would be the case that A would be the main lineage of this clan (say they were snakes), and that its house would hold the snake-clan fetishes and provide the snake priests. But the order of segmentation would probably be lost, and all the other lineages would be linked simply by the knowledge that they sprang from the original snake.

This shows how the difference between lineage and clan is a technical one. In the literature, these words slip about and the rigorous definitions are not adhered to, but in the Chinese case we should speak of a very large lineage with great depth and span, and in the Hopi case of a clan.

We have taken as our model here one particular kind of drift process that has been christened the 'spinal cord' method of segmentation. Here the 'senior' lineage – lineage A – is the spinal cord from which the others radiate like nerves; their seniority is reckoned in terms of their nearness to the central 'cord', i.e. the senior lineage. Some central Africans fit this model well, where the senior lineage is the lineage of the royal house, for example. But it is doubtful if these implications of seniority are always present in the Chinese lineage system; it is sometimes the case, but it is also likely that a lineage sometimes simply splits into two (or more) sub-lineages, without any notion of seniority. If this always happened then we would get an 'equal and opposite' system:

Diagram 22

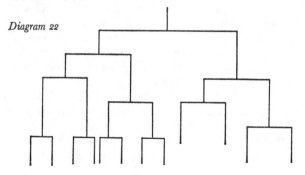

The Chinese seems to be a mixture, with some lineages splitting 'equal and opposite' and others splitting into senior and junior branches. (This is a mixture of both systems, of course.)

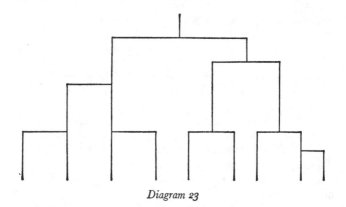

Diagram 23

In fact in south-eastern China, it is often the case that the lineages that split off from the main branch are the rich and powerful ones that can afford to build their own ancestral halls and assert their distinctiveness. The mass of the poor members of the super-lineage remain attached to the original hall. This is almost the reverse of the principle of seniority as it works in Central Africa or among the Nayar.

Both large lineages and large clans are subject to the segmentation process; the difference lies in whether or not they either (a) remember the exact links or at least the order of segmentation, or (b) do not remember them. The first kind has been called a 'merging segmentary series' of lineages, because one can go on tracing the relationships between lineages back until one reaches the founder; the second case has been called a 'linear series' of lineages, because they do not 'merge' but simply stand side by side as it were, knowing only that they share common blood, but not knowing the segmentary details. You may be asking why they want to know the details of segmentation, and the answer is as usual – for many reasons. These may be ritual, economic or political, but they usually involve some notion of seniority, of preference. The 'nearer' a lineage is in order of segmentation to the senior lineage, for example, the higher may be its precedence in ritual, economic or political matters. Take, for example, the succession to the chieftainship that may be held in this lineage. If the line of A should die out, then to whom should the chieftainship revert? Well, clearly it should go to B. Alternatively, if D^3 were to die out, who would get its lands? It should be D^2 in terms of 'next of kin', but, of course, the clan may have some other rule in this case. Closeness of cooperation; responsibility in bloodfeuds; homicide payments – all these may involve a knowledge of one's 'next closest' lineage. For all these and other reasons, the order of segmentation is important. In circumstances where much weight is given to the lineage organization in the social structure, then this segmentary process can be put to many important uses. It is not our purpose here to look into all these uses; a study of these properly belongs to the area of institutional analysis concerned – politics, economics, religion, etc. We are more concerned to look at the logic of the process.

The 'drift' method of segmentation can work fairly well for both patrilineal and matrilineal systems, and so far we have not differentiated these, but another method, which we might perhaps call 'perpetual' or 'automatic' segmentation – a version of the 'equal and opposite' method – does not work equally well in each case. Even with the drift method, however, there are problems for a matrilineal system not shared by its opposite number.

For the patrilineal system, the 'splitting' process (usually called 'fission' in anthropology only if it involves a complete break) is relatively easy. If a man has two sons, then on the man's death they can split up, each son can get a wife, and each start his own lineage. At any point in lineage development an individual male member can split off and start up a lineage (theoretically – there may be practical reasons preventing him). With the matrilineal, however, this is more difficult. We saw how, amongst the Nayar, a man 'and his favourite sister(s)' might split off – and this is the crux of the matter. If a man splits off from a patrilineage, then he only has to get hold of a wife and he can raise up future generations; but a man splitting from a matrilineage has to get hold of a *sister* and get *her* a husband, if he wishes to set up in business on his own. Now, if there were an equal sex ratio in all families and each brother could be assigned a sister, then this would be easy. But such a situation is rare. If a family, has, say, three sons and one daughter, then how can the sons split up? They cannot divide their sister between them. Equally, if there are three daughters and one son, then the daughters might have difficulty splitting up as they have not a brother each to take over the male role in any lineage they might found. And if Principle 3 holds good, then the women could not really found lineages anyway (although technically in a matrilineal society a lineage is always 'founded' by an ancestress, of course).

Let us look at perpetual segmentation in the patrilineal setting. The principle here is that every man is the potential founder of a lineage. Diagram 24 shows how this works.

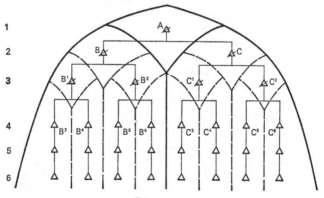

Diagram 24

This is a very schematic representation of a patrilineage over six generations. A had two sons B and C. On A's death they each founded a lineage. They in turn had two sons each (B¹ B² C¹ C²). On the death of B and C they each formed separate lineages from themselves and their sons and grandsons. When they died, the automatic segmentation process came into action again and the present set-up shows lineages B³ to B⁶ and C³ to C⁶. As these men die, their descendants (not differentiated on the diagram) will split up in their turn. Thus, each man becomes his own lineage-head on the death of his father.

I have said that this is very schematic, and, of course, the real situation would depend on how many sons each man had, and on how long he lived. For example, if B³ died well before all the other lineage heads, then his sons would split up and form lineages before the other Bs and Cs began the process – and so on. But schematic as it is, it is the way many tribes practising this form of segmentation actually conceptualize their system. That is, they see it as progressing regularly from generation to generation in this way even if there have been hitches along the route. Thus, for example, B¹ may only have had one son, and the splitting of the lineage may not have occurred until his grandsons (B³ and B⁴) split up. So the son of B¹ is simply ignored in the system – he is forgotten, and B³ and B⁴ treated as though they were the sons of B¹. Thus, genealogies are 'adjusted' in order to preserve the symmetry of the system.

The relations of the lineages in such a system are brought out best in ancestor worship. Thus, C³ and C⁴ combine to worship C¹. All the descendants of C¹ and C² combine to worship C; and finally all the descendants of B and C combine to worship the ultimate ancestor A. Thus, ancestor worship provides what Fortes has called for the Tallensi – who run such a show – the 'calculus of the lineage system'. Another well-known patrilineal society, the Nuer of the Sudan, use such a system as the basis of political alignments between territorial groups. Thus every lineage from B³ to C⁶ would be the focus of a local territorial group.

These groups are often in dispute with each other. Thus B³ may be quarrelling with B⁴; but if B⁴ gets involved in a dispute with B⁵, then B³ and B⁴ must sink their differences and, as the lineage of B¹, stand together. B⁶ would similarly stick by B⁵. Ultimately B would fight C, and the whole group combine against another lineage, if necessary. Evans-Pritchard describes this as the 'relativity' of the system. Thus, the lineages do not exist in their own right, but only relative to – in opposition to – other lineages.

So, patrilineal societies can put their segmentary process to work in a quite spectacular fashion. Sometimes, the final lineage is the whole nation and all the lineages of the nation merge into one ultimate ancestor. All the Somali, for example, who are divided into numerous patrilineages, are supposed to be descended from one common ancestor *Samaale*, who lived some thirty generations back. All the patrilineal Bedouin are similarly derived. (We have already noted the depth of Chinese genealogies.) Now, this can be achieved either by the system of 'perpetual' segmentation (each man his own lineage) or by the 'drift' method. For a matrilineal society, however, while the drift method can work (and does) with perhaps some difficulty, the perpetual method is a bit hopeless in any situation where Principle 3 holds with any force.

If the property of the matrilineage is primarily held by the women, and the men have not much property but simply wish to exert, shall we say, ritual control over their nephews, then the problem is not so great. We could draw a diagram the exact opposite of the patrilineal, with women instead of men. Then, if a man had three sisters, and on the death of his mother these three set up separate households and so founded three new lineages, he could still carry out his brother/uncle role towards the women and children of all three, providing he was not too far away from them to make this practical. I have seen this happen in the matrilineal village of Cochiti. But where property becomes important, then the answer is not so simple, for, as we have seen, while in the patrilineal system the men of the lineage can segment without any reference to the women, in a matrilineal system, one has not only got to segment the women, but the men as well. For every segmenting sister there must be a brother. This is particularly so if *individual* property is involved. Thus, we might expect that in matrilineal societies there will be a tendency to keep the lineage as a whole together longer, and, if segmentation occurs, for it to be of the drift kind. A man of a matrilineage can of course split off, and then try to attract some of his sisters' sons to him with land or wealth. This does happen, and is perhaps one root of the avunculocal system. It leads to an unhappy situation in which men compete for power and influence by trying to attract matrilineally related youths to their villages, and so build up a strong lineage village. Needless to say, this does not always make for a harmonious social system, and a great deal of energy has to be expended to deal with its problems.

Once again, we find matrilineal systems tending to flounder when dealing with the problem of continuity. Again, the Nayar seem to have it nailed rather better than the others. This does not mean that patrilineal systems do not have their problems with segmentation, but again these are less built into the system, less directly derived from its internal logic. The joker in the pack is of course the problem of reconciling the needs of Principle 3 with the principle of descent through females.

II

One of the mistakes of the early evolutionists was to imagine that these forms of descent were mutually exclusive; societies that were, say, patrilineal could only have emerged from a previous matrilineal stage – the two could not live together. However, we have seen that these descent principles can be put to many uses, and that there is no reason why a society should not have matrilineal descent groups for some purposes, and patrilineal for others. Anthropologists refer to this as a *double descent* system, and while it is perfectly feasible, it is rare and presents some difficulties. Even though we do not accept the evolutionary view that these two types of descent group are mutually exclusive, it is hard to resist the idea that double-descent systems are transitional; the Central African examples that we cited clearly are. Here, a situation that was previously exclusively matrilineal has been invaded by the patrilineal principle, and patrilineal local groups founded with the matriclans dispersed. It may be that this is always the way in which double-descent systems originate, but this is hard to say. If a society *starts* with patrilineal descent groups, then how might it develop matrilineal groups at a later stage? Or how might a society develop both forms of descent group together from scratch?

Well, all these things are possible, but we lack the data to help us decide. Among the Ashanti, despite the overall matrilineal nature of the system, there is a belief that *ntoro*, or spirit, is passed on patrilineally, and hence a shallow patrilineal descent group of men sharing the same *ntoro* exists. The reverse can happen in patrilineal societies, and a belief that some essence is transmitted through the female line may lead to the setting up of descent groups on a matrilineal basis.

Here we must exercise some caution. I have stressed that it is the existence of *both kinds of descent groups*, that really qualifies a system to be called 'double descent'. Thus, there must exist identifiable descent groups of both kinds. I feel this is necessary for, otherwise, we run into great confusion by calling all kinds of systems by the same name when they are in fact very different. For instance, even in a patrilineal system, a man has matrilateral relatives, and it is often the case that they are very important in his life. Thus, a man may have important relationships with the men of his mother's patrilineage – as among the Tallensi – but this does not create both types of descent group. Equally, among the Hopi, a man has important relationships with the members of his father's matrilineage, but again this does not make a double-descent system. It is sometimes the case that a man's mother's brother in a patrilineal system has very important duties to perform for his sister's son. It is often for precisely the reason that he is *not* in his sister's son's lineage that he has these duties. He has no legal power or economic rights over his maternal nephew, and is therefore an ideal relative for the performance of some ceremonial and other duties in the nephew's life. It is often the case that relations within the patrilineage are very strained, and that there is quarrelling and competition between brothers and other agnates over inheritance and succession. It may be that a man will turn to his mother's patrilineage for support in these circumstances. This turning to the mother's male relatives may crystallize over a period of time into customs of support and privileged behaviour between them. Thus, in South Africa, many tribes have the custom whereby a man is allowed to play jokes on his mother's brother, steal his property, and generally behave freely with him. As Eggan nicely demonstrates for the Hopi, a man has a similar relationship with his father's sisters in the matrilineal situation.

Thus in any society with established unilineal descent groups, an individual usually has important relationships with relatives other than those in his own descent group, and in particular with the relatives of the parent other than the one through whom he gains his descent-group membership. Fortes has called this, 'complementary filiation'. Thus, in a patrilineal society, although a man gains his descent-group status through his father, he is still his mother's child; he therefore has a 'complementary' relationship with his mother's agnates, and in particular with his mother's brothers. Another way of looking at this is to see it not as a result of 'filiation' – of being the child of one's mother – but as resulting from the marriage tie itself. Thus, when a man marries he sets up an affinal relationship between his lineage and that of his wife. His son – this is a patrilineal example – is a member of his lineage and so shares with him in this affinal relationship. Thus the son does not have special relationships with his maternal uncles because they are his mother's brothers, but because they are the brothers of his father's wife. This may seem like two ways of saying the same thing, but a lot of hot anthropological ink has been spilled in controversy over the merits of one or other of these views of the situation. The full significance of this distinction should be clearer when we come to consider descent and marriage in detail.

Another caution should be entered here. Many societies have groups which recruit by kinship; thus, a man may join his mother's group for some purposes and his father's for others. We might imagine a situation here, for example, in which a man got his religion from his mother and his politics from his father: he might be maternally a Methodist and paternally a Socialist, or an Anglican through his mother and a Liberal through his father and so on. This is a method of *affiliating* people to groups or organizations through kinship links. But it does not carry any implications of *descent*. All the members of such a group do not necessarily regard themselves as descended from a common ancestor, or even from sub-groups descended unilineally from a common ancestor. Thus, they are not unilineal descent groups, even though they recruit unilineally (i.e. through one sex only). A society in which a man gained descent-group membership through his father, but was affiliated to a religious group through his mother, would not then, on our definition, be a double-descent society. Such modes of recruitment and their relations with 'true' double-descent systems are well worth investigating; but for present purposes they do not constitute systems of double descent. Where an individual can be doubly affiliated in the manner discussed above, we should perhaps talk about *dual-affiliation*. It may turn out that a lot of groups described as 'clans' in the literature are, in fact, based on affiliation rather than descent – thus resembling 'clubs' or 'cults' rather than lineages.

At the moment we must simply note that neither dual affiliation, nor affinal alliances, nor complementary filiation create double descent, if by the latter we mean that the society recognizes both types of lineages. Each sets up a personal set of relationships for a particular ego, that is all. We can perhaps clinch this by pointing out that if a man has two sisters and one marries into patrilineage A, another into patrilineage B, then the man will have sisters' sons in both these patrilineages. But the nephews in A and those in B, will have no relationship *to each other*. In a truly matrilineal system, they would both be members of the same matrilineage. Even if the relationship is extended from ego to his mother's brother's mother's brother (ego's mother's mother's brother), and still further, the situation is the same. We have an *ego-centred* group of matrilineally related people, but not a matrilineage. Thus, we must not confuse the important fact that in unilineal systems people have relationships of great importance with relatives outside their own unilineal groups, with the situation where a society has institutionalized both kinds of descent group for different purposes. Let us look at an example of the latter, before discussing the more abstract problems that double descent presents.

The Yako of Nigeria are perhaps the best documented double-descent society in existence. They live mostly in one large town – Umor – with a population of 11,000. This is divided into wards and each ward is inhabited by a patriclan (*kepun*), which is exogamous and conducts rites in a central assembly house. The clan is composed of a number of separate lineages (*yeponama*: singular *eponama*), which own land within the clan territory and the members of which live with their wives and children in a single compound. (*Eponama* means 'urethra', thus stressing the biological link between agnates.) The *kepun* is not a segmentary clan, and lineages only trace their genealogies for a few generations. A man's rights to house, land and to some extent protection, then, lie in the patriclan and patrilineage. Umor is however also divided into matriclans (*yajima*: singular *lejima*). These are obviously dispersed because of patrilocal residence and the rule of patriclan exogamy. The matriclan is divided into lineages of shallow depth (*yajimafat*: singular *lejimafat*). Exogamy is only now enforced within these lineages although previously it operated for the matriclan as a whole. Each matriclan has a shrine to its spirit, and a priest, who is a man of great authority. But the most striking feature of matrilineal kinship is that all movable goods and inheritable wealth are passed matrilineally. Thus, for an individual man inheritance is divided; he gets his house and land and all other immovables from his father, but it is from his mother's brothers that he gets money and livestock and all movable property. Looked at another way, on a man's death his land and house go to his own sons or other close agnates, while his money and cattle will go to his sisters' sons or other close uterine relatives. One result of this is probably the maintenance of the equality of the patrilineages. A patrilineage (or clan) cannot build up a commanding position over others, because its wealth is always being redistributed over the other patrilineages on the death of a member.

The matriclans are also very important as ritual groups and are expected to 'keep the peace' of the village. This can be seen as stemming from the fact that they cross-cut the territorially defined patriclans and so in a sense bring them together. But the matriclan spirits and priests are more powerful and prestigious than those of the patriclans. This leads me to think that the Yako may once have been wholly matrilineal and suffered patrilineal intrusions of the kind we have looked at earlier. (The Yako practise general polygyny.) The move to patrilocal residence may have weakened the matriclans somewhat, but before this went too far the Yako came together in very large settlements like Umor in which the members of the matriclan could easily keep in touch. Thus, they retained their precedence and some of their functions such as the inheritance of movable wealth, but patriclans grew up out of the new territorial alignments and not unnaturally controlled the real estate. This is wild surmise, but it might be the explanation for this interesting system which illustrates so beautifully how a society can use both systems of descent for different purposes.

It might also explain another anomaly in the system. If a man is killed amongst the Yako then his matriclan can demand compensation but not his patriclan. The matriclan of the murdered man can go so far as to demand for itself a woman of the killer's matriclan. Now this is not really intelligible in material terms as Forde, ethnographer of the Yako, points out. If the woman claimed in compensation bears children, then these will belong to the dead man's matriclan. But this is overcompensation; had he lived and had children *these* would not have belonged to his matriclan but his patriclan – it is the latter that has lost potential new members by his death. If we add to this the fact that bride-price for a woman is paid to her matriclan not her patriclan, then we can, I think, be left in little doubt that the matriclan is the original unit and retains these functions in changed circumstances which logically do not require them.

There are many other features of the Yako system which it would be fascinating to deal with, but we must leave it at this brief sketch and pass on to a more general discussion of double descent.

Any double-descent system can work provided it gives each principle different work to do. With the Yako this is very neatly arranged; the men do not move so the immovables pass through men: the women do move so the movables pass through women. At the ritual and legal level it is not so clear cut, and the logic fails somewhat. In most double-descent systems, the residential group is the patrilineage. This is most reasonable as this is the easiest type of residential group to arrange. The reader can try to imagine a double-descent system based on some kind of residential matrilineal group and see why this would be difficult, though not impossible, to run. It may, however, be the historical fact that double descent often arises from matrilineal descent through a change to patrilocal residence, that explains this arrangement.

All the things that we have said about the problems and difficulties of unilineal descent-groups – matrilineal and patrilineal – remain true when these are combined in a double-descent system. If we simply take the viewpoint of the matrilineage, then it is still true that it is concerned that its women should be impregnated, and that it should have control over their children for whatever purposes it is to fulfil; the matriclan priests of the Yako, for example, are anxious to have sister's sons to follow them in office. It is also still true that the patrilineages want to 'unload' their consanguine women and acquire wives in order to produce sons. To this end, they have institutionalized polygyny and brideprice – although the latter is not always effective in asserting the rights of the pater over the genitor.

What is different about the double-descent system is that these purposes can be brought into happy conjunction by marriage. At one stroke the matrilineage gets its women impregnated and the patrilineage obtains a wife and hence sons. The matrilineage, amongst the Yako, is to some extent the gainer here. It receives brideprice from the man's patrilineage for the privilege of the use of the woman's fertility, but it does not lose its own claims on her children thereby – that is, it retains its own rights in her fertility. In ideological terms, then, the matriclan controls ritually the fertility of its women, although, as we have seen, the place of the man in procreation is fully acknowledged. But in any such system, the same would be true; both matrilineage and patrilineage gain by the marriage. This does not mean that conjugal relations need be stable, although some degree of stability is advantageous to the patrilineage. Divorce is possible amongst the Yako, but polygyny and remarriage make up for this. If a woman is pregnant and leaves her husband, then the child will be his and belong to his patriclan. But here again the patrilineage loses out somewhat, and it would be better if the payment of brideprice gave a man absolute rights over his wife's offspring. It is here perhaps, as in the question of homicide payments, that the two principles rub a little and fail to achieve an equilibrium. But what it does illustrate, and this too must be true for all double-descent systems, is that the matrilineage is able to flourish under such a regime despite its dispersal, and it may even get the better of the deal, not being dependent on marriage in the way the patrilineage is.

If we look at this from the point of view of roles, then we see that the system has another interesting aspect: it allows

an individual to play a fuller set of roles than in a simple
unilineal system. Thus, a man is a 'father' in his patrilineage
and produces its new members, and he is also a 'brother'
in his matrilineage with rights over his sister's sons and claims
on his mother's brothers. A woman can at one and the same
time produce sons for her husband's patrilineage – play the
role of wife – and produce sisters's sons and daughters for
her own matrilineage – play the role of 'sister'. A man is
both a son and 'sister's son', a father and 'mother's brother'.
As far as an individual's total behaviour and total rights and
duties are concerned, then, participation in a double-
descent system is very different from participation in one
recognizing only one principle of unilineality. As far as the
total system is concerned, a lot depends on what the two
sets of descent groups are given to *do*. This, of course, is a
product of historical development, and cannot always work
smoothly. Given a rational plan, a smooth solution could
no doubt be worked out, but societies do not plan their
institutions in this way and double-descent systems, like
other systems, are built up on accidental foundations. The
circumstances under which they arise and the situations in
which they work efficiently or, alternatively, fail to adapt,
have yet to be worked out.

III

Up to now we have taken the sibling group as our starting
point in the discussion of descent groups, but some of those
awkward ethnographic facts may have to make us revise
our decision. The trouble with these particular facts is that
they are somewhat enigmatic and we cannot always be
sure that we are dealing with groups and not just categories,
or modes of affiliation rather than descent.

The Mundugamor of New Guinea, according to Margaret
Mead, pass on land patrilineally, but this is plentiful and
there is no problem over inheritance. All other goods,
including the sacred flutes, which the Mundugamor put
great store by, are passed from father to daughter and
mother to son. These 'lines' of inheritance are called 'ropes'

by the natives. Mead traces this to the hostility between people of the same sex. Fathers hate sons, and brothers hate brothers. Sister-exchange is the common form of marriage (which is polygynous), but fathers sometimes exchange their daughters for young wives thus robbing sons of their chances. Thus, a man will only trust either his mother or his daughter and is at war with his other male relatives. This is carried to the lengths of having the father and daughter sleep in the same mosquito basket until the girl is married.

It is difficult to see in what way these 'ropes' are descent groups. When a father dies, his goods go to his daughters. These then marry and retain the goods until they have sons to whom they pass them. It is a form of individual inheritance, but it does not seem to produce any form of descent group. The Mundugamor tried, evidently, to form a kind of cognatic descent group by uniting the descendants of a brother and sister who would have been separated by the 'rope' system. But this broke down. As no residential or other groups seem to have emerged from this system we can leave it aside. But it is worth noting for its interest and for the fact that it cannot be deduced from anything about the 'natural' tie of siblings. It formally links people across the generations, but leaves the cross-sex sibling bond out of account. It is noteworthy however, that when the Mundugamor attempted to evolve a system that overcame some of the difficulties – to 'entwine the ropes' as Mead puts it – they utilized the sibling tie.

Another method of arranging descent, that this time does seem to result in groupings, is that reported for the Apinayé of Brazil. Here the notion that descent groups contain both sexes goes by the board and there are matrilineal groups of females and patrilineal groups of males, a system which has been christened 'parallel descent'. This is perfectly feasible providing the *purposes* for which the female groups exist are fairly limited. Thus, we saw that in some matrilineal-matrilocal tribes, the property was more or less in the hands of the matrilineally related groups of females in the residential group. A parallel development of 'male' property could produce the Apinayé situation. But this, like the Mundugamor case, cuts across the brother-sister tie that we have made our starting point. It can only be classified and dealt with if we take the four roles – father/husband, mother/wife, brother/son, sister/daughter – and look at the possibilities these give us of forming groupings. This is a purely formal analysis and unlike our other starting point tells us little about how descent groups originate.

There are, as I see it, nine possible ways of arranging these relationships – of linking these roles, if we add the two possibilities of combined roles, that is, parents on the one hand and children on the other.

1 Father to children
2 Mother to children
3 Father to son
4 Mother to daughter
5 Father to daughter
6 Mother to son
7 Parents to children
8 Parents to son
9 Parents to daughter

If consistently followed, 1 and 2 would produce patrilineal and matrilineal reckoning respectively; 3 and 4 would produce the Apinayé situation; 5 and 6 the Mundugamor 'ropes'; and 7 a cognatic system of reckoning. This latter brings out my point about the cognatic system 'ignoring sex'; in the other cases the differentiation by sex has been essential (either father from mother and/or son from daughter). Now, 8 and 9 present a problem. We can see how both children can be 'filiated' to the father or the mother, but how can one child be filiated to the parents and not the other? Well, if we follow out the logic of our extreme patrilineal case then this is what happens in a sense. In the patrilineal case, we see that the links that make up the system are between father and son and mother. Where is the daughter? She is off playing the 'mother' role elsewhere: there is no role of daughter. This is in the extreme case in which sisters really are 'rubbish' and are sloughed off to act as mothers elsewhere. Insofar as they are kept as members (non-reproductive) of the lineage, then it is pattern 1 that pertains, not pattern 8. Pattern 8 involves the incorporation of the 'mother' into the group of the father and son, as we argued was the case in China. We can perhaps illustrate it as follows:

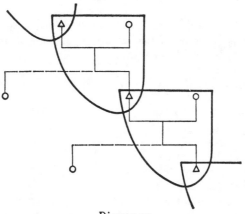

Diagram 25

What in fact then possibility 8 gives us is the alternative 'model' of a patrilineal system to possibility 1. Possibility 9, which would be the matrilineal opposite, does not occur, for all the reasons that we have previously dwelt on regarding the differences between matrilineal and patrilineal descent groups.

The thing that interests me about this analysis is this: one could not logically deduce systems 3, 4, 5, and 6 from our starting point of the 'natural' group and its perpetuation, which we used in Chapter 1 to arrive at the three systems of descent. These four cases all require us to take the four roles of the 'nuclear family' and see how each generation is differentiated by sex and filiated to the preceding generation. And yet, these four which require the roles of the 'nuclear family' – logically – for their generation, cover *only two known cases* in the whole of ethnography. In the system of analysis by familial roles that we have used here, they are equal *possibilities* with the rest; yet only one example of each is known. I am not sure that I am justified from this in concluding that my strictures about not taking the nuclear family as 'central' or 'basic' are justified; but in a logical sense, if not for all the other reasons advanced in Chapter 1, it is barely necessary to introduce it.

This little excursion into kinship logic in order to accommodate two awkward types of descent principle may seem, by now, to be an unnecessary irrelevance. But it is important because I think that to most kinship analysts it would have been the logical and natural *starting place*. If, therefore, I have dethroned it to the status of an arid aside, I am more than satisfied. I think that even most laymen would want to start the study of kinship with an approach like 'given the family, then there are X number of possible ways of affiliating one generation with the next'. To this, then, my answer would be, 'True, but only if you want to include the Mundugamor and Apinayé; the rest of the world can manage without an assumption of the nuclear family as central and necessary, and we can deduce the various forms of kinship system without having to consider it.' And, of course, logical considerations aside, even in the two societies mentioned it does not follow that the 'nuclear family' need exist as a unit! All that needs to exist is an acknowledged 'father' and an acknowledged mother for each child; or put another way, a legal husband for the mother.

NOTE. Since I wrote the above I have discovered that when viewed from the angle of the internal marriage arrangements of the tribe the Apinayé system is not out of line with our theories at all. The tribe is divided into four 'groups': let us call them A, B, C, and D. Now the marriage rule is that men of A marry women of B, men of B marry women of C, men of C marry women of D and men of D marry women of A. Using large letters for males and small for females we can see how this works:

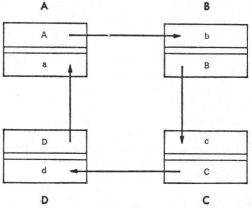

Diagram 26

A woman joins her mother's group and a man his father's.
So what we have in effect is four *endogamous* groups Ab,
Bc, Cd, and Da. A man's sister will be in his affinal group,
but he should not marry her. He should marry the daughter
of a woman other than his mother, in his affinal group.
This process is illustrated below:

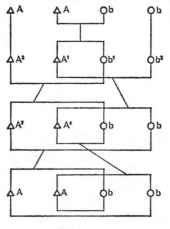

Diagram 27

Here a man of A married a woman of B (b). Their children were assigned respectively males to A and females to B. Now the sons of the marriage (the A^{1}s) cannot marry their sisters (the b^{1}s) but they can marry other girls of B (the b^{2}s). The daughters of the marriage cannot marry their brothers but they can marry other men of A (the A^{2}s). In subsequent generations there is nothing to stop the children of these two sets of marriages (who would be cousins of course) from marrying each other. Thus, in a sense, what is happening is that the males of A are 'exchanging sisters' with each other – and this goes for the males of all the other groups.

The reader need not puzzle over this but should return to it after reading Chapters seven and eight. It will then be seen as a species of 'elementary' marriage arrangement and should make more sense. For the moment he need only take the point that notions of the affiliation of parents and children in the family do not get us very far with a system like this. But insofar as the men are exchanging sisters, then the brother-sister relationship is still central and the system makes a kind of 'patrilineal' sense: one exchanges sisters for wives, rubbish for reproductive capacity. Membership in the categories A, B, C, and D is based on 'affiliation', and is simply the way the Apinayé phrase the system. It really has nothing to do with 'parallel descent' but with marriage arrangements.

CHAPTER SIX

Cognatic Descent and Ego-centred Groups

I

In Chapter One, we contrasted the unilineal and cognatic methods of recruitment with respect to the forming of descent groups. The unilineal method, we saw, had the advantage of assigning individuals to one group only (father's or mother's) and so creating discrete, that is non-overlapping groups. We can perhaps visualize this as below:

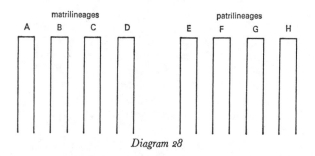

Diagram 28

When both unilineal principles are used, the same remains true and a man is a member of one matrilineage and one patrilineage and these exist for different purposes. Either unilineal system produces a discrete series of descent groups – lineages or clans – and an individual is assigned to one of these only. In a double-descent system, the units of the system are still discrete and non-overlapping patrilineages on the one hand and matrilineages on the other, although there will be members of all the matrilineages in each of the patrilineages and vice versa. As the matrilineages and patrilineages exist for different purposes, this does not matter, although as we saw for the Yako, it might if not skilfully 'meshed' produce some problems. We might illustrate it as below:

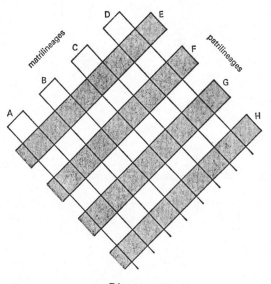

Diagram 29

When we come to cognatic descent groups, however, the picture changes. No longer is the society composed of discrete non-overlapping groups, for as we saw, by their very nature the cognatic lineages are bound to overlap in membership, and a man will be a member of several similar-purpose groups at the same time. Clearly, then, these must present different structural problems from unilineal groups, although, like the latter, they are composed of the descendants of a common ancestor. In the cognatic case, however, this descent is not limited by sex, but *all* the ancestor's descendants are included in his group. It represents the third alternative open to our sibling group: allow both men and women to reproduce the group. We might illustrate it as follows:

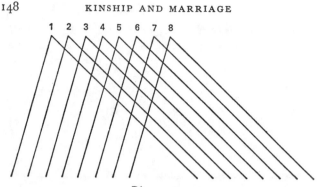

Diagram 30

Here, at some time in the past, a number of descent groups were founded, and every descendant of each founder remains a member of the founder's group.

If we look at it from the point of view of an individual, we can diagram simply the difference between his group membership under double descent and under cognatic descent:

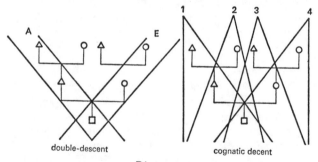

double-descent   cognatic decent

Diagram 31

Under double descent, he is a member of one matrilineage and one patrilineage, while under cognatic he is a member of as many cognatic lineages as he has lineal ancestors who were members. Taking it as we have done to the grand-parental level gives him four; taking it to the great-grand-parental level would give him eight ... and so on. This model assumes all his four grandparents came from different groups, but, of course, they might not have done. It is usually rare for cognatic descent groups to be exogamous, and indeed it would be impractical; sometimes there is even an endogamic preference and 'cousins' are encouraged to marry just in order to avoid too great an overlapping. Thus, a man's parents might both come from the same group, or at least his grandparents might. Thus, if in our example his father's parents had both come from group 1, this would cut down the number of allegiances that ego was faced with. If there is a limited number of such descent groups in the society – say there is a fixed number of named groups – then the likelihood of at least two of his grandparents coming from the same group is quite high. If there are, for example, only eight such groups, then he will perhaps be a member of four or five of them. This all depends on how far back he traces his genealogy of course. If he can remember the group affiliations of his eight great-grandparents, this gives him eight chances of membership; but the chances of his remembering the affiliations of his sixteen great-great-grandparents are perhaps slim. If these were in fact named groups like clans, then he would simply remember the names he inherited. He would know, for example, that he bore names 1, 3, 5, 6, and 8. But if his wife say, was a member of 2, 4, and 7, then she would pass on these and their children would be members of all eight groups.

This is a limited model, but theoretically it is possible under such a system for everybody to be a member of every group in the society! If the descent groups are likened to clans in which affiliation is cognatic, a man might easily be able to trace a cognatic link to every 'clan' in the society. If, however, the model is not that of clanship but of lineage membership, where exact genealogical links merging towards a common ancestor are involved, then the individual cannot so easily exhaust the system; but, even so, his membership can be spread pretty thinly.

Now clearly such a system is radically different from the unilineal, if it is logically pursued. Cognatic descent groups of this kind cannot really serve the same kind of function as unilineal descent groups. They cannot, to take a simple example, ever be residential groups. If one of these lineages decided to keep all its members together, then it could only do so at the expense of other lineages, by depriving them of members. It could keep a core of members together and compete with other lineages for the allegiance of the absent ones – and we have seen that something like this can happen in some matrilineal societies – but there cannot be a *rule* that all members of the lineage reside together. We cannot, in fact, predict what rules of residence there will be. As these groups are almost bound to be dispersed, then they could go with *any* rule of residence, or more likely with *no* fixed rule. To take another example, they could not act as vengeance groups – a common function of unilineal lineages. If a man of lineage A killed a man of lineage B, in our unilineal examples, then B could revenge itself by killing a member of A. This is easy because the membership of B is quite distinct from that of A. But if a man of 1 killed a man of 2, in our cognatic example, then how could 2 revenge itself on 1 when members of 1 are also members of 2 and vice versa? One could go on adding examples of the problems that overlapping brings in its wake. So devastating have these seemed to some theorists that they have denied that cognatic descent groups could possibly exist and treated them – because Principle 3 holds good here and the men are in charge – as patrilineal groups in a state of flux. We will see why this is later.

II

There is nothing wrong with being a member by birth of several groups. Indeed, it might even have positive advantages. But it does follow that unless they are modified in some way these cognatic descent groups cannot function like unilineal lineages. They share with the latter the charac-teristic of being groups based on descent from a common ancestor, but in accepting the cognatic mode of recruitment they have lost the discreteness that is the unilineal descent group's trump card in social effectiveness.

But the fact that they cannot function quite like unilineal descent groups should not blind us to their possible functions, and, in some circumstances, they may even have survival value that unilineal groups lack. But let us first say that what we have been discussing above, in an abstract way, are what anthropologists have come to term 'unrestricted' cognatic descent groups; that is, those that admit to membership *all* the descendants of the founding ancestor. It is possible to restrict membership in such groups on criteria other than sex, and produce groups that can function like their unilineal opposite numbers. But for the moment let us stick to the ruthlessly cognatic version.

We could imagine a situation in which these were ceremonial groups, as is in fact the case with the Sagada Igorots of the Philippines. If group 1 called its members together for a ceremony, then it would be no matter that they were all also members of other groups who had other ceremonies; the only clash would be over *time*: they could not hold different ceremonies at the same time. But another circumstance that is easily imagined might get over this problem. Say, there were in the society several areas of grazing land, and these areas had been owned originally by men who instituted the rule that all their descendants could graze their cattle on them. It would again be no matter that a man had grazing rights on more than one of these – in fact it might be a very good thing. The Igorots mentioned above provide examples of this. Their ancestors entered the territory they now hold about eight to ten generations ago. Some prominent men among these early migrants cleared certain hillsides of trees and *all* the descendants of each man have a right to cultivate on the patch of hillside he cleared. Similarly, clusters of pine trees that were first claimed by a man are the possession of all his descendants who appoint a 'warden' to regulate the gathering of wood. Again, take inheritance. If there were a rule that all a man's children shared in his inheritance, then this would go on being divided down the generations and his heirs could form a cognatic lineage. This 'potential' lineage may never in fact amount to very much except that links would have to be kept up in the case of the dying out of one branch of it and a consequent 'reversion' of property. This would all depend on the nature of the property. If it were, say, cattle – which could easily be divided and shared – then there would be perhaps less need for the group to stick together; but if the inheritance were impartible – say undividable land – then, of course, the group would have to have some unity in order jointly to exploit it.

This latter point raises the question of residence again. If the property of the group is a territory, how can the group reside in and exploit this territory? We have already suggested a slight modification of the system that will allow for this: a core of members could reside there, while the absent members could retain rights in the land without actually being on it; they could come and live on it if they wanted to. This method could be pushed a little harder. The group could be defined as all the descendants of the ultimate ancestor *who elected to live on the lineage lands.* Those who elected to live elsewhere would lose rights to membership in the lineage. If some such qualification is made, then the group is known as a 'restricted' cognatic descent group. The cognatic principle still holds – all the descendants of the ultimate ancestor have a *right* to the land of the group; but unless they exercise this right, then they lose it. This means that a man must *choose* which lineage to belong to of the many to which he claims a link. In our example (p. 148), then, ego must choose whether to affiliate with 1, 2, 3, or 4, and must, in fact, take only one of these. The result of such a system would be groups as discrete as unilineal descent groups, but instead of achieving this discreteness by restricting recruitment to one or other *sex* of the group, they achieve it by a restriction on *residence*: only those who reside with the group are members of it.

Thus it is that while still holding to the cognatic principle (a man can join *either* father's *or* mother's group etc.), a series of discrete non-overlapping groups can be formed. The great adaptational advantage that these groups have is *flexibility.* In a society where, say, patrilineages each live on a limited amount of land, it is likely that demographic pressures can result in some lineages becoming far too large for the amount of land they hold, while in others the ratio of land to members may drop over a few generations. We saw earlier how unilineal descent groups had this chink in their armour – they were subject to demographic fluctuations. When this happens, the neatness and precision of the unilineal principle which is fine for recruitment purposes becomes a built-in rigidity which can throw the system off balance. The cognatic system, on the other hand, can deal with this contingency quite easily. If one group threatens to become far too large for its land, then many of its members will be members of other such groups and can take up their land rights in these, thus redistributing the population evenly amongst the holdings. The fact that cognatic descent groups seem most popular in small island communities may be due to this fact – population pressure on a small area of land. The cognatic system here allows for flexibility, while a unilineal system might well break down under demographic strain. In fact, unilineal systems do exist in small island communities but they have to be ready to make adjustments in the face of the pressures we have described. This leads some commentators to see the systems we have called 'cognatic lineages' as results of the breakdown of a patrilineal system. In fact, they often have a patrilineal tinge. There is a strain towards keeping men together – fathers, sons and brothers – for purposes of defence and solidarity in work etc. This means that residence is often predominantly patrilocal: of the choices open to him, a man most readily chooses to live with his father's group. Whether we regard this as the result of a breakdown of patriliny – or, as other observers have seen it, as the beginnings of a patrilineal system – depends perhaps on our views of the nature of social evolution and change. My own opinion is that the cognatic lineage method is in all probability an independent type, but that it could in some cases result from unilineal breakdown. It could also rigidify into unilineality in some cases, depending on whether circumstances led to the adoption of a matrilocal or patrilocal system of residence.

A lot here depends on the ideology of the system. The Mae-Enga of New Guinea have a predominantly patrilineal ideology – they believe in the 'closeness of relationship' of agnates and they have patrilineal clans and lineages etc. But a lineage will allow cognates to farm its lands, when there is not too much pressure on these. Thus, a man will give land to his sister's sons and daughter's sons if they need it. When pressure builds up, however, preference is given to agnates. Now the Maori of New Zealand, on the other hand, have a cognatic ideology. The social unit is the *hapu*, a territorial group, and a man is a member of as many *hapu* as he has lineal ancestors who were members. But here, *de facto*, he has to reside in only one at a time. This does not mean that he loses rights in the others as he would in a truly restricted system, but that, in effect, he is stuck with the one he chooses first. Here most men choose to stay near their fathers and join the father's *hapu*. Also, the Maori are great keepers of genealogies which run to enormous lengths. The more *males* a man has in his genealogy the more prestigious it is, although to trace a link through a female who was a great princess does not disgrace him. All these facts give a strong patrilineal tinge to the *hapu*, but nevertheless, a man may without prejudice join his mother's or grandmother's *hapu* and he does so quite often. In terms then of the situation on the ground, with both the Mae-Enga and the Maori we have groups of cognates who are primarily agnates using a territory and its lands. A statistical survey may well show that composition of local groups is more or less identical between the two societies – yet one is 'patrilineal' and the other 'cognatic'.

It may be argued that the Mae-Enga cognates do not become *members* of the agnatic lineages to which they attach themselves. This is true, but an example we have already discussed may push the argument a little further. The Yako are divided into territorially based patriclans and a man is supposed to reside in and be a member of the patriclan of his father – by definition it seems. But the Yako leave a loop-hole. A man may, if he wishes, leave and join the patriclan of his mother's brother. He is adopted by the latter and be-comes his mother's brother's 'son' by adoption. (This has an enormous advantage as he is then his mother's brother's heir both matrilineally and patrilineally and he has his cake and eats it at the same time. A considerable proportion of the Yako take advantage of this stratagem.) Thus, in any patri-lineage there may be men who are in fact cognates by birth ('sister's sons') but who have been adopted in. In what sense is this system different then from the Maori? The answer lies at the ideological rather than the practical level. What we have in all these cases are land-holding corporations; one can get membership in these (or, at least, some rights) in various ways. In all three cases, the commonest and surest way is by being one's father's child. In the Mae-Enga and the Yako, one can sue for membership in virtue of a cognatic connexion; but amongst the Maori, one has a *right* to membership by virtue of a cognatic connexion. This may seem a small difference, but it is very important.

However, this discussion should make us wary of trying to force systems too rigidly into the categories of 'patrilineal' 'cognatic' and 'matrilineal'. Some 'patrilineal' systems may in fact be much more like some 'cognatic' than they are like other patrilineal systems. We must always look care-fully at all the rights and obligations that people can hold in property, group membership and in each other, and see how these are distributed. Very often, the lines of division be-come blurred when this is done, but at least we escape the fallacy that having said of a system that it is 'patrilineal' we have disposed of the most important question about it. We have, in fact, only just begun. All systems are in a sense 'transitional'; change is the law of life in society, as well as in nature. If a system is faced with changing circumstances, then it either changes and adapts to these, or dies. Thus, some cognatic systems as we see them operating may be the result of adaptational changes by patrilineal systems, but the opposite may be equally true. This sobering fact should perhaps turn us from asking simply, 'into what structural category should we place system X', to asking, 'what are the trends in system X; from where is it coming and where does it seem to be going?'

III

We have seen, then, that cognatic descent groups can be of three kinds:

1. *Unrestricted.* In these, all the descendants of the ultimate or founding ancestor are members.

2. *Restricted.* In these, all the descendants of the founder have a right to membership, but can only exercise this right if they choose, say, to live in the founder's territory.

3. What we might call *pragmatically restricted.* In these all the descendants remain members, but in practice they cannot take up membership in all the groups they belong to, as these are territorial. So they have to choose which one to affiliate with, but this is not immutable.

The important thing here is that the restricted variety can, in fact, function with the same effectiveness as unilineal descent groups, and also have an added flexibility that might turn out in some circumstances to be a positive advantage. Let us look at some examples of these kinds of groups in action in order to see just what they can do. We have discussed the third type under the Maori, so we can leave that aside for the moment.

Let us turn to the Gilbert Islanders in the Pacific to see an elaborate cognatic system at work. The Gilbert Islanders have several kinds of kinship group but we will concern ourselves with their cognatic descent groups. The most all-inclusive of these is an unrestricted cognatic descent group known charmingly as the *oo*. Both men and women hold land and on the death of an individual his land is divided between all his children. (His daughters may have received their share on marriage.) As this process continues, a tract of land is divided and subdivided amongst the descendants of the original owner. The *oo* regards itself as in a sense jointly responsible for all the land, and members of the *oo* may not sell land without the permission of all the others. If any line of the *oo* dies out, then the land reverts to the *oo* generally and is redistributed among the members. Members who leave the area in which the descent group owns land, do not thereby lose rights in it. Any one who is descended from the original owner keeps his rights in the land and passes these on to his children. The fact that the *oo* are bound to overlap means that an individual may hold rights in several of them. In such a system the various plots of land that an individual holds in the various *oo* territories must not be too far from each other or he could not work them. On small islands, such a system of landholding is feasible. The Maori *hapu*, on the other hand, were not so compact, and so multiple inheritance was relatively impossible.

Another important descent group on the Gilbert Islands is the *bwoti*. This is a segment of an *oo* which is concerned with seating-rights in the community meeting-houses. These rights are very important to the Gilbertese. Each meeting house is marked out, and certain areas of it belong to the descendants of men who owned particular plots of land. Now *all* the descendants of one of these men would be an *oo*, but not all would have inherited a piece of his land. When a man died his land would be divided amongst his children, and he would bequeath the land in one of his *oo* to one child, that in another *oo* to another child ... and so on. Thus a child might be a member of an *oo* but not necessarily have inherited any of its property; hence he would not be able to sit with the *bwoti* associated with the *oo*. He would, however, have got some land in at least one *oo* that had *bwoti* rights in one of the meeting houses. A person would so distribute his property to his heirs that each of them obtained such a right. The division of inheritance is such that men got much more than women, and in consequence a man is more likely to get *bwoti* membership from his father than his mother. This gives the *bwoti* a patrilineal tinge. Early writers often described it as a patrilineage.

The *bwoti* is then a common descent group whose membership is restricted to those descendants of a common ancestor who have acquired rights in a particular plot of land.

Thirdly, the Gilbertese have the *kainga*. Now, every ancestor who founds a *bwoti*, also founds a *kainga*, but the membership rules are different, so that although each *kainga* is associated with a *bwoti*, their membership is not coterminous. The rule for *kainga* membership is again hitched to landholding. The original ancestor had lived on a certain tract of land. Some of his descendants continued to reside there but others moved away. Those who continued to reside there *plus* those who had been born and raised there but had moved away after marriage, formed the *kainga*. Thus, those who were born on the land inherited membership even if they moved away; but if they moved away their *children* did not inherit membership. Thus, if a man's parents were living patrilocally he would belong to his father's *kainga*: if they were living matrilocally he would belong to his mother's. It was thus in a sense *parental* residence choice that determined an individual's *kainga* membership. Since residence was predominantly patrilocal most people belonged to the father's *kainga*. Leadership of the *kainga* was passed on patrilineally. This was worked by having the eligible successor reside patrilocally so that his son would be eligible to succeed him and so on. Thus, the *kainga* very much resembled a patrilineage, but this resemblance was arrived at by a route far different from the simple rule of patrilineal succession.

Goodenough, who describes this system sums it up thus: '. . . all three descent groups are somehow connected with land. An ancestor having established ownership of a tract was the founder of all three. All of his descendants formed an *oo*. Those in actual possession of a share in the land are eligible to membership in a *bwoti*. Those whose parents resided on it form a *kainga*.' Thus the *oo* is concerned with *rights* in the land; the *bwoti* with actual *possession* of a piece of it; and the *kainga* with *residence* on it.

Similar groups to these three – particularly the *oo* and the *bwoti* – are found in the Philippines, the Solomon Islands, Samoa, Polynesia generally and, of course, New Zealand. The Scottish 'clan' was a form of cognatic descent group, *clann* in Gaelic simply meaning 'children' or descendants. Because of a preference for endogamy and patrilocal residence it, too, had a strong patrilineal tinge as is evidenced in the inheritance of surnames. But note that every true Highland Scot bears two names: his father's and his mother's. Thus Robert McAlpine McKinnon is a McKinnon through his father and a McAlpine through his mother – and he may belong to other clans 'by birth'. This system no longer functions except for sentimental reasons, but in some of the more remote Celtic parts of the British Isles, a descent group like the *oo*, with very similar functions, is still in existence. It would be described with the old Gaelic word too – as 'Clann Eoghain' for example: the children or descendants of Owen, over as many as eight or more generations.

At this point, the reader might like to refer back to Chapter three and look at case 5. In discussing the possible environmental pressures that might produce various kinds of grouping, I suggested that 'transferability of skills' in males, and the need to distribute a population over agricultural plots might lead to a situation in which either the men or the women moved on marriage, thus creating ambilocal residence. In the examples we have just looked at, we can see how this has happened in a number of cases. The residential group that we would get in case 5 would be the core of the Gilbertese *kainga* (with the spouses of members). If those members who were born there and subsequently moved away on marriage continued to have rights in the land of the group, then a true *kainga* could easily come into being. Such a combination of groups that we get in the Gilberts and elsewhere on small islands, however, are very tied to plots of land and localities. This is fine for small islands, but clearly it would be of little use to desert nomads or expanding warrior tribes. For these, a patrilineal system has obvious advantages and such a system of groups as we find on the Gilberts would not be workable. They represent a rather fine adjustment to ecological pressures: an exploitation of our third option which human biology offers for the recruitment of groups on a kinship basis.

Before leaving cognatic descent groups, we should perhaps look at one for which case 5 in Chapter three can serve as the exact model. The Iban of Borneo live in 'longhouses' and each longhouse may contain anything up to 50 families each living in its own apartment. These families, known as *bilek* after the name of the apartment, are the real units of the society, rather than the longhouse as such. When a couple marry, they must decide whether to live in the *bilek* of the man or that of the woman. This is a momentous choice, because they become members of the one they live in and lose membership in the one they turn down. If a man chooses to go to his wife's *bilek* and farm the land that it owns (part of the longhouse land), then he loses all rights to the land of his natal *bilek* and is thoroughly incorporated into his wife's. (The *bilek* family is exogamous.) A *bilek* family consists, then, of all the descendants of the original owner of the apartment, except those that have moved away and their children, but includes the spouses of natal members who continue to reside in it. Here an individual does not choose whether or not to live in the mother's or father's group, but in the natal group (whether this be mother's or father's), or the spouse's group. It is a kind of cognatic version of the Chinese practice of incorporating the wife of a man into his lineage. It is interesting because virilocal and uxorilocal residence are equally balanced in Iban society, and it therefore gives us an example of cognatic recruitment which is not predominantly patrilocal. The Iban are rice farmers, and one rice farm is very much like another, so labour and skills are easily transferable. A couple on marriage therefore must judge which is the best bet – his *bilek* or hers.

We can see that out of a situation such as we envisaged in case 5, a number of possibilities could emerge. Predominantly patrilocal residence and continuing rights in the land on the part of those who left would lead to a Gilbertian

situation, while a more rigidly residential rule of membership would give us something like the *bilek* of the Iban. That
such groups as the *oo* and the *kainga* seem confined to small
islands is perhaps significant, but we should not lose sight of
the Maori – a numerous, sophisticated and warlike people –
who show that a cognatic principle of descent-group formation need not be confined to atolls.

I have approached the problem of cognatic descent
groups backwards in comparison with the approach used
for unilineal groups. With the latter, I tried to show how the
principle of unilineal descent-group organization could arise
out of a simple residence situation: in the present case I
started with the principle of group organization and ended
with a rather tame reference to residence. The main reason
for this was that I wanted to align these groups firmly with
unilineal groups in the common category of *descent* groups.
Hence, I started by exploring the possibility of having all the
descendants of an ancestor as members of his group. This
gives us a continuum: at one end we have the unrestricted
cognatic descent group in which all the descendants of the
ancestor are members; then we have cognatic descent
groups restricted in membership in terms of residence; then
we have descent groups restricted in terms of sex – that is,
only allowing the members of one sex to recruit the group.
Thus unilineal groups are seen simply as one type of restricted descent group rather than as a completely separate type
of group altogether from the cognatic. All these groups share
in being common-descent groups – their focal point is an ancestor from whom all the members ultimately trace descent.

The second reason that I approached this problem backwards was because I am less sure of the connexion between
residence and descent in this case. As we saw earlier, the
cognatic descent group seems to be compatible with any
kind of residence principle – it really depends on what the
purpose of the group is. Where, as is usually the case, it is
concerned with the inheritance and control of land, then
perhaps we can more easily see tnat residence on the land
might have something to do with it. The circumstances that

favour the development of ambilocal residence (case 5) might well favour the growth of cognatic descent groups. Given the transferability of skills and a subsistence-agriculture economy with a pressure on land, then a system of cognatic descent groups would provide a reasonable solution in that it allowed for a redistribution of population amongst the scarce plots. A system like the Gilbertese is an admirable answer to the problem. The unrestricted descent group operates in relation to *claims* on the founder's plot, while the restricted descent groups operate with respect to the actual ownership of parts of it, or residence on it. Such a system can have its problems of course, not least that of fragmentation, and the product may be small, scattered holdings which are uneconomical and difficult to farm.

If residence is ambilocal, and the areas of land concerned are distinct, then the members and their children who leave can either retain rights in the land or lose them, thus producing unrestricted or restricted descent groups. If, however, the people live in large settlements and not on their land, and residence rules are flexible, how then do such groups arise? The full set of determinants for these groups has not yet been worked out, and it may be that an independent ideology of the equal rights of all children to inheritance is involved. But it is hard to believe that the ideology would survive in the face of environmental pressures that made it non-adaptational. Ideological factors cannot be ruled out, however, because it is possible – with suitable adjustments – for unilineal systems to survive in much the same circumstances as seem to breed cognatic systems. Ecology sometimes sets hard and fast limits, but very often it allows a large amount of 'play', and so different systems can flourish in the same conditions. But we must not forget the theorists who insist that cognatic systems are breakdowns of unilineal systems in the face of environmental pressures. Thus they may represent an adjustment of a unilineal system. Alternatively they may simply be the breeding ground of unilineal systems. On this subject, we have a long way yet to go.

My reason for wanting to put these cognatic groups firmly into the category of 'descent groups' is largely due to the fact that anthropologists have tended to ignore them until recently. Most students of kinship, following Radcliffe-Brown, have been bemused by the hard, clean beauty of the unilineal principle and have seen in such things as the *hapu* only sports and oddities. They have either tried to assimilate them to unilineal systems, or have just ignored their existence. Thus, the 'descent-group theory' that gets much talked about really means 'unilineal descent-group theory'. Radcliffe-Brown thought the advantages of the unilineal solutions to be so obvious that he could hardly imagine how any society could get by without adopting one or the other of them. Quite a number, however, have managed to stagger along despite this handicap, and we are now becoming better equipped to see why and how.

There has also been another confusion. Anthropologists have thought that the cognatic principle could not be effectively used to form *descent* groups – those based on descent from a common ancestor – and have thought that it was solely concerned with the formation of *ego-centred* or *personal* groups. It is to these that we must now turn.

IV

Descent groups have certain characteristics in common whatever their form. They all consist of the descendants of a common ancestor; all the members are therefore related to each other in respect of such descent. They are usually 'corporate' groups, that is, groups that exist independently of the individuals composing them. They exist 'in perpetuity'; individual members come and go, but the group goes on. Corporateness also implies that they act 'as a body'; thus if one of their members kills a man, the group as a whole is held responsible for the killing; or, as is often the case with land, this cannot be alienated by an individual member but belongs to the group as a whole and must only pass from one member of the group to another. Descent groups are not always corporate in this latter sense, but they always are groups that exist in perpetuity. They are commonly exogamous, but this is not universally the case. It is the relation by common descent of all the members to each other, and corporateness in the sense of perpetuity of existence that characterizes all descent groups. Bearing this in mind, we can now look at ego-centricity.

We saw earlier that there were two ways of looking at any kinship system: from the angle of the kin-groups composing the society and from the angle of the individual and his kin. Thus, we saw that looked at from the first angle we may only see a society composed of patriclans; but that in such a society an individual may recognize cognates up to a certain degree as relatives, and have important relationships with matrilateral relatives . . . and so on. Now, this is true of all kinship systems. Goodenough has christened these two angles the *ancestor-focus* and the *ego-focus*. Now, while all kinship systems can be viewed from either focus, only some make use of the ancestor-focus in the formation of groups – descent groups; others make use of the ego-focus in group formation and it is this formation of groups on the basis of the ego-focus that we must now look at. Let us note that these are not mutually exclusive methods, and a society can have more than one kind of kinship group operating in it.

Groups formed on the ego-focus must, of necessity, be very different from those based on the ancestor-focus. They consist not necessarily of people who have an ancestor in common, but of people who have a *relative* (ego) in common who is not an ancestor of theirs. The best known of such groups is the *kindred*. This is recruited on the basis of the degree of relationship of its members to a common ego rather than a common ancestor. The best way to illustrate this is by the familiar English notion of cousinship. Thus, all ego's cognates up to, say, second cousins, could be counted as his kindred. Diagram 32 illustrates this by using the neutral square to mean 'person(s) of either sex' – which stresses the cognatic nature of the group. But it is very different from a cognatic descent group. The men born of the kindred are not all related to each whereas they are all related to ego.

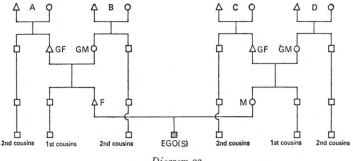

Diagram 32

All the members of it do not have an ancestor in common; all they have in common is ego himself (or herself). Thus, every person in the society has such a group, and each group is relative to that person. No two people except siblings will have the same kindred, and kindreds will thus endlessly overlap. We can illustrate this as below:

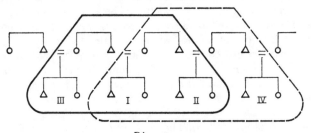

Diagram 33

(solid line = I's kindred; dotted line = II's kindred)

Here we have a simple kindred of first-cousin range. II and III are members of I's kindred; I and IV are members of II's kindred; but IV is not a member of I's kindred ... and so on. If we carry the analysis lineally – over the generations – then we would find that ego's kindred was different from the kindred of his father, and that of his mother. Such groups clearly then cannot function except in relation to the ego who is their focus. They cannot be 'corporate' in the sense of existing in perpetuity, because once ego dies (and here siblings are counted as a collective ego), the group ceases to exist. This is not true of a descent group. Nor do ego's children inherit his kindred. The kindred then is a purely *personal* group.

It is easy to see that such a group cannot perform the same functions as a descent group. It cannot be a landholding corporation passing on land to its descendants. It cannot be in any sense a 'constituent' unit of the society, because it comes in and out of existence as its focal egos are born and die. What does it do then and how does it work? Well clearly it would be a useful group to have in societies where people operate independently, but need on occasion to call in help for some purposes. The Iban, for example, have made the *bilek* family their domestic and economic unit. They lack any form of descent group that is more inclusive than the *bilek*, and the longhouse is not a corporate unit. But the Iban put out quite spectacular raiding and trading parties of considerable size. These are recruited by means of the kindred principle. The Iban surround ego with a kindred of up to second cousin range. Thus each Iban has a body of people – all those related to him up to the degree of second cousin – on whom he can call for some services to himself and who have some obligations to him. He himself of course is a member of several such kindreds – those of his first and second cousins. Now when an Iban wants to take out a head-hunting party, he calls on the members of his kindred. They in turn can call on the members of their kindreds who are not members of the original ego's kindred, who in turn can call on the members of their kindreds ... and so on until the requisite number of men are mustered. Thus, in our diagram 33, (assuming that these are second-cousin range kindreds rather than first) I would call on II and III; II would call upon IV, who would in turn call on his kindred mates other than II ... and so on. This body would then go on the hunt and share the spoils between them.

It is also possible to make ego's kin in some degree responsible for him. Thus, in the payment of blood money, it could well be the kindred that was the operative unit rather than the clan or lineage. If a man killed another, then all his kindred would have to pay out blood money to the kindred of the dead man who would share it between them. Amongst the ancient Teutons this is supposed to have been the case, with the nearest kin to the murderer paying most, and the nearest kin of the dead man receiving most. In some systems (England under King Alfred for example), the patrilateral relatives paid and received more than the matrilateral. The kindred here was known as the *sib* – a word that has been wrongly appropriated by some writers for application to unilineal descent groups. Amongst the Teutonic peoples, the *sib* was the exogamic unit, and this method of fixing the degree within which marriage was forbidden was adopted by the Christian church.

The kindred could also be used for purposes of inheritance, even if it could not be a property-owning group itself. Thus, if a man died without heirs, his land could revert to his kindred for distribution amongst its members – perhaps again on the basis of 'nearness'.

The essence of the kindred then is that all ego's cognates up to a certain degree are recognized as having some duties towards him and some claims on him. It is perhaps wrong to call this a 'group' at all, but rather should we call it a 'category' of persons. It is never a residential unit nor is it corporate, and it only comes to life, as it were, when the purpose for which it exists arises – like headhunting or the payment of blood money, or the regulation of marriage. (In the latter case it need not exist as a group at all. All ego need know is that he must not marry within a certain degree of relationship.) It is, then, a category out of which a group can be recruited by ego for some purposes.

If we look back to the Gilbert Islanders, we will find that among their kin-groups they have, in addition to the *oo*, *bwoti* and *kainga*, a kindred called the *utuu*. Their Malayo-Polynesian relatives in the Northern Philippines whom we have mentioned as having cognatic descent groups, also combine these with personal kindreds of third-cousin range. The descent groups regulate ceremony and the use of land sites; the kindreds deal with homicide payments and regulate exogamy. They also come to the aid of an individual in trouble, but because of the overlapping of kindreds, this is only really effective if the trouble is between two people so distantly related that their kindreds do not overlap. Clearly, if the two kindreds do overlap then some members will have divided loyalties as they will be equally members of the kindreds of the two combatants. This, in fact, can be quite effective as these 'overlap' members will then make strenuous efforts to bring about a settlement. There are many other examples of the co-existence of descent groups and kindreds, each serving different social purposes. Kindreds can and do co-exist quite easily with unilineal descent groups too, but we do not need elaborate examples of this to see how it could work. I must again stress that the kindred is not really a *group* in the sociological sense. The fact that amongst the patrilineal Zulu a man may not marry any woman descended from his great-grandparents established that each Zulu has an exogamous kindred of second-cousin range. But that is all. Nothing else follows from this, and the kindred has no other functions.

We should perhaps clear up one point that has caused some confusion. One way that the kindred was reckoned amongst the Teutons, and one way that it can always be calculated is in terms of *stocks*. Now a stock is all the descendants of a person or of a married pair. Thus, a kindred of second-cousin range such as we have drawn on diagram 32, will consist of four stocks – the descendants of ego's four pairs of great-grandparents. (A, B, C, and D on our diagram.) A kindred of third-cousin range, such as that of the northern Philippines, would consist of eight stocks ... and so on. The trouble with the definition of the stock is that it is the same as the definition of cognatic lineage, and this causes confusion. Some writers have called the 'stocks' of the Teutonic sib 'non-unilinear descent groups' for example. The reader should be able to see what the confusion is here. The essential difference is of course that the cognatic lineage, in common with other descent groups, is founded at a point in time and persists over time from then on; the stock of a kindred exists only in relation to a particular ego and it disappears when he dies. If a member of a cognatic lineage dies, the lineage still continues; when the focal ego of a kindred dies, then the stocks are no more. The lineage then is defined relative to an ancestor who remains a fixed point of reference; the stocks of a kindred are defined relative to an ego. The stocks of a kindred then *are*, like cognatic lineages, *all* the descendants of a person (or couple); but unlike cognatic lineages they are not independant entities, but only part of the circle of kin around an ego. Thus a cognatic lineage is a stock, but a stock is not necessarily a cognatic lineage, and when it is simply a constituent of a kindred it is really nothing like such a lineage.

V

We have concentrated above on the *cognatic* kindred. Indeed I have not yet bothered to mention that there is any other form. I wanted to deal with this form of the kindred first, because of the confusion that has arisen in anthropology from dividing the world into societies with unilineal kinship and those with cognatic, and assuming that the only form of kinship organization compatible with the latter was the personal cognatic kindred. We have seen that what matters is not so much the division into unilineal and cognatic, as the difference between the *ego-focus* on the one hand with its personal 'groups', and the *ancestor-focus* on the other with its descent groups. We can clinch this by showing that other forms of personal kindred exist than the cognatic – forms which employ a unilineal principle in recruitment, if we use unilineal as synonymous with 'unisexual'.

The kindred can be broadly defined as 'ego's relatives up to a certain fixed degree'. What matters is how this 'degree' is defined. It need not be defined cognatically (or 'bilaterally' as it is usually called in the literature). The Kalmuk

Mongols, for example, have a personal kindred consisting of all the people related to ego *through males* within a fixed degree. This is illustrated below:

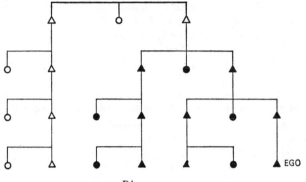

Diagram 34

Say the fixed degree involved is that of second cousinship – all the descendants through males of his great-grandfather (father's father's father). Then ego's kindred would be those people on the diagram who are shaded. You might immediately object that this is a lineage – all the descendants through males of a common ancestor. So it is, but like the stock of a kindred it is not a lineage decided upon in terms of descent from an ancestor, but in terms of the degree of the relationship of its members to ego. Thus, all the people on the diagram are the descendants of a common ancestor, but they are not all members of ego's kindred. Those in white however are members of ego's *father's* kindred. Thus the point of reference for membership is ego and not an ancestor as a fixed point of reference. To confuse this group – known as a patrilateral kindred – with a patrilineage is to fall into the same error as we discovered in the confusing of cognatic lineages with the stocks of a cognatic kindred.

The Kalmuk case should underline the fact that the real distinction is between the two foci – ego and ancestor: between *descent groups* and *personal groups*. Even when ego-centred groups recruit unisexually they are still more like cognatic kindreds than they are like unilineal lineages. The fact that they recruit unisexually has some important effects that makes them different from cognatic kindreds, it is true, but it does not turn them into lineages.

As long as a recognized category of persons exists in the society which has as its point of reference an ego to whom all the category are related, then whatever its composition such a group will be of the kindred type, even if it is not symmetrical and cognatic. Thus, on the island of Truk in the Pacific, where the corporate units are matrilineages, each ego is surrounded by a group of relatives, which is named, and composed thus:

1. Ego's grandparents and grandchildren
2. The members of his matrilineage
3. The members of his father's matrilineage
4. The children and grandchildren of the members of his matrilineage
5. The children and grandchildren of the members of his father's matrilineage.

This group, as I said, has a name, and certain rights and duties towards ego; it is constant only for siblings, and its membership is fixed by degree of relationship to ego. Here it is not so much a case of an ego-centred group co-existing with unilineal grouping: the ego-centred group absorbs ego's unilineal groups. In a number of unilineal societies, such clusterings of kin around ego exist, but they are not always by any means formalized and given a name and duties towards ego. This example stresses then the difference between analysing a kinship system from the ego-focus – which can be done for any kinship system – and the system itself using the ego-focus as a means of forming groups or categories of kin for various social purposes.

There is a great deal more that we could go into here, but space and probably the reader's patience forbid. Enough perhaps to have grasped these essential points:

1. That the division between groups descended from an ancestor and groups based on degree of relationship to an ego is fundamental.

2. That both kinds of group can recruit either cognatically or unisexually.

3. That these modes of grouping are not mutually exclusive and can co-exist in one society serving different purposes.

The fact that two otherwise different systems both use, say, the cognatic principle of recruitment, is important and makes it worth comparing them. But it should not lead us to lump them together on this one criterion. To help clarify this point I offer diagram 35. Here the intersection of two factors – focus, and mode of recruitment – gives us our types of grouping.

Recruitment		Focus	
		ego	ancestor
Unrestricted		cognatic kindred	unrestricted cognatic lineage
Restricted	by sex	'unilateral' kindred	unilineal lineage
	other	?	restricted cognatic lineage

Diagram 35

The blank cell could be filled by an example of an ego-centred group restricted on the basis of residence with ego, although I know of none at the moment.

Obviously the system of cognatic kindreds rings a bell for most readers as it resembles our own kinship system which is however, unformalized and lacks named kindreds. We simply recognize that relatives on both 'sides' of the family are our kin, and we may interact with these, invite them to ceremonies etc. Unless the personal kin-group is formalized in some way, it is perhaps better to speak simply of ego's kinship *network*, and to spell out its form and functions.

Our own system is primarily concerned with the nuclear family as its basic unit, and continuity over time is not of great importance. At ego's marriage two families are linked – his own and his wife's. The family he is born into is sometimes called by sociologists his 'family of orientation', (a barbarous usage – 'disorientation' might be more appropriate in many cases). The family he forms at marriage is his 'family of procreation' (very ambiguous but now accepted). Thus, our 'kindred' consists of linked nuclear families – ego's family of orientation, his family of procreation, his wife's family of orientation, the families of procreation of his siblings and children, and so on.

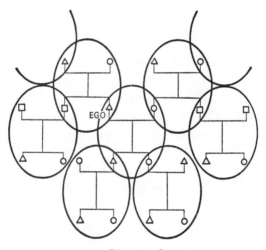

Diagram 36

The limit of recognition of 'nuclear-family' linkage tends to be narrow. This system is more reminiscent of the Shoshone or some Eskimo than of the more elaborate systems we have been discussing here. Cognatic descent groups can form on an *ad hoc* basis if property is involved, but there is not, above the level of the family, any extended kinship group to which people must belong. If such groups arise, it is to meet specific eventualities; they are not constituent units of the social structure with legal status.

CHAPTER SEVEN

Exogamy and Direct Exchange

I

AFTER the uphill struggle of the last chapter it will perhaps be refreshing to turn back to the fundamental topic of exogamy; a topic we have been taking for granted up to now. We saw in Chapter two how prohibitions on incest automatically produced exogamy – because of the association of sex and marriage – but that the reverse was not necessarily true. In consequence, we could not accept that all exogamic regulations were simply 'extensions' of incest prohibitions. We saw in the subsequent chapters how exogamy presented a problem to those descent groups that practised it, because it made them look outside themselves for brides, and so forced them into relationships with other descent groups.

Now 'forced' here is simply a figurative way of speaking about the situation, and it may be misleading. Why should the descent groups not actively *want* to marry women other than their own? In many cases they will not think too consciously about it; the rule of exogamy, whether it applies to lineage or clan or both, is, like the incest taboo, a part of cultural inheritance. But, unlike the incest taboo, its benefits are more obvious to the people practising it, and they can often verbalize these quite cogently. It may here be the case that the continuing benefits of the rule may in fact be closely connected with its origin – which was not the case with the incest taboo. Like a good preacher, I will offer you a text for my sermon on exogamy:

'Then will we give our daughters unto you, and we will take your daughters to us, and we will dwell with you, and we will become one people.' (Genesis 34:16.)

I am not original in offering this text; the anthropologist

E. B. Tylor used it in 1888, and prefixed it with these words:

'Again and again in the world's history, savage tribes must have had plainly before their minds the simple practical alternative between marrying-out and being killed-out.'

We might call this the 'hostage' theory of exogamy. Our palaeolithic hunting-and-gathering bands – patrilocal bands in all probability – exchanged women in order to live at peace with each other. If it were made a firm rule that no man of the band must marry any woman of it – or rather that each man should marry a woman of some other band, then each band would become dependent on the other bands for marriage partners. This would form bonds of 'alliance' between the bands. They would enter into a *connubium* – a system of marital exchanges. Thus, two categories of band would be set up: those with whom we had a connubium, and those with whom we did not.

This theory sees the rule of exogamy not as a negative outcome of incest extensions – 'do not marry women of the band because you cannot have sexual relations with them', but as a positive outcome of the need for survival – 'enter into marital alliances with other groups in order to live at peace with them'. This prohibition need not extend to sexual relationships, but clearly it is more clear cut if it does so. Also, there may be other factors such as the premium on the girl's virginity at marriage that operates in many tribes. If she loses her virginity, she may be unmarriageable, or a poor marriage bargain, and consequently the band may lose the chance of a good alliance. This may lead to fierce sanctions against intra-band sexuality that make it indistinguishable from the intra-familial incest taboo, and the two may be called by the same term.

We have seen how descent can regulate relationship *within* descent groups of often very large size; what comes out of this theory of exogamy is that the exogamic rule is a positive rule for regulating relations *between* descent groups by means of connubium. But you might ask why they could not have exchanged something else. I think the answer, perhaps, is that in the beginning there was precious little else to exchange. These were hunters and gatherers, not traders; they had their weapons and their skills which were not exchangeable, and their women who were. The hunting-bands of males stuck together but one woman was very much like another – her skills were transferable – so it was she who was passed on in exchange for another. We cannot of course know exactly why the earliest groups of men decided to exchange women, but we can perhaps see the consequences of their not doing so. Pre-human primate groups are obviously well-ordered internally – the dominance hierarchy sees to that; but relations between primate groups are either non-existent, unordered or plainly hostile. At the sub-human primate level, this does not matter too much, but with the advent of man the organized predator, things changed. The *weapon* is to some extent the characteristic of Man; he is the weapon-bearing ape – the killer primate. Relations between non-weapon-bearing bands of apes are bad enough, but with the advent of the axe and the spear and the large cunning brain that went with them, there must have been a danger that proto-human bands would rapidly extinguish each other. If they were to exploit the same area of country, then they had to come to some agreement: form some relationship other than the simply hostile. Nature had already provided within the structure of the primate bands, along with the principle of 'dominance' which we will take up later, the ideas of 'sharing' and 'cooperation'; the basic idea of 'reciprocity' – give and take. (The very expression 'I'll scratch your back and you scratch mine' perfectly expresses one of the most fundamental of primate cooperative relationships – grooming!) It only needed the extension of the idea of reciprocity across the band boundaries to provide for some form of inter-band cooperative relationship. You would not try to exterminate a band whose wives were your daughters and whose daughters were your potential wives; you would become, in one sense at least, 'one people'; you would be *dependent* on each other for your continuity and survival. All species which develop fighting instincts and efficient means of killing in the struggle for survival, have the problem of not using these means to wipe themselves out in intra-species warfare. Nature develops many means to this end, and exogamy was the human species' answer to the universal problem. In that it had survival value, it flourished. Larger and larger groups of cooperating bands exploiting larger and larger territories speeded up their domination of other animals, with the results we see today.

Of course, it had to have some boundaries. It could not, for practical if no other reasons, extend indefinitely. Groups speaking the same language and being alike in other ways might well exchange wives amongst themselves – but the connubium stopped at the boundaries of the language, territory, or colour, or whatever marked 'us' off from 'them'. The boundary between those with whom we had connubium and those with whom we did not, was probably the original 'tribal' boundary. But even though there was no general connubium across tribal boundaries, 'dynastic' marriages might still carry the idea into the international field. To settle a treaty with a marriage is a common enough practice in European history; and it is usually the woman who moves. Here instead of using all one's women as diplomatic pawns, one uses some of one's most important high-ranking women. As bands were not stratified in this way, such a modified solution was not possible.

I do not mean here to imply that groups which exchanged women always lived in perfect amity. The opposite was usually true. Many tribes have a proverb along the lines of 'we marry our enemies' or 'we marry those we fight'. Often the brides are taken from their people by a ceremonial 'capture' which has uncomfortably real overtones and sometimes ends in an actual fight or at least a skirmish. (This is the custom of 'bride capture' that sparked off McLennan's interest in kinship. See Introduction.) Nevertheless, the fact that the capture is ceremonialized is indicative of the restraint that exogamy introduces into inter-group relations. The groups concerned may be hostile and see each other as enemies, but they are still dependent on each other for their very continuity, and hence have to come to terms, however uneasy, in order to replenish each other's stock of reproductive capacity. In animal species other than man it is precisely *because* the individuals or groups are in a state of permanent hostility that they have to develop ritualized means of settling disputes or risk killing off the species by internecine strife. It does not always work, of course, in either human or non-human populations, but the basic tendency is there. Many novels and plays depend for their plots on the ending of a feud by a marriage.

There are many examples from primitive peoples of the conscious recognition of these principles and benefits of exogamy. They are as conscious of its benefits as is the king who sees the benefit of marrying his daughter to a foreign prince, and of himself taking a foreign queen. 'Arranged' marriages between noble families, or between great families and rich business-houses are similarly familiar. If they offend our romantic notions of the true 'love-match', it is just too bad. We are not here discussing their morality but their efficiency; and without 'arranged' marriages we would perhaps not be here to discuss the problem – so we must treat them with some respect.

As culture advanced and goods became more varied and more common, the women ceased, of course, to be the only scarce goods – the only liquid assets of the group. It became possible to evaluate a woman, and instead of directly exchanging women, the groups could offer the equivalent in goods to the value of a woman. This system would have marked advantages as it would iron out demographic problems caused by sex-ratio imbalance. A group, for example, might not have enough women to do enough 'straight swops' to provide for all its men. Yet another group might have a surplus of women. The under-stocked groups could offer goods instead of women in exchange for the women of other bands. This, like the introduction of any currency system, made for an easier and more rational flow and distribution of goods than the simple barter method. Thus was bride-wealth (bride-price) born; but, like so many of these brilliant cultural inventions, it lived to serve far more varied purposes than those which brought about its innovation.

I could go on for many more pages about the fundamental importance of exogamy and its origins and functions, but it would perhaps be best to look now at some examples of it in action. We will start with some examples of systematic exchange of women and try to unravel the complexities of the structures of marriage and descent that this involves.

II

Systematic exchange of women has advantages in terms of stability, sureness of supply etc. But often it is the only feasible form of exchange. We saw how amongst the Shoshone it was the practice for men to exchange sisters; or, put another way, for the children of one family to marry the children of another. Now this 'sister exchange' is of course the simplest and easiest form of marital exchange. We might cavil at the use of 'sister' exchange on the grounds that it is usually the senior generation that manages these things, so that 'daughter exchange' might be better – as the biblical quotation suggests. But if we use 'sister' loosely to mean 'consanguine woman of the band or descent group', as we have been using it, then the term is reasonable. The model of sister exchange is easy to grasp:

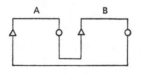

Diagram 37

The men of A give their sisters to the men of B and take the sisters of the men of B in return. Now the Shoshone were constantly splitting up into small nuclear family units, and there was no regular group over and above the nuclear family. But a slight variation in conditions would have produced the patrilocal band. If the exogamic unit were the patrilocal

EXOGAMY AND DIRECT EXCHANGE

band and not the nuclear family, and the practice of sister exchange were carried on over the generations, then our model would look like this:

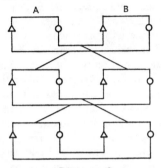

Diagram 38

Thus, A and B are two patrilocal bands. In each generation the men of A exchange sisters with the men of B. The two local groups then become the men of A plus the women of B and the men of B plus the women of A. The local group situation can be illustrated thus:

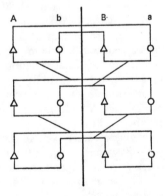

Diagram 39

There are two local groups of men, A and B, who exchange their sisters a and b. The local groups then are Ab and Ba.

For the rest of the exposition we will stick to the first model (Diagram 38) as it illustrates well the situation not only for a localized horde, but for any patrilineal group. The two groups could be patrilineages A and B, or patriclans A and B, with the symbols standing for 'men of A', 'women of B' ... and so on. If the tribe as a whole is divided into two such groups which exchange women in the manner shown, then these divisions are termed *moieties*. (Note: the model would not be affected if matrilineal rather than patrilineal descent operated. The reader could redraw the diagrams for matrilineal descent as an exercise.) There may of course be smaller divisions within the moieties – lineages, or clans, or local groups – which actually arrange the marriages and do the exchanging. The model will serve to illustrate either the total process of reciprocity between moieties, or any of the reciprocal-exchange arrangements between lower-order groups.

Moieties probably grow up in the way we have described for the development of clans etc. Two local hordes begin by exchanging women. These hordes then grow and segment, splitting up into clans or lineages but retaining their identity. Moieties are often named, like clans, after natural phenomena or places of origin, so that identity is easy to maintain. They are in fact a particular kind of phratry. They form a neat way of organizing a tribe, and a simple division of labour or ritual function can often be achieved. The moieties can rotate ritual or other functions season by season for example – and indeed sometimes they are called the 'winter people' and the 'summer people' – but this is running ahead a bit.

We can then imagine a moiety system having arisen in which the A's exchange women with the B's. If we are still at a rather primitive stage of hunting and gathering, then our local groups will still be small bands of males with their wives. The two moieties will then consist of a number of local bands $A^1, A^2, A^3 \ldots A^n$, and $B^1, B^2, B^3 \ldots B^n$. A local group then, may not just arrange exchanges with *one* group of the opposite moiety, but may have exchange arrangements with several. Thus A¹ may exchange with B¹, B³ and B⁵, while B¹ may exchange with A¹ and A³ ... and so on. A series of reciprocal exchanges will then be set up, perhaps as follows (for a small part of the system):

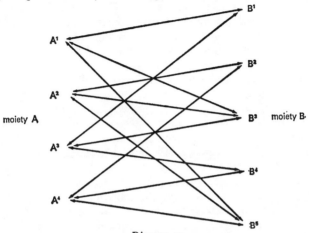

Diagram 40

If the operative groups are clans to which several hordes may belong, then the same model will serve. What matters is that if a horde or clan exchanges women with another horde or clan in one generation, it continues to do so in the next and subsequent generations. Thus, for any A and B groups that enter into relationships of marriage, the model of Diagram 38 will hold. Exactly which groups will make alliances with which, will probably depend on distance.

I have stressed that this can work in the context of a hunting-and-gathering ecology with the band as the local group: – in fact it works very well in such circumstances, because this is the ecological context of the Australian Aborigines. The model I have just put forward is the basic model for the understanding of the kinship-marriage system of most of the Aboriginal Australians. This has been described as the most difficult and complex kinship system in the world; and the great paradox is that it occurs in such a simple stone-age economy. The Australians certainly manage to introduce some elaborations to the basic model, but they are all logical developments of it. The joke is usually made that these natives have elaborated their kinship systems because there was not much else to do. There was in fact a good deal else to do – staying alive in fact; and the Australian was not the man to waste time elaborating a kinship system for the fun of it unless such a system had a high survival value.

Our model should show two things: firstly, that the kinship system is not all that complex (we will see later why anthropologists have thought it is); secondly, that it has to do with the very basic process on which the survival of the human race probably depended amongst our stone-age ancestors – the exchange of women between groups. It is, thus, not at all strange that the stone-age Australians should have developed and stuck by it. Centuries of evolutionary development have led them to modify and elaborate, and even have fun with it; but, in essentials, it represents the primeval answer to the challenge of possible extinction: reciprocal exogamy.

III

To see why it has been thought an impossibly difficult system and to examine a little of its elaboration, we must switch our focus to ego. So far, you will notice, we have not spoken of the system from ego's point of view; we have stuck to seeing how the constituent groups in the society go about exchanging women. It is because anthropologists have consistently looked at the problem from the ego-focus that they have been baffled by it. They have placed ego at the centre of his kinship network and tried to work the system out in terms of his personal relationships. Thus phrased, it does become more difficult to understand, but even so I think we can follow it.

The system we have just described with its two patrimoieties is sometimes called the *Kariera* system, as that particular Australian tribe is the best known exponent of it; we will therefore stick by this name for identification. The Kariera system has been said to be based on the rule that a man marries a woman who is a 'double (or 'bilateral') cross-cousin'. We must pause for a moment and examine this. Ego's first cousins are divided into two types – *cross-cousins*, and *parallel-cousins*: cross-cousins are the children of siblings of opposite sex, parallel-cousins are the children of siblings of the same sex. Thus, ego's father's sister's children, and his mother's brother's children are his cross-cousins; his father's brother's children and his mother's sister's children are his parallel-cousins. To make this quite clear we will diagram it as below and this will introduce us to the anthropological symbols for types of kin which are as follows: F = father, M = mother, B = brother, Z = sister, S = son, D = daughter. Secondary relatives are indicated by combinations of these – e.g. MM = mother's mother, FZ = father's sister. Affines are H = husband, W = wife.

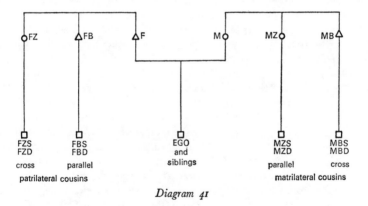

Diagram 41

Now if the Kariera rule is what it is said to be, then a male ego marries a double (bilateral) cross-cousin: one who is his FZD *and* his MBD. If we look to the diagram again and treat the symbols as *individuals* rather than just as 'men of A', 'women of B' etc., then we can see that this is so.

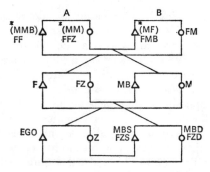

Diagram 42

*The significance of this will appear later

The system of sister exchange means that ego's father's sister has married his mother's brother; thus their child – who is ego's wife again by sister exchange – is both his MBD and his FZD. But this may well be a deduction of the anthropologist's rather than an idea in the aboriginal mind. It is the logical outcome of the exchange of 'sisters' over the generations. To say that the system is based on the rule of double cross-cousin marriage is to substitute what is analytically true for what is operationally true. The Kariera do not need to know the difference between cross- and parallel-cousins, all they need to do is to exchange 'sisters'.

We have been using 'sisters' in the loose sense indicated. It is not necessary that men actually exchange their true sisters, but simply that the reciprocal alliances between the A and B units be kept up. Thus, if the units are patriclans, 'sister-exchange' simply means that two patriclans which have exchanged women at one time go on doing so in subsequent generations. Thus, if there is an exchange arrangement between patriclan A¹, and patriclan B¹, all a man of A¹ has to do is make sure he marries a woman of B¹. There is no need for this woman to be genealogically his *actual* MBD/FZD. Now, it is true that in Australia the actual exchange of sisters does take place, so sometimes ego's wife will indeed be of this category, but there is no necessity for it. It is simply that A¹ and B¹ have an exchange relationship, that is all. The smaller the actual exchanging units are, the more likely is ego to marry an actual first cousin; but in many cases it is simply a woman of a reciprocal clan that he marries. We usually refer to these as 'classificatory' (as opposed to 'real') cross-cousins, because they are 'classified' with the real cross-cousins. The two points here are then, (1) that the Kariera are not necessarily pursuing a 'rule' of cross-cousin marriage; they are simply exchanging women between local or descent units; (2) it is not even necessary that actual first cousins marry, and indeed it is unlikely in many cases that they will.

One thing that has puzzled anthropologists here is the kinship terminology – the subject of Chapter nine. The kinship terminology has been assumed to describe actual genealogical relationships. Thus, there is a term that has been translated as 'mother's brother's daughter/father's sister's daughter'. But this term is in fact not a description of genealogical relationship, but a term covering the category of 'marriageable women'; it is a 'classificatory' term. The category includes of course his real FZD/MBD's, but it includes all the other potential mates as well. Thus, if ego of A^1 has his mother in B^1, then his classificatory 'cross-cousins' will be the daughters of all the men of B^1 of the same generation as his mother – all his mother's 'clan brothers'. A marriage to any one of these will satisfy the reciprocal arrangements. Thus, in their terminology and their own view of the situation, the Australians are nearer to our model than to the notion of 'cross-cousins' seeking each other in marriage.

The idea that this is a form of 'cross-cousin marriage' has been attractive to anthropologists because there are tribes where such a form of marriage is practised consciously. Cross-cousins have the advantage of being outside ego's lineage/clan under either unilineal descent system. They are therefore ideal mates if ego wants to marry a close relative. One set of parallel cousins is always a member of ego's unilineal descent group.

So far this slight misinterpretation has not been too

bothersome, but in an attempt to explain this 'cross-cousin marriage' phenomenon in Australia, anthropologists have resorted to more extreme interpretations. The Australians have not helped by introducing a complication which is now called the *section* system. It used to be called the 'marriage-class system', and was thought to regulate marriage. It is in fact a way of dividing the tribe up into ceremonial groups and although it results from the marriage arrangements, it does not in any way govern them. Let us spell it out.

In a *four-section* system the tribe is divided up into four sets of people – let us just use numbers for the moment: 1, 2, 3, and 4. The 'marriage rule' is said to be that 1 can only marry 2, and 3 can only marry 4. If a man of 1 marries a woman of 2, their children are 3; if a man of 2 marries a woman of 1, their children are 4. If a man of 3 marries a woman of 4, their children are 1; if a man of 4 marries a woman of 3, their children are 2. It is usually diagrammed as follows:

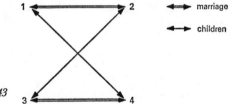

Diagram 43

But this obscures the fact that what is involved is that members of alternate generations will be in the same pair of sections:

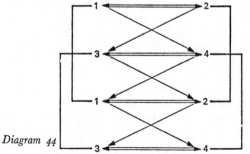

Diagram 44

The reader will see immediately that this can be neatly superimposed on the model of the Kariera system. The idea of sister exchange implies that it is only women of the same generation who can be exchanged; and the two factors of generation and patrimoiety can accommodate the section system. Let us call the adjacent generations X and Y, and using capital letters for males and small for females, set out the system in terms of our model.

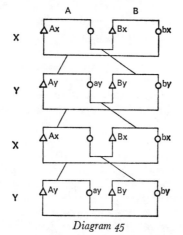

Diagram 45

Thus, an Ax marries a bx and their children are Ay(ay); a Bx marries an ax and their children are By(by). This is simply another way of describing reciprocal exogamy. Let us set out the equations here between our two models, and add the native terms to show how the four-section system works:

Ax(ax) = 1 (Burung)
Bx(bx) = 2 (Banaka)
Ay(ay) = 3 (Karimera)
By(by) = 4 (Palyeri)

Thus, Burung and Karimera are adjacent generations in moiety A, and Banaka and Palyeri are adjacent generations in moiety B. Alternating generations of the same moiety are, of course, in the same section. Thus, ego's father's father (FF) will be in his section, along with all the men of that generation in ego's moiety. Thus, if ego is Burung, then his FF and his ss – his grandparental and grandchild generations of agnates – will be in his section, and will cooperate with him in ceremonial activities. If he is Burung, then he will automatically marry a woman who is Banaka, and a male Banaka will marry his sister. This follows from the reciprocal exogamic arrangements – it is not a cause of them. These arrangements result in the stratification of society in terms of generation, and in its vertical division into two moieties. These elementary results of reciprocal exogamy have been used by the people to construct a simple system of grouping people for ceremonial purposes – but they cannot have resulted from what they have created. This is obvious because the marriage-class interpretation ignores the fact that for any ego, women of his grandparental and grandchild generations will be members of the section he marries into – but he does not marry them. Nor does he marry just any woman of the appropriate generation and section; his choice will be largely governed by the reciprocal alliances formed previously by his patriclan or local group.

The 'marriage-class' interpretation has led to a curious theory that has held sway for some time. This says that the 'cross-cousin marriage' rule and 'marriage-class system' results from there being in fact *two* sets of moieties – matrimoieties as well as patrimoieties – *even if the natives don't realize it*! This is ingeniously proved as follows:

Assume there are two patrimoieties A and B, and two matrimoieties C and D. Ego, therefore, belongs to a matrimoiety and a patrimoiety, *both* of which are exogamous. He must therefore marry someone who is of neither his own patrimoiety nor his own matrimoiety. We can diagram this as follows:

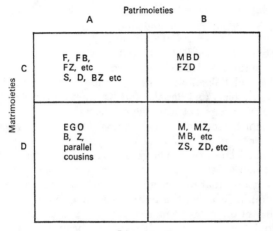

Diagram 46

Ego is a member of matrimoiety D and patrimoiety A. He must marry someone therefore who is of patrimoiety B and matrimoiety C. The only people this leaves are his cross-cousins. You will remember that this was the salient point about cross-cousins: under any unilineal system they will not be members of ego's descent group. The present theory says that what we have here is a 'double-descent' system, which rules out all ego's parallel cousins, but leaves his cross-cousins as marriage partners. It ties up with the marriage-class theory quite neatly. If ego is Burung, for example, then those of his relatives who are members both of his patrimoiety and his matrimoiety will also be Burung – those who are AD on our diagram. He will marry Banaka (BC), but will not be able to marry Karimera (AC) or Palyeri (BD). Karimera, on this scheme, will include those people who are members of his patrimoiety but not his matrimoiety, and Palyeri those who are members of his matrimoiety but not his patrimoiety. To complete the equations then:

$$Ax(ax) = 1 = AD \text{ (Burung)}$$
$$Bx(bx) = 2 = BC \text{ (Banaka)}$$
$$Ay(ay) = 3 = AC \text{ (Karimera)}$$
$$By(by) = 4 = BD \text{ (Palyeri)}$$

Thus, Burung and Karimera form one patrimoiety, and Banaka and Palyeri the other; Burung and Palyeri form one matrimoiety and Banaka and Karimera the other. The form of marriage between these 'classes' then is, on this theory, the outcome of the intersecting of two moiety systems. It is like a large double-descent system with only two large matriclans and two large patriclans. Now, this theory has the merit of seeing that it is not the rule of marriage with a cross-cousin that produces the system. Marriage with the cross-cousin (whether she be the true first cousin or just a member of the relevant moiety and generation) *results from* the double moiety system. It would be beautiful if it were true. But the truth is that the supposed double-moiety system itself results from the simple reciprocal-exogamy rule.

Look at it this way. There are two classes of people that ego may not marry on our simple model: he may not marry members of his own patrimoiety, and he may not marry members of adjacent generations. This leaves only members of the same generation and the opposite moiety. Now, as a result of this simple rule, and the system of 'sections' that is erected on the moiety-generation basis, ego finds that his own section, and that of the adjacent generations in the opposite moiety, together form a body of matrilineally related people who may not marry each other. If he is Burung, as we have seen, then he and his section mates together with the people who are Palyeri, form a matrilineal group. Again taking our symbols to mean 'the men etc. of the moiety' we can see in Diagram 47 how this works out.

If we carried this over more generations, we would see that alternate generations of the same patrimoiety were matrilineally related. This follows for they are of the same section, and members of the same section must be both matrilineally and patrilineally related. Thus, for example, ego's father's

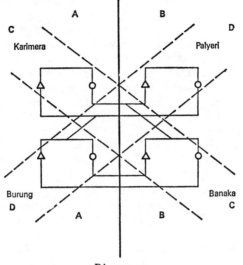

Diagram 47

father (FF) is also his mother's mother's brother (MMB) – a senior matrilineal relative. This has led to much elaborate talk of matrilineal descent 'cycling' through the generations and such like, but again it is a simple outcome of the original system.

And this is my point. If one has a simple system in which patrilineal groups exchange women systematically over the generations, then one produces a system as shown on our original model. If one then adds to this the 'section' idea; that is, arranges together and names all the people of the same moiety and generation, then it follows from the logic of the system that two pairs of sections will contain patrilineally related people, and two other pairs will contain matrilineally related people. Thus, from the societal point of view it is organized into two patrimoieties automatically – and there are potentially two matrimoieties if it wants them. For ego, his relatives are divided into those related to him patrilineally and – because of the nature of the system –

those related to him matrilineally (these latter including his patrilineal relatives of alternate generations.) The moiety system then is latent in the reciprocal-exogamy system. The advent of sections – a very simple mnemonic device for knowing which moiety and generation a person is in – brings this latent fact out into the open because a linking of two pairs of sections produces two matrilineal groups. Now, sometimes the Australians have seen this potential and have used it for further ceremonial purposes and even named the matrimoieties so produced; some have seen that these latent matrimoieties exist but have not utilized them; others have simply ignored the possibility. The theory of 'double-descent' through 'dual moieties' would have us believe that the dual-moiety system is basic and that it produces the section system and the marriage rule – but that sometimes the natives fail to recognize that this is the case and in consequence there is only an 'implicit' matrimoiety system. If everywhere there are patrilineal groups which exchange women, then we must take this as basic. Many Australian tribes have realized the potential for group organization that is latent in the reciprocal-exogamy situation, and have utilized it; but all these elaborations are derivations of the logic of the simple situation. It is all there in the situation of our two simple hunting bands that agree to exchange their sisters and become 'one people' – the two halves of a moiety system inseparably bound into one tribe.

Before passing on, we should note that, from ego's point of view, the system groups his near relatives into the two bodies of matrilineal and patrilineal relatives. As we saw in Chapter five, a man's matrilateral relatives might have important duties in his life in a patrilineal system – particularly his mother's brother. This is true in Australia, and should not be lost sight of. In the system we have just described, it is not so elaborated, because of the considerable overlap of patrilineal and matrilineal relatives in this case. It is hard to give these two logically different groups different functions to perform for ego when they physically overlap so much. But in the next system we will discuss,

this possibility is more fully exploited because ego's matrilineal and patrilineal relatives are more clearly differentiated.

For the moment, the reader can forget the dispute we
have just dealt with about what is basic to the system, and
return to the simple model (Diagram 38), and the details
of ego's personal relations in Diagram 42 on p. 186. With
these in mind, we can move on to the complexities of the
eight-class (or eight-section) systems that have caused sink-
ing feelings of incomprehension in many undergraduates –
and if the truth be told, in their teachers as well.

IV

In the Kariera model, a man marries where his father
married. He marries into his mother's lineage or clan, in
other words. Now, in an 'eight-class' system he is not
allowed to do this. Quite why this should be so we do not
know. It may be that he does not wish to become involved
in the complexities of mother-in-law avoidance. The
Australians are not unique in avoiding their mothers-in-law
– it is a widespread practice. Even if we do not actually
avoid them in a systematic and ritualized way, we still
maintain an ambivalent attitude towards our mothers-in-
law; the mother-in-law joke is still the oldest in the world.
Now, in a Kariera system, the mother-in-law is in fact the
father's sister, who has married the mother's brother. It
may be then that some societies which have a strong avoidance taboo find it awkward to have men avoiding women of
their own patrilineal group. Hence, while sticking with the
principle of reciprocal exchange, such societies oblige men
to look farther afield for a spouse. It may not be this problem, but something to do with the rivalry of adjacent
generations that decrees that a man must not marry where
his father married. The natives themselves say that a first
cousin (real or classificatory) is 'too close', and that a second
cross-cousin should be married. We will see that such a
cousin will come from a patrilineal group that is allied,
not to men of the father's generation of ego's clan, but to

men of the father's father's generation. We have already seen
that alternate generations are closely linked.

The kind of system we are discussing is usually called after
the Aranda tribe, and we will stick to the 'Aranda' system
here. The rule is simple: a man must not marry a first cross-
cousin – MBD/FZD – but a second cross-cousin: a MMBDD
who is also a FMBSD. Let us see how this works out.

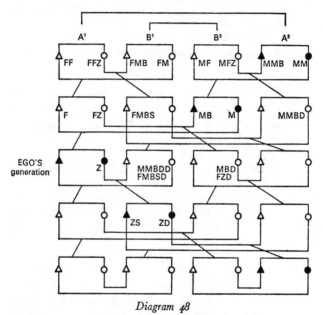

Diagram 48

This shows how the system would operate between any four
patrilineal units working the system (we need at least four
in this case). There are two units from moiety A and two
from moiety B. In the first generation A¹ exchanges women
with B¹ and A² with B². Now, if this were a Kariera system
they would continue this relationship over the generations,
but with the Aranda this is not allowed. In the next generation, the men of A¹ may not marry into their mother's
clan/lineage – they have to look elsewhere. Hence, they

marry into B^2 and vice versa - B^2 men take brides from A^1. Similarly B^1 and A^2 exchange women. In the subsequent generation – which we have taken as ego's – the men of A^1 cannot exchange with B^2; this is where their 'fathers' have alliances, so they revert to B^1 again; that is, they exchange with the clan from which their fathers' fathers took wives.

The reader can, as an exercise, do several things. He can trace out the actual 'path' of relationship and see that by following this simple variant of the Kariera rule, a man actually does marry his classificatory or real MMBDD/ FMBSD, and that this fearsome-seeming combination is simply a consequence of 'marrying where grandad married' and nothing more. He can also see how this produces eight 'classes' or 'sections', and how these will make up two sub-moieties in each patrimoiety and two sub-moieties in each matrimoiety (if such a division is recognized). I have shaded in the matrilineal relatives of ego's generation, and again one can see how his matrilineal relatives fall in alternate generations of his own moiety. Thus, ego's MMB is the senior member of ego's matrilineal lineage, and also a senior member of ego's own patrimoiety. This relative tends to loom large in ego's life and is often the chief functionary in arranging his marriage. In the Kariera system, you will remember, ego's MMB and his FF were one and the same person. In the Aranda system they are not; and in such a system ego's matrilineal kin – 'cycling' as they do through the four descent groups – play a large role in his life and, in particular, in his marriage. The matrilineal kin, after all, are drawn from *both* sides of the alliance and hence are the appropriate unit for arranging the marriage.

The Aranda system is, in fact, only a slight variation on the Kariera system, and the overall set of alliances in an Aranda system will look much the same as those in a Kariera shown on Diagram 40. A^1 will in fact have a number of clans/lineages with which it is allied, not just two. In principle, the systems should differ not in the overall scheme of alliances but in the mechanics of the alliances;

that is, whereas in the Kariera system the clans in B to which A^1 is linked continue to be linked in successive adjacent generations, in the Aranda system the B clans would be linked in alternate generations:

$$A^1x = B^1x + B^3x + B^5x$$
$$A^1y = B^2y + B^4y + B^6y \text{ etc.}$$

Thus A^1 would be allied with $B^1 + B^2 + B^3 + B^4 + B^5 + B^6$, as would A^2. It is the way in which they are linked that differs. Clearly such a system requires a larger number of units than a Kariera (unless it is going to run on only four clans and this never happens). It may, indeed, be a response to a growth in population or the amalgamation of a number of tribes or bands, or anything that increased the numbers of 'alliance units'. It preserves the moiety system, but brings a larger number of clans into alliance relationships.

In effect, it works out much the same as a Kariera system at the total system level. A clans exchange with B clans; ego looks for a wife in a clan with which his own clan has made previous exchanges – preferably with the clan into which his own FF has married. It is conceivable that this might be ruled out and he might be sent even further afield to marry a third cross-cousin and produce sixteen classes or sections and so on up the geometric scale. Some observers think they have found thirty-two-section systems. But this might strain genealogical knowledge in these societies to breaking point.

The Aranda system can, in fact, approximate even closer to a Kariera model in that for demographic reasons appropriate spouses may not be available for members of a clan and then they have to make a 'wrong' marriage. Old men are often polygynous, and so have to look for second and third wives for example. In this case, the first cross-cousin is sometimes allowed, and hence ego may marry where his father married. If this is repeated in subsequent generations – even on the second cousin pattern – then it will mean that A^1, for example, would be linked in each generation with B^1. In fact, when Aranda-type communities become large and mixed, rather than territorially spaced out – as has happened in modern conditions – then the 'rules' become simply an ordering of marriage preferences as far as ego is concerned and less a matter of alliances between patriunits. He has a 'first claim' on his MMBDD in the marriage race. If she marries anyone else, it can only be by his consent.

We started here from the simple business of swapping sisters or daughters. Nothing could be simpler: give and take, live at peace. (At least that is the hope; as often as not it has the opposite effect and leads to quarrels over women. Two clans of A for example may both have claims on the women of one clan of B, and may fight each other for these women. At least they are locked in conflict, I suppose, which is a kind of integration.) But once one adds to this simple tendency to perpetuate relationships by the direct exchange of women, the feature of unilocal residence or unilineal descent, then relationship systems of some complexity can be erected on the simple base of reciprocal exchange. But in pursuing sections and sub-sections, moieties and MMBDDs, we must never lose sight of the almost absurdly simple basis on which this elaboration is built. The elaborations are fascinating and, as we have seen, to add even slightly new wrinkles to the basic system may result in a scheme of enormous complexity; but the system is still in essence the same at bottom – 'let's swap women'.

Anthropologists sometimes say that such systems are characterized by 'positive' marriage rules. They not only say whom one may *not* marry, they specify also whom one *should* marry. This contrasts with 'negative' rules which simply lay down whom one should not marry but have no rule about the actual choice of partner. We will take up the implications of this distinction later.

v

The model we have just been investigating has several distinct features: there is no distinction in it between kin and affines, or kin and non-kin; all one's affines are kinsmen and all one's kinsmen are affines. Thus, one's father-in-law is one's mother's brother, one's wife is one's cousin, one's brother-in-law is one's father's sister's child and so on. (Always remembering of course that these relatives can be 'classificatory'.) Thus, one cannot marry anyone who is not already a relative. The second important feature is that the system rests on the exchange of women between groups. There is *direct* reciprocity: we give you women and you give us women back. In the model examined here, this reciprocity involves clans and moieties in systematic exchange, but the same basic *idea* of reciprocity by a direct return occurs in societies where this systematic method is not carried out. Thus in societies lacking groups such as clans and moieties, there can still be 'cross-cousin marriage'. In fact, it is in such societies that one can really talk of cross-cousin marriage, i.e. people really do marry cross-cousins and this is not just a way of saying that a man must marry a woman of a certain age and generation in another clan or moiety.

In such a society – like the Shoshone for example, or the Ojibwa of eastern Canada, or in Ceylon and parts of southern India – the 'preferred spouse' is a cross-cousin: a bilateral cross-cousin. As we have seen, persistent sister-exchange will produce such a system, but for obvious demographic reasons *real* sister exchange is not always easy to achieve. Thus, a society of this type will usually only be able to achieve a certain statistical level of such 'direct' exchanges.

The difference between these two types of direct exchange – what I have loosely called the 'systematic' and the 'statistical' – really lies in the nature of the groups involved. In the 'systematic' type, it is the overall exchange between such large groups as clans, lineages and moieties that is involved. Clan A takes women from clan B and gives women back – and so on. Thus, although a man may like to marry his double cross-cousin (MBD/FZD), it does not matter if he does not, and, in fact, very few probably do so. All he has to do is to marry a woman of the right clan and generation: a clan to which his 'fathers' have given sisters and from which they have received wives in return. In a statistical system on the other hand, it is 'true' relatives which are involved. If a Shoshone family has managed a sister-exchange with another in one generation, then the ideal thing in the next generation would be for the children of this arrangement to again marry each other. But sex ratios being what they are, this may not be possible and some of the boys and girls will have to look elsewhere than to their cross-cousins for marriage partners. There would be no 'equivalents' to cross-cousins here, i.e. classificatory cousins of the same clan or moiety as the real cross-cousin. Thus, there can only be a statistical trend in the direction of direct exchange, and a large number of marriages would be with 'non-kin' – previously unrelated people.

However, it would not do to exaggerate the difference, for the 'principle' involved is the same: there is a strain in the system towards direct exchange of women between the groups that organize the exchanges, be they moieties or individual families. At the actual organizational level, much the same problems may face families and lineages in the systematic type as occur in the statistical – but that would be too long a story.

One kind of variant on this direct-exchange principle – the 'swapping principle' of marriage – is something that has again been labelled as a form of cross-cousin marriage – *patrilateral* cross-cousin marriage. You will remember that we separated out the two kinds of cross-cousins – mother's brother's children and father's sister's children – but said that any form of real or classificatory 'sister exchange' would result in these two being the same person (because the father's sister would have married the mother's brother). However, wherever sister-exchange does not prevail – in the real sense – then the father's sisters will have married people other than the mother's brothers and so ego will have two lots of cross-cousins: the children of his paternal aunt and those of the maternal uncle – a situation we are quite familiar with. Under these circumstances, he has the choice of marrying either of these cousins, and it might not seem at first glance to matter much which one it is – but it does, in fact, matter very much, so much, indeed, that some tribes have stern laws which forbid marriage with one or the other type of cross-cousin.

I have said that marriage with the patrilateral cross-cousin (FZD) is a form of direct exchange – a swap in fact. How does this work? Imagine this situation: A society composed of lineages (patrilineal or matrilineal – it makes no difference) has a rule as follows: If a lineage has given a woman to another lineage, then the receivers 'owe' a woman to the givers and must, at some time, repay this debt. Now, this is exactly the case with sister-exchange, only here the debt is paid at once and so cancelled as it were; the two groups are immediately on an equal footing. It may not suit the society however to have the groups on such an equal footing all the time, and here we must look at a seemingly widespread rule in the exogamy game: *wife-givers are usually superior to wife-takers* (the exception being where wives are 'tribute'). If we give you a wife then you are in our debt – many mothers-in-law never let their daughters' husbands forget this fact! Now, there are several things the receivers can do about this: they can reciprocate immediately either in kind or in payment of some sort, or they can, as it were, write out an I.O.U. for the woman and promise to make a return at some future date.

The French anthropologist Mauss saw this exogamic principle as part of a wide principle operating in human affairs. In all societies and at all times, the giving and receiving of gifts has been a feature that has often been fantastically elaborated. Often the gift-exchanging seems to have no economic function; indeed it was this that drove Mauss to inquire into it, because it seemed that otherwise completely self-sufficient groups, such as clans and even whole tribes, would go to enormous lengths to exchange extremely valuable gifts of one kind or another with other like units. Why, if they were self sufficient, should they bother? The answer seemed to lie in the same direction as that proposed for exogamy: they exchanged to express, cement, or create alliances. This was true from the personal level up to that of exchange between nations. And always there was this compulsion to make a return. If you did not make a return you were not an ally but a beggar: you were one-down and inferior. The reader need only examine his own attitude to such simple things as Christmas cards and buying rounds of drinks to see the force of this. Thus wife-exchanging was a species of gift-exchanging; wives were the primitive gifts. Reciprocation was here very necessary, because unlike manufactured goods, women were necessary for the sheer physical continuity of the group; if we gave away our goods, we could presumably make some more, but if we give away our women – the essence of exogamy – then we must get others or we cannot reproduce ourselves. If I part with my sisters, I must have wives.

We seem to have got away from patrilateral cross-cousin marriage somewhat, but let us follow through the logic of our thoughts. We have assumed that for some reason or other, the groups involved in the exchanges of women are not too concerned with immediately wiping out the debts. Indeed, it may be that a dominant-subordinate relationship has its attractions and that to have people in our debt may have advantages. If we are involved in wife-exchanges with several groups, there will always be repayments coming in, so we can afford to lord it over some groups who have not reciprocated. At the same time, of course, we will be in the debt of groups to whom we owe women. It may be, of course, that we do not want to be indefinitely in the debt of, and so inferior to, other groups, and so we eventually pay them back and the whole thing starts again.

This seems to be the secret of 'patrilateral cross-cousin marriage'. What it amounts to is this: there is a rule that *a girl should ideally marry into the group from which her mother came*. That is, if A receives a woman from B in one generation, it should give one back *in the next generation*. For one generation B would be superior to A, and the position would be reversed in the succeeding generation.

How does the patrilateral cross-cousin come in? Consider the following model (Diagram 49): here we have two patri-lineages (for the sake of argument), and in the first generation A gives to B and in the second B gives to A and so on down the generations.

If you take any of these men who are marrying, you will see that the 'type relative' that is being married is consistently his father's sister's daughter. This follows from the rule that a woman should marry into the group her mother came from, which is a simple variant on the rule that the wife-receivers owe a woman to the wife-givers. It can be called *delayed* direct exchange, and so operates to allow inferiority and superiority to alternate rather than allowing the debt always to be automatically cancelled.

It will be immediately clear that, unlike the sister-exchange model, this one is incomplete. We have to marry off all the people in A and B who are not married. If in the first generation A gives a woman to B, then A males cannot take B females and so they have to marry elsewhere; similarly B females must marry other than into A. We can envisage the system as in Diagram 50. There is nothing to stop C and D from being the same group, so three lineages could form a closed system, sending women one way round in one generation and the other way round in the next (Diagram 51).

Again we have seen how important it is to get away from the restrictive notion of 'cross-cousin marriage' when discussing these features. What only appears to be a bizarre oddity – the rule that one should marry one cousin and not another – becomes quite clear in the light of inter-group marital exchanges. Ego's father's sister's daughters are the prototype spouses in this case as they are his nearest relatives of the right category; that is, they are women of the group to which his group gave a woman in the previous generation, and hence from which it must take a woman in his generation. He probably calls all such women – including his 'real' FZD – by the same term, and can marry any of them in

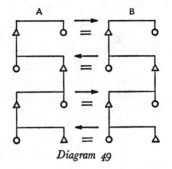

Diagram 49

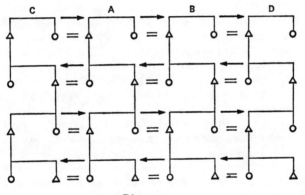

Diagram 50

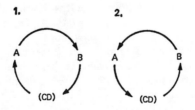

Diagram 51

principle, although of course who he actually marries will be a matter of negotiation, distance etc. etc.

The trouble with this whole issue is that material from the Highlands of New Guinea where systematic forms of such marriage are reported, is sparse and contradictory. However, several experts seem to agree that something like the above analysis is probably the best interpretation of the facts. Again, a non-systematic or 'preferential' form of this marriage is common elsewhere. As with the sister-exchange situation, it is often the case that there is a preference for marriage with the FZD, although there is no systematic swapping of women in alternate generations between groups such as lineages. Again, what one will get in these cases is a statistical trend in patrilateral cross-cousin direction, without the development of any elaborate exchange mechanism. In many of these cases, it does seem to be the *chiefly* lineages that are involved, and we are probably in the field of 'dynastic' marriages again here. Thus, noble or chiefly lineages will play the alternating-status game with each other, using just a few of their women as pawns.

Before leaving this subject and going on to explore the 'matrilateral' alternative in the next chapter, we might make this point: one must always keep clear at what level of social organization one is talking when using words like 'exchange' and 'inferior'. Thus, in the New Guinea case, it may well be that at the level of the clan or larger community, all that is happening is simple direct exchange: A is giving women to B and B to A, and they are passing back and forth all the time. At the level of the local lineage however, if A^1 is giving to B^1, then it will be another generation before B^1 reciprocates with another wife for A^1. At this level it will be delayed exchange that is working. A^1 of course, while giving wives to B^1 can be recouping past debts from B^2, B^3 ... and so on. Thus, at the clan level – direct exchange, and at the lineage level – delayed exchange.

The basic question, of course, is why in these types of system there is a shift away from direct reciprocity between the wife-giving and wife-taking groups? Why should the lineages want to play at one-upmanship in this way? One theory is that these societies are egalitarian but competitive. Lineages do not accept that any other lineage is superior to any other in the long run, but in the short run – often for political reasons – they want to dominate other lineages or to be the clients of other lineages. The 'patrilateral cross-cousin marriage' system therefore suits them very well. After all, a 'generation' in these circumstances may amount to anything up to 20 years depending on the age of marriage of the women and the age at which they bear their first children. Thus, there is no rapid alternation of lineage status, but rather an undulation over the years. Often the marriages are, in fact, only part of a much more elaborate set of ceremonial exchanges – as we might expect on Mauss's theory – and do not stand in isolation in what is essentially the political system of the tribe.

In this chapter, then, we have looked at two ways of exchanging women – the direct and the delayed direct – and seen some of the complications that arise when they are followed. It may seem absurd to call these 'simple' or 'elementary' as anthropologists tend to do, but this is in fact not a bad description. Our own system of moving women around the society in marriage is technically much more 'complex'. But at this point, and remembering the relative status of 'wife-givers' and 'wife-takers' we must move on to the much discussed 'matrilateral' alternative – remembering that in 'systematic' exchange the actual cross-cousin is only one of a class of 'potential spouses' and it is the class that we must seek out if we are to understand the system.

CHAPTER EIGHT

Asymmetrical and Complex Systems

I

THE systems we have described as 'direct exchange' are often designated 'symmetrical' by anthropologists. In them, the exchange balances out: we give you women, you give us women. It is true that the patrilateral system involves temporary asymmetry, but in the long run the balance is achieved; a man gives his daughter to the group from which he got a wife. (The exchange here may be delayed in terms of generation, but direct in terms of time. Thus, an older man who already has a wife and daughter may be looking for a second wife and give his daughter in return for one.) We are now going to look at some 'asymmetrical' systems – those characterized by the 'indirect exchange' of women. The principle involved here is again 'elementary' in both the loose and the strict senses of the term. It may be simply stated thus: wife-givers cannot be wife-takers; a group cannot *give* women to a group from which it has *taken* women. This appears to be the radical opposite to the symmetrical, direct-exchange principle, and indeed it is hard at first to see how it can be dubbed 'exchange' at all.

In such a system, if group B takes women from group A, then it must give women to group C, which in turn must give women to a group other than B. It could of course give them to A, and here is where the exchange comes in. The women could 'cycle' round the three groups. A→B→C→A . . . Of course, many more than three groups could join in – as many as the social and demographic strains could stand in fact.

We saw that in the 'patrilateral' system the women would circulate round three or more groups *in one generation*. But they would then circulate *back* again in the next generation. In the asymmetrical system, this could not happen.

Women move the same way in each generation. If B takes from A, it can *never* give back to A. From the point of view of an individual, he is trying to marry a woman of his mother's group, i.e. the group that gave a wife to his father. Failing this, he can take a wife from any of the clans/ lineages which have previously given wives to his group. The world is divided up for him into 'wife-giving' groups from which he may take a woman, and 'wife-taking' groups from which he may not.

This is often called 'matrilateral cross-cousin marriage', that is, marriage with the 'mother's brother's daughter', just as the delayed exchange system was called 'patrilateral cross-cousin marriage' – marriage with the FZD. We saw with the latter that although the actual FZDs were the ideal spouses, the system in no way depended on marriage with them. A man simply married a woman of a group which had previously given women to his group and he probably called all these 'potential spouses' by the same classificatory term as he called his FZD. Similarly, with the asymmetrical case, a marriage with the real mother's brother's daughter would be ideal in many respects; but any women of a 'wife-giving' group of the right generation would be equally eligible. It is, perhaps, very likely that a man would approach his mother's brothers and ask them to help him find a wife, but this is not necessary to the system.

For comparison with the patrilateral case and the systems of direct exchange, we will illustrate the asymmetrical case as it would pertain between four units – in this case patri-lineages:

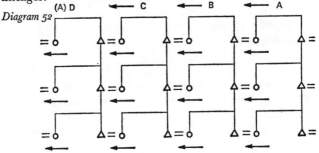

Diagram 52

(A) D   C   B   A

Again the 'type relative' that is being married is indeed the MBD, and obviously the FZD must be banned. If a man married her, he would be taking back a wife from the group to which he had previously given one, thus contravening the basic asymmetric rule.

There is no reason why in this system C should not give women to A. It has not taken women from A. Hence A, B and C could marry in a circle. Thus, they would 'exchange' women amongst themselves although this would never be a direct exchange between any two groups.

The basic model then is A → B → C → A ... But there may be many more than three groups involved, and A, for example, may take women from other groups than C, provided it does not give them back.

For example, the Purum, a tribe of Manipur on the eastern border of India, numbered only 303 individuals in 1932, but practised a system such as we have been analysing. They were divided into five exogamous patriclans, but these were not the 'alliance units'. Alliances were formed between named lineages and there were thirteen of these. Thus, for any one of the lineages the rest were divided up into 'lineages of our own clan', 'those from whom we take women' and 'those to whom we give women'. Thao-kung lineage, for example, of the Thao clan, took women from the two lineages of the Makan clan, and gave women to the two lineages of the Kheyang clan and the Rim-ke-lek lineage of the Marrim clan. As another example, we might take the Rimphunchong lineage of the Marrim clan which took women from the two lineages of the Kheyang clan and the Kankung lineage of the Makan clan; it gave women to the Makan-te lineage of the Makan clan and to the Parpa clan (which had only one lineage). Here we see that between two clans – Marrim and Makan – there is exchange, but the clans are dispersed exogamous units and are not the units that form alliances. A lineage that has taken women from another does not give them back. Only if demographic pressures force this solution is it ever adopted, and then several subterfuges may be resorted to, such as splitting a lineage in two and so creating a whole new lineage to which it is legitimate to give women. This may be the reason why clans are split up into named lineages. Thus, at one point, Marrim may have given to Makan but not vice versa. When they wanted to 'exchange' Makan split into Kankung and Makan-te lineages. Thus, Marrim could take from Kankung and give to Makan-te and so preserve the asymmetrical A→B→C rule.

The number of possible 'cycles' that can be run through with 13 lineages is dauntingly large. Let us take a system of eight lineages – A to H – and run through some of the possibilities. Let us say that

A gives women to lineages BHF and takes from DEGC

E gives women to lineages ADG and takes from BFC

B gives women to lineages ECF and takes from HA

We will stop here and look at some of the 'cycles' that this produces. Thus, A gives to B gives to E gives to A again: this is one cycle. We will list some of the others:

A→B →C→A
A→B →F →E →A
A→H→B →E →A
A→H→B →C →A
A→F →E →G→A   and so on.

We can quickly see the possible cycles by drawing a 'flow diagram'.

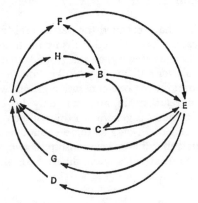

Diagram 53

We can see from this that there is a cycle $E \rightarrow G \rightarrow A$ $\rightarrow H \rightarrow B \rightarrow E$, for example, and many others. As an example of how the system can expand, let us suppose that D begins to take wives from G. It may do so as it has never given wives to G. We would then draw an arrow from G to D. This would give us some new cycles such as $G \rightarrow D$ $\rightarrow A \rightarrow H \rightarrow B \rightarrow E \rightarrow G$, and several others. We could also, of course, as the Purum do, split up a group into two units and create more cycles.

The main thing to note here is that in sharp contrast to the direct exchange systems, the 'debt' is never wiped out. B never gives back a woman to A. If wife-givers are superior to wife-takers, then A will always be superior to B. However, no one is absolutely inferior in such a system; a group will always be a debtor to some groups but a creditor to others. Very often the 'debt' will be in a sense cancelled by the payment of bride-wealth. This does not alter the dominant-subordinate relationship. The bride-wealth becomes a kind of 'tribute' paid by an inferior to a superior. But this is not an hierarchical system. There is a 'peck order' but it is not linear. In a linear peck-order, A pecks B who pecks C who pecks no one. In our peck-order, A is superior to B who is superior to C who is superior to A. It is a cyclical peck-order, a kind of caucus race. Between any *two* lineages however, there can only be a dominant-subordinate relationship, and this is very different from direct exchange.

Some writers have counted the patrilateral (FZD) case as 'asymmetrical'. I have placed it firmly in the symmetrical or direct exchange category, on the grounds that the debt is repaid even if after a delay. If you like, you can see it as a half-way house; during one generation groups will be in an asymmetrical relationship and can only be linked in a 'cycle', but in the next generation this will be reversed and the debt cancelled. Insofar as there cannot be a *permanent* superordinate-subordinate relationship between any two groups, the patrilateral system differs radically from its matrilateral 'opposite'. If we simply take the marriage rule, then they are both asymmetrical as opposed to the direct-exchange model; if we take the nature of the exchange relationship, however, then the 'bilateral' and 'patrilateral' fall together as 'direct', and are distinct from the 'matrilateral'.

Insofar as the peck order is cyclical, such a system must be to some extent 'democratic'; no one group can dominate all the others. But the superior-inferior relationship that is built into the system does allow for hierarchical tendencies to develop which are inimical to the direct-exchange model. The Kachin of northern Burma who number some 300,000, for example, are stratified into three classes – Chiefs, Aristocrats and Commoners. Within each class, patrilineages marry on the asymmetric model. Wife givers are called *mayu*, wife takers *dama*. Now, although most marriages take place within the classes, some women pass between them in marriage. As you might expect, lineages from a superior class give women to lineages from an inferior. Thus, for example, chiefly lineage A, which rules over a certain domain, will marry with other chiefly lineages which rule other domains, but it will be *mayu* to at least one aristocratic lineage in its own domain. The Aristocrats of A's domain will largely marry amongst themselves, but at least one of them will be *mayu* to a commoner lineage. Thus, an alliance link is established between the classes. Women pass 'down' the system and wealth passes 'up' it, as bride wealth is paid by *dama* groups to their *mayu*. As the chiefs are expected to give lavish feasts for their retainers, some of the wealth that flows up to them is redistributed in this way. The ideal model of the system can be drawn as follows:

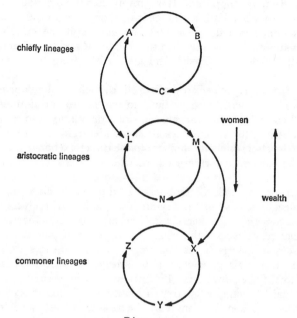

Diagram 54

Here, in A's domain there are three aristocratic lineages,
L, M, N. A is *mayu* to L. There are three commoner lineages,
X, Y, Z. M is *mayu* to X. Thus within the classes the system
is circular and 'democratic'; between the classes it is
hierarchical. No system of direct exchange could achieve this
degree of political elaboration.

II

We have drawn a sharp distinction here between the direct
and indirect principles of exchange, so we must pause to
consider a system that has puzzled anthropologists because
it seems to combine both principles. To understand this,
we must remember our warning at the end of Chapter Seven.

Here we said that the kind of exchange operating depended on the level of social organization that was at issue. Thus, in the patrilateral case we said that at the clan level it might simply be that women were passing back and forward; that is, a system of direct exchange. At the local lineage level, however, the method of exchange might be 'delayed direct', with women passing back and forth in alternate generations. Also, we saw how among the Purum, at the clan level women might pass back and forth, but never between the same lineages. Thus, in clans A and B there may be lineages A^1 and A^2, B^1 and B^2. If A^1 gives to B^1 then the latter cannot reciprocate, but it can give to A^2. Thus, the four lineages could marry in a circle $A^1 \rightarrow B^1 \rightarrow A^2 \rightarrow B^2 \rightarrow A^1$. Between the two clans, however, there would be 'exchange' thus:

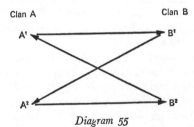

Diagram 55

However, we know that among the Purum the clans are not really the units involved in the exchange; they are simply dispersed exogamous groups. It is interesting, however, that both the Purum (300 persons) and the Kachin (300,000 persons), have *five* patriclans. These are ideally exogamous, but among the Kachin this exogamy is not rigorously observed (it is among the Purum). Each society ideally sees itself as composed of five clans which marry in a circle. This may have been true at one time, but is true no longer and the lineages are, as we have seen, the operative units. However, the odd number of 'ideal' units is interesting. Any number of units can marry in a circle, but the 'direct' exchange system ideally can only work with even numbers. I stress that this is at the ideological level, for as we have seen in the Kariera case there can in fact be almost any number of alliance groups involved.

This difference between the ideal view of the system and the way in which it works has caused some confusion in the case of the Murngin, a tribe of northern Australia. The 'formal' system of the Murngin looks very 'Australian' and is, like that of the Aranda, based on two moieties and eight 'sections' and a number of clans. Yet the rule of marriage is that a man should marry a real or classificatory MBD; that is, it is an asymmetrical system.

Here then is the problem: clans of the opposite moieties exchange women, indeed they have traditional relationships of exchange between particular pairs of clans, and the ritual system runs on eight sections – a system we have previously linked firmly with 'sister exchange'. Yet the rule is uncompromisingly that the MBD should be married and the FZD is banned as a spouse.

The Purum however, have given us the clue. We saw how it was possible for two clans to exchange women without the rule of asymmetrical marriage being breached, as long as no two *lineages* actually exchanged women. Now, exactly the same rule operates for the Murngin. Clans of the two moieties 'exchange' (and of course the moieties themselves 'exchange') but the smaller local units that actually operate the system always pass women 'one way'. The little model we have used for the two Purum clans will work exactly for any two Murngin clans of opposite moiety which exchange women. At the clan level, the exchange is 'direct' – but as far as the actual alliance units are concerned, it is indirect. If A^1 gives women to B^1, then it must take women back from B^2 (or B^3, B^4, B^5... etc.) For purposes of comparison, I have set out the Murngin system opposite in the same manner as the Aranda earlier. Readers will see how the moieties and clans can exchange women even though the MBD rule operates. They will also see how the eight 'sections' can be fitted onto this system.

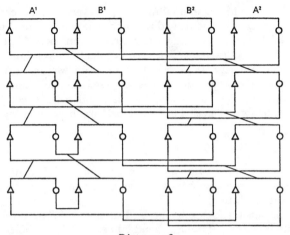

Diagram 56

There is good reason to believe that the 'section' system is new to the Murngin and that they borrowed it from neighbouring tribes. There are documented instances of tribes in Australia adopting the ritual divisions of other tribes. This probably helped large-scale ritual cooperation. It was advantageous to have the same set of categories as one's neighbours in case of ritual collaboration. Thus, some 'Kariera' tribes have consciously tried to adjust their marriage rules to fit the 'Aranda' pattern. The picture of the Murngin then is of a 'Purum' type community with clans but with lineages as the operating units marrying asymmetrically, who adopted the section system and divided the clans up between the two moieties. But as among the Purum and Kachin, the clans are not the actual units involved in the marriage exchanges: nor with the Murngin are the moieties. These are dispersed ritual-exogamic units, and most confusion has come from trying to see the 'sections' as actual groups arranging marriages. If this were the system, then it must involve 'direct' exchange, and how is this reconcilable with the marriage rule? Well, we have seen that it is.

What the Murngin do illustrate, however, is that the two principles, while radically different at one level – that of the actual lineages operating the system – can merge into a simple 'direct exchange' pattern at a higher level – that of clan and moiety. What we have to do in each case is to identify the 'operational' as opposed to the 'formal' groups. With all our examples, clan and moiety seem to be at the formal level. The 'operators' are the local lineages.

III

We must now pause and take stock of the 'elementary' systems of exchange that we have been considering. What are they all 'about'?

The answer is 'exchange and alliance'. Whatever the units involved – families, bands, lineages, clans, moieties, tribes – they enter into relations of exchange with each other, and form alliances. Once an alliance has been formed, it is perpetuated. That is what elementary systems of marital alliance are about: the perpetuation through time of alliances. Once we have given you women, we continue to give you women; once we have taken women from you we continue to take them in perpetuity. This has the effect of laying down not only the category of persons whom one may *not* marry (same clan or family, parallel cousins etc.) but also that into which one *must* marry (opposite moiety, *dama* lineages, 'mother's brother's daughters' etc.) This is what anthropologists mean by saying that elementary systems are characterized by a 'positive' marriage rule as well as a negative.

The systems differ in the ways in which they organize this positive marriage rule. Basically this boils down to two alternatives: as far as any unit is concerned, its 'wife givers' are either the same as its 'wife takers', or they are different. If they are the same, then we are working on the principle of 'straight swaps': if they are different, then we are not directly exchanging women, but 'circulating' them.

Lévi-Strauss has characterized the first kind of system as 'restricted exchange' and the second as 'generalized exchange'. Exchange is 'restricted' where it has to involve two groups who exchange directly. Such a system can only 'grow' by splitting into four, eight, sixteen etc. groups and by continuing to exchange directly. This might suit small populations with a small number of groups, but it is difficult to run it with large and complex societies. The 'generalized' method, on the other hand, can expand indefinitely. As we have seen, any number of groups and any number of 'cycles' can be involved. This interpretation is open to some objections, but basically it seems sound. Direct exchange does seem confined to small populations, while 'generalized' or indirect exchange can accomodate huge populations if necessary. But, as I have said *ad nauseam*, one must be careful at what level one is talking here. The 300,000 Kachin *could* in fact be organized on a moiety basis and still operate indirect exchange on the 'matrilateral' model. But this would mean that for any group at least *half* the other groups in the society would be out as marriage-alliance partners. Without the moiety system or a system of a small number of exogamous clans, the number of groups with which alliances can be formed increases enormously. Thus, it is interesting that among the Purum the clan is still exogamous, but among the Kachin it is not.

Lévi-Strauss argues that it is this capacity to integrate large populations efficiently that explains the preponderance of indirect exchange systems. Direct exchange suits small isolated populations, but breaks down in large and complex ones – especially if, like the Kachin, the latter are stratified into castes or estates or classes. Thus, by dropping their moieties the Murngin could presumably expand on the Kachin model, while the Aranda are 'stuck' with their direct exchange system.

Logically, this expansion of small systems can occur in two ways: a system of direct exchange must change into indirect, or the small system must have developed indigenous indirect exchange in the first place. In the latter case, the indirect exchange system can be regarded as a kind of 'mutation' which is favourable to the development of expansion. It just happened to go that way and was advantageous in adaptation. Many anthropologists would be happy to leave it at that. After all, they argue, there are only the two possibilities – direct and indirect – and a close decision could go either way. We don't know why one system should occur rather than another.

Other anthropologists are not so sanguine and have tried to work out why it might be that indirect exchange originates. Direct exchange is easy: one swaps 'sisters' or 'daughters'. This is perfectly straightforward and must have been an easy and obvious choice for two bands or tribes, as the Bible testifies. But why should the indirect and rather complicated principle arise? It could be a consequence of a pre-existing system of status in which groups were ranked. When they came then to exchange women, the superior would not take from the inferior. But this is implausible as the system operates among non-ranked lineages, for example. Another and more plausible theory is that the system did originate in true 'cousin marriage'. In primitive conditions, in which our units – bands, lineages etc – are small and dispersed and not very 'deep' genealogically, we can imagine them at first marrying amongst themselves in a rather random fashion. The argument then goes like this: in such societies there is usually a considerable age discrepancy between men and women at marriage. Particularly where polygyny is allowed, men are much older than women when they marry. Now, our ego has two choices if he wants a relative of the older generation to find him a bride. We will assume that the tendency to a 'positive' rule is there, that is, that ego will want to marry into a group where his own group has previously established alliances. This will be particularly essential if the groups are small and scattered and exogamous and there is competition for wives. To whom should he go? He can go to his mother's group and ask her brothers to help him, or he can go to the group where his father's sisters have married and claim a woman from them. In other words, he can ask for a MBD or a FZD. One might imagine that his chances of getting either were equal, but they are not. The age discrepancy at marriage will mean that his father's sisters will have married well before his mother's brothers. Most of his father's sisters' daughters then will be likely to be older than himself, while most of his mother's brother's daughters will be younger. Insofar as he marries a younger woman, he will try to marry a MBD then. And in any case, his FZDs will all have been snapped up by the time he comes to marry. Given this age discrepancy and the fact that ego looks to a senior-generation relative for help in finding a bride (which is simply a graphic way of putting it – the arrangement may well be made by ego's parents of course) then this demographic argument may well account for the origin in some small scale systems of a matrilateral trend in exchange which is the basis for a widescale system of indirect exchange.

The reader need not worry too much about the possible origins of the systems. They are variations on the basic exchange theme, and again illustrate how a seemingly small variation can have far-reaching consequences. The difference between them in the long run is not as important as their basic similarity. Once one grasps the picture of small exogamous groups intermarrying amongst themselves, then the various patterns that this intermarrying can form should fall into place. The patterns we have been looking at are based on a premise that goes beyond simple exogamy: it is the premise of reciprocity, of systematic exchange, of perpetual alliance. This produces the 'positive' marriage rule. We must now move on to examine those systems that dispense with this luxury and work on the negative rule only; namely, the 'complex' systems.

IV

We have been working on an implicit classification of marriage systems:

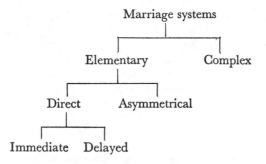

As with George Orwell's animals, all complex systems are complex, but some are more complex than others. We are not so far advanced in this area of analysis as we are with elementary systems, and although anthropologists seem to be working with two 'types' of complexity in mind, it is not all that easy to characterize these. While, as we have seen, it is possible to characterize the elementary rule as either $A \longleftrightarrow B$, or $A \rightarrow B \rightarrow C \rightarrow (A)$ (whatever kind of units A, B and C represent) it is only possible to characterize the complex rule as something like $A \rightarrow ?, B \rightarrow ?, n \rightarrow ?$. In other words, the system lays down whom we shall not marry (if we are A's, then everyone in the category A), but it does not make a formal rule about whom we must marry. We can only replace the question marks by statistical probabilities. Thus, in our own complex system the law decrees that we shall not marry certain relatives (look in the back of the *Book of Common Prayer* for a handy list of prohibitions). This prohibited category fluctuates: for instance, the deceased wife's sister used to be banned, but is no longer. However, outside this ban we can only determine whom a person might marry by knowing his life history, social position, personal preferences etc. We might be able to say with some confidence, for example, that if our ego were a royal prince, it would be pretty certain that he would marry a royal princess or at least an aristocrat. If he were a dustman, we might predict that he would marry a working-class girl from his own neighbourhood. If he were a film star, he would probably marry another film star, and so on. But there is no category laid down; there are only statistical probabilities.

In our own system, and in other systems which lack corporate kin-groups as the basic units of the society, then the prohibited relatives tend to be an ego-centred group of kin. These are either a motley collection such as our own, or a well-defined kindred (usually symmetrical); for example, all ego's kin up to second cousins or something such. As long as ego marries outside this category then there is no prescription applying to his marriage choice. The effect of this is, to put it graphically, to send people shooting off in all directions at once, and to link together many kindreds in a complex way. This is really the radical opposite to the elementary principle. If I release my sisters/daughters to other men, I do not demand their sisters and daughters in return, as I would under a direct exchange system. It is more like an asymmetrical system in some ways: I take a wife from one group, but I send my daughters to another. The difference is that the 'other' is not specified. Of course, there is nothing to stop groups, in a system like ours which allows cousin marriages, from exchanging women. Two 'families' could link each other over the generations by successive marriages. This used to be fairly common in noble families, and in some large business 'houses', but even that form is now lapsed. And in any case, it was never a matter of a formal rule, but of self-interested strategy. In the society at large, the rate of consanguineous marriages (i.e. with cousins) tends to be less than 1 per cent, except in some fairly endogamous rural areas.

We then have rules of exogamy, but no rules of alliance. Many 'primitive' societies can be characterized in the same way, but because they are societies composed of corporate kinship groups – clans, lineages, phratries etc. – they work somewhat differently. Again, there are no positive rules and the simplest of them have only the rule of clan exogamy – thou shalt not marry members of thine own clan. Any other clan is a potential provider of marriage partners, and within

such a system every clan will in all probability be linked to
every other clan. 'Preferences' can certainly arise, and it is
common to get pairs of clans between which the network of
marriages is 'denser' than between others. Thus, if clans are
residential units, then two which are close to each other may
well prefer to intermarry. As with royal marriages in Europe,
there is often a 'strain' towards alliance, towards the setting
up of perpetual relationships. But the only rule is the
negative one: marry out of own clan.

This is somewhat different in degree if not in principle
from our own complex system in that the units here are
corporate, discrete descent groups. If these comprise, say,
five clans, then we can at least represent the marriage
choices thus:

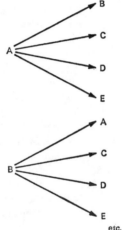

Diagram 57

Some systems with unilineal descent groups, however, go a
little further than this. They make a rule of this kind: in a
matrilineal system, a man may not marry in his own clan,
nor his father's clan, nor his mother's father's clan: in a
patrilineal system he may not marry in his own clan, his
mother's clan, nor his father's mother's clan. These rules

usually apply at the level of the clan, but they may apply to either lineage or even phratry. The matrilineal case is often called a 'Crow' system and the patrilineal an 'Omaha' system, after two American Indian tribes which have similar rules.

Now, this system is in a sense 'complex'; it does not lay down rules about whom one should marry. But at the same time it has some features of an elementary system about it.

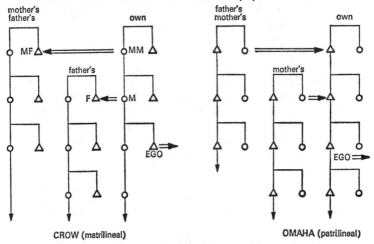

Diagram 58

If we take the Crow system as our example, then we see that ego's clan (phratry) 'gave' a woman to his father's clan, and before that to his mother's father's clan. Ego, therefore, cannot take a woman from either of these 'wife-taking' clans. As far as he is concerned, the world must look pretty much as it looks to an individual Purum: it is divided up into 'wife-taking' clans which are banned to him, and 'wife-giving' clans; that is, those into which he may marry. Again, let us suppose that there are five clans and ego is in clan A, his father is from clan B and his mother's father clan C. For this particular ego we can characterize the system as $(D, E) \rightarrow A \rightarrow (B + C)$, and he must take a wife from the 'wife-giving' clans D and E. This looks like a system of indirect exchange, but of course *it applies only to individuals and not to whole groups*. Thus while our ego cannot marry into B and C, there is nothing to stop other members of his clan doing so providing their mothers and mothers' mothers have not previously married into them. We can imagine another ego of clan A whose mother had indeed married into B, but whose mother's mother married into E. For this man, then, the rule would read $(C, D) \rightarrow A \rightarrow (B + E)$. Looked at from the clan level then, all the clans marry into all the other clans, but at the same time, because of the exogamic rule, any individual's marriage choice will be limited to a 'category' of women which is circumscribed by the previous marriage arrangements of his mother and mother's mother. The direction of this choice is of the 'asymmetrical' or $A \rightarrow B \rightarrow C$ type, although there is no necessary rule of MBD marriage, and, indeed, this is often forbidden. To use the language of elementary systems, clans would be linked by both 'cycles' and 'direct reciprocity'. We might represent it thus:

$$A \longleftrightarrow B \longleftrightarrow C \longleftrightarrow (A)$$

Now, amongst the Purums and the Murngin, we saw that clans might be linked by direct exchange, but that between lineages there was only indirect exchange and 'cycles' of alliance. In Crow-Omaha systems, there is no such distinction. We get both forms of exchange simultaneously at the same level. And this is because the rules pertain to individuals, not whole groups, Thus, if A gives a woman to B, it is only the children of that woman who may not marry into B; other A's will be similarly governed by their mothers' marriages. If this were a true elementary system, then once A had given a woman to B, it would continue to do so and all A men would be banned from marrying B women.

These Crow-Omaha systems, then, seem to stand half-way between elementary and complex systems. In that there is no positive rule, we have to classify them as complex, but their negative rules do tend to push them in an 'elementary' direction. If we can characterize marriage choice in complex systems such as our own as 'probabalistic', then in Crow-Omaha systems it is less probabalistic than in other complex sysems. As we have found before, it is often inadequate to try to classify systems on one dimension only. And, in any case, there is no necessary rigid distinction between types but maybe a 'cline' from extremely elementary to extremely complex with various stages on the way. Whether or not these are 'evolutionary' stages we do not know, but some of us are working on the theory that Crow-Omaha systems are 'elementary' systems which have changed in certain characteristic ways in a 'complex' direction.

The distribution of these systems in space is interesting. Truly elementary systems seem to be clustered in South-east Asia (including Australia and New Guinea) and possibly South America; Crow-Omaha systems are characteristic of North America; complex systems occur in Africa and among the Indo-Europeans. Most areas contain examples of all types, but this is where the main clusterings occur. Complex systems are not confined by any means to 'advanced' countries or cultures, but occur throughout the range of social types. Truly elementary systems, however, do not seem compatible with large industrial social structures.

The effects of the two systems are what differ and what matter in analysis. Elementary systems – whatever their type – strain towards the perpetuation of alliances over the generations. This is seen at its 'purest' in true bilateral cross-cousin marriage, where the children of brothers and sisters continually remarry each other over the generations, thus keeping marriage in the family, as it were. Complex systems, on the other hand, do not favour the constant renewal of links, but distribute people widely around the society. Thus, at one extreme, although ego must marry out of his nuclear family of birth, it is almost a matter of random chance into which other family he will marry. It could, theoretically, be any other in the society. Whatever patterns emerge will not be the result of positive rules of alliance, and can only be discerned by the demographers.

V

It will be obvious by now that what started as simply an attempt to understand exogamy has ended as a completely new way of looking at kinship systems. In the first part of the book, we were almost exclusively concerned with the way in which kin groups *recruited* members; that is, with descent. In this perspective, kinship systems were seen as mechanisms for the formation and recruitment of property-owning groups, residential groups, political units etc. One basic problem was to see how these units were held together over time. In the first part of the book, we concentrated on what one might call the 'genetic' model for such integration; that is, the linking of groups on the basis of their real or assumed common ancestry. Thus, clanship and segmentary lineage-organization were seen as devices to this end.

In this latter part of the book, we have switched focus. We have looked at kinship systems as mechanisms for distributing women between groups and integrating groups by the creation of perpetual alliances. In the genetic model, group A is linked in perpetuity to group B because they are the descendants of the same ancestor: in the alliance model they are linked by ties of affinity as 'wife givers' and 'wife takers'.

Both models can be used in the discussion of all kinship systems as we have seen, but some systems – notably in South-east Asia – put their money heavily on alliance as the integrative mechanism, while others – notably in Africa – put theirs on descent. Marriage in most African societies has been described as simply the 'residue of exogamy' – which is a nice way of phrasing the negative rule. In many South-east Asian and most Australian societies on the other hand, the 'kinship system' *is* the system of marriage alliances as we have seen.

What the 'alliance' model enables us to do is to put all systems on the same continuum. If we stick to the descent model only (with marriage as simply the residue of exogamy) then we have no way of adequately dealing with, for example, the Australians. On the other hand, the 'descent' societies such as the African can be seen as a variant of 'complex' marriage patterns. It is natural, of course, that anthropologists specializing in South-east Asia should favour an 'alliance' view of societies; that is, they look at them to see how women are distributed in marriage between kinship units. Specialists in Africa, on the other hand, prefer to look at the composition and recruitment of kinship groups – particularly unilineal groups. As we saw in Chapter Six this led to difficulties in handling cognatic systems; it leads to even greater difficulties in handling, say, the Australians. Some anthropologists were prepared to regard 'section' systems etc. as oddities (after all there are only a few of them), but as we have seen, in the 'alliance' perspective they become one extreme of a continuum, of which societies such as our own are the other extreme.

Most British anthropologists have worked in Africa and have tended to see the world through African spectacles. To those like myself who have either dealt with variants of the Crow system (as in New Mexico) or with cognatic and 'complex' systems (as in western Ireland), the alliance theory has its attractions. No one likes to have his fieldwork material dismissed as an oddity, and after a while, when it appears that the 'odd' cases number more than 50 per cent of the total, one begins to suspect the usefulness of the theory.

The theories, of course, are not at all incompatible. We should, in fact, look at all systems from the point of view of both recruitment and alliance. The only danger comes in stressing one at the expense of the other. If we put them together, we can effect a very satisfactory overall view of systems of kinship and marriage as mechanisms of social integration.

From an evolutionary point of view, such an overall perspective is essential. Primate communities, as we have seen, are closed and undifferentiated. One of the great breakthroughs from primate to human existence was the elaboration

of a mechanism for holding together different groups –
for bringing them into some kind of perpetual and dependent relationship. Only in this way was it possible to make the
evolutionary leap-forward that led to truly human communities. The two models show how this must have happened.
As proto-hominid groups, for example, grew too large and
split up, connexion between them could be maintained insofar as they recognized and symbolized their common descent. Hence, for example, the clan with its distinctive name
and its emblems, rituals, and exogamy. Exogamy keeps it
distinctive, but also means that it must form alliances with
other groups, and again there is a mechanism for integration. The simplest of these mechanisms, as we have seen, is
the swapping of women. But in a sense, any system of exogamy makes groups dependent on each other for women, and
so weaves them together in an alliance network. This can
vary from the very simple network of the Kariera, with only
two 'ends' tied by one knot, to the incredibly complicated
network of a complex system such as ours, with millions of
ends and millions of knots joining them.

Another important evolutionary feature is the genetic
consequences of these systems. Elementary systems, after all,
are methods of systematic in-breeding, while in complex
systems the mating arrangements can be almost random.
Elementary systems do seem able to control population growth
in a way that complex ones cannot manage. What the consequences for heredity and fertility of these systems are, we are
not quite sure. But research on this may help to crack many
problems of human social and physical evolution.

VI

Let us end this all too brief section on marriage, exogamy
and alliance, by looking at some 'kinship' customs in the
light of the two theories.

A classical argument in anthropology has concerned the
interpretation of the custom of privileged relationship between a man and his mother's brother. Particularly in patri-

lineal systems, a man is allowed to joke freely with his MB, to steal his goods, to insult him, and even to sleep with his wife. The MB in his turn often has special duties and responsibilities towards his maternal nephew.

The older evolutionary anthropologists saw this as evidence of a previous state of 'matriarchy' in which the MB was the authority over ego; but it was rightly pointed out that this did not make sense in that the 'avunculate' in patrilineal systems concerned an *indulgent* relationship between a man and his maternal nephew. Radcliffe-Brown pointed out that in matrilineal systems a man had a similar relationship with his father's sister. Thus, he argued, what was involved was a contrast between authority relationships (those within the lineage) and indulgent relationships (those outside the lineage). In a patrilineal system, authority over a man was in his father's lineage, so he looked for indulgence to his mother's and to the men of the mother's lineage: in a matrilineal system the authority over ego was in his mother's lineage, so he looked to the women of his father's lineage for indulgence. This was the source of the customs.

Fortes, as we saw in Chapter four, pointed out that the Tallensi take a different view of the matter. They say that the son of a woman of the patrilineage is a kind of member of it. It is not, they say, the woman's fault that she was born a woman, and she should not be wholly deprived of her privileges because of this. Thus, her son is accorded some privileges in his mother's lineage, and hence has some claims on the indulgence of his mother's brothers.

To explain this, Fortes contrasts 'descent' with 'filiation'. A child is 'filiated' to both parents, but he is only descended from one of them in a unilineal system. (Unless of course it is a double-unilineal system.) Thus, he is equally the child of both parents, but he only derives his 'legal and political' status from one of them – father in a patrilineal and mother in a matrilineal system. However, even in, say, a patrilineal system the fact that a man is only descended from his father does not mean that his tie of 'filiation' with his mother is lost. He is still her child and has some rights as a result of this. Fortes, as we saw earlier, refers to this as 'complementary' filiation; that is, the ties a man has through the parent who does not give him his 'descent' status.

This is looking at it from the point of view of the individual. From the point of view of the lineage it has two types of 'members': those who are members by descent (the children of men in a patrilineal system and the children of women in a matrilineal), and those who are the children of 'residual siblings' (the children of women in a patrilineal system and of men in a matrilineal).

In all this argument the whole system is seen as 'based on' the lineage and hence on descent. Everything else about the system is an attempt to accommodate the awkward fact that ego has two parents to the needs of the descent system. Alliance theorists argue that this is putting the cart before the horse. What is being ignored in this theory is the *marriage*. Descent theorists are stressing all the time the relationships between the generations and forgetting the *structural* importance of the marriage. They may recognize the importance of marriage in many ways, but they do not regard marriages as part of the structure of the system. Marriage is simply the residue of exogamy.

Both sides would agree that in all marriages in primitive societies (and many others) the union is a matter not of the linking of two individuals, but of the linking of two groups. Very often, the bride-wealth payments and the counter gifts to them are of enormous value. They may take years to pay. Sometimes children even inherit the bride-wealth debts of their parental generation. But how does putting the emphasis on alliance – seeing the system as essentially one of marital rather than descent arrangements – help in settling the vexed question of the mother's brother and his curious relationship to his sister's son?

The alliance theorists would say this: A man from lineage A marries a woman from lineage B, and thus the two lineages come into an alliance relationship. Bride-wealth, for example, will be collected from all the members of A and distributed to all the members of B. (Some of the more tedious sections of books on tribal marriage consist in the listing of the details of this distribution and collection. The obsession with this kind of thing has been called 'the right foreleg of the ox' school of anthropology.) Now, as a result of this marriage all the members of patrilineage A will stand in an alliance relationship to all members of patrilineage B. Look at this from the point of view of ego: his father has married a woman of B, therefore he, along with his father, has an alliance relationship with the men of B, including his mother's brothers. This relationship was set up by the marriage. It was there before he was, in the relationship between his father and *his* wife's brothers. Ego's privileged relationship with his mother's brother is simply an extension of this alliance relationship. It often extends to the privilege of asking the MB for his daughter in marriage and hence a 'strain' towards asymmetrical alliance common in Africa. The bride-wealth a man obtains for his sister gets him, in turn, a wife. He gets this bride-wealth from the sister's husband and hence a kind of alliance 'chain' is set up: A man gets bride-wealth for his sister and with this gets another man's sister for a wife, this other man in turn getting himself a wife and so on. Thus, there is this linkage between lineages set up, and a very special relationship between brothers-in-law i.e. between a man and his wife's brother. This special relationship extends therefore to the son of the wife's brother, and hence the 'avunculate'. Thus, it is not really a relationship between a man and his MB, according to alliance theory, but a relationship between a man and his father's wife's brother. This view of it takes proper account of the role of the marriage and does not 'disguise' it under the term 'complementary filiation' – which is simply another way of saying that a marriage took place and was fruitful. So say the men of alliance.

To sum up, we can indicate this roughly by a diagram:

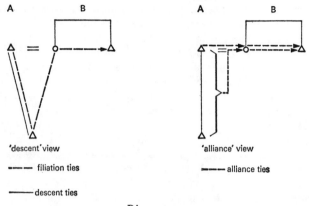

'descent' view

---- filiation ties

——— descent ties

'alliance' view

---- alliance ties

Diagram 59

The descent view and the alliance view deal with the same four roles, but they would phrase them differently. Thus, the descent view sees them as F, S, M, and MB; the alliance view as F, S, FW and FWB. In many African societies, the 'strain' towards alliance is reinforced by the custom of allowing a man to have first choice in marriage of his wife's brother's daughters. This, from the alliance viewpoint is simply a variant on matrilateral cross-cousin marriage whereby two lineages are asymmetrically linked:

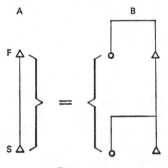

Diagram 60

Here either F marries his WBD, or s marries his MBD (FWBD). In either case the alliance is renewed.

Alliance theorists would argue, I think, that their model took account of *all* the elements of the role system involved including the marriage, whereas descent theory had to smuggle in marriage by the back door.

Customs such as the *levirate* and *sororate* are open to both explanations. In the levirate, when a man dies one of his brothers has the right and obligation to marry the wife and raise children ' to the name of' the dead man. In the sororate, when a woman dies, then a younger sister is sent to replace her. To descent theory, these are clearly devices to preserve the continuity of the lineage: to alliance theory, they are ways of perpetuating the alliance.

There is, of course, as we have seen, no incompatibility between the theories. Most African systems have been looked at in descent terms, and it does help to switch focus and ask ' how are alliances created, expressed and perpetuated, and how are women moved around the system?' This gives a different focus: the facts are the same. The only danger comes in trying to force facts too much into one mould – trying to explain everything about a system from the point of view of its recruitment mechanisms, for example. The more one looks at African systems, the more one can see the strains towards alliance-structures in them. In only one that we know of – the Lovedu of the Transvaal – is there a thorough-going asymmetrical alliance system, but as we have seen, many customs of preferential and secondary marriage are moves in the direction of the creation of ' elementary' systems. Some others approximate to Crow patterns, yet others are undoubtedly complex. But by putting them in the alliance framework we are able to see them as variations on the same theme as the Australians and the Kachins and the Crow, and so to compare them in a meaningful way.

Let us end with one more example. In his account of the Trobriand Islanders Malinowski pointed out the strains that were 'inherent' in the matrilineal system between a man and his wife's brothers. These were the strains between 'mother right' or the rules of matrilineal descent, and 'father love' or the natural desire of a man to further the interests of his children. Thus, a man had no rights over his own children as these were vested in their mother's lineage and hence in their mother's brother. This has been dubbed the 'matrilineal problem', and put down as one of the peculiar strains of matriliny.

Alliance theories counter that men have brothers-in-law in all societies and that this is a basic situation that is simply 'stretched' somewhat in matrilineal societies. After all, for alliance theory the 'basic situation' is neither the nuclear family nor the mother-child bond, but the brother and sister and the sister's husband. The basic situation is the 'releasing' of sisters to other men, whatever the system. This creates an alliance and all alliances are liable to strain – 'we marry our enemies'.

The three positions can be diagrammed as follows:

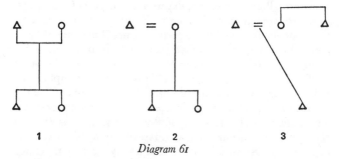

1   2   3
Diagram 61

1 is the traditional starting point for kinship theory – the nuclear family and the choice between 'descent' from one parent or the other or both, and of filiation 'filling in' the gaps left by descent. 2 is our starting point in this book, which approaches an alliance position while being cautious about it. Insofar, however, as we took the fate of the brother-sister bond as in some ways 'central' to the elaboration of kinship systems, we anticipated 3, which is the alliance position as illustrated by Lévi-Strauss. He sees this as the basic element or 'atom' of all kinship, and argues that, for

example, in times of strife when systems break down, they revert to this atomic situation. A man's special relation to his mother's brother – as opposed to his father's brother – is built in from the start. It was the MB who released the M in marriage and so produced the son. The relation of the S then to FB and MB is not symmetrical – the maternal uncle is a very special person. Medieval songs evidently celebrate this relationship at length. We are in anthropology only just beginning to explore the consequences of such thinking for the study of kinship. I hope this discussion has done something to give the flavour of the debate.

It may well be that a study of English history and contemporary society from the viewpoint of the 'circulation' of spouses in the system will be rewarding. In a complex system we want to know how far marriage choice departs from randomness and in what directions. Clearly the extent of both territorial and class mobility affect this deeply. One thing demographers have tried to do is to determine the average size of the 'pool' of people who marry among themselves. Clearly, in any fairly stable population where there are no large immigrations and emigrations, and where territorial mobility is limited, people will marry spouses from a restricted area. Over the years, then, the population of the area will be complexly intermarried within itself, and most people will be marrying spouses with whom they share *some* degree of consanguinity, however remote. (This is also true, of course, of the nation at large. After all, if a good many of my ancestors had not married each other, I would have had more ancestors alive in 1066 than there were people in England then – roughly 2^{40}!) Now the average size of this 'pool' or 'isolate' as it is called – which is the category from which any person 'at risk of marriage' (as the demographers delightfully put it) is likely to find a spouse – is surprisingly small. It varies from about nine hundred to just over two thousand people; the kind of variation in population size we find for the most elementary of elementary systems. The average effective range of marriage choice for a man, then, is not as he might like to think, the several million unmarried women in the nation, but probably, at best, not more than a thousand or so. Thus in a fairly loose way the same thing is true of our complex system as is true for the Crow-Omaha: a man's category of 'potential spouses' is to some extent determined by the previous marriage choices of his ancestral consanguines. The difference is that in Crow-Omaha systems this is absolutely fixed in terms of descent groups, as we have seen.

Another interesting feature here is the different patterns of social mobility that involve marriage. The English aristo-cracy, while being largely endogamous, has nevertheless 'married down' a good deal. Younger sons have often married heiresses to boost the family fortunes. The various patterns that this involved have largely been explored by novelists – Jane Austen is a great favourite with anthropolo-gists – but there is obviously room for research on the circu-lation of wealth and women in the dowry system. The dowry is a very 'Indo-European' institution and is in many ways the opposite of bride-wealth. We never get round to calling it 'groomprice' or 'groomwealth', but that is often how it functions. In many parts of peasant Europe, such as Ireland and Greece, it still survives, and families can ruin themselves in providing suitable dowries for their daughters. Descent theory I think would have great difficulty in hand-ling this phenomenon, but it might be susceptible of an alliance analysis.

In contemporary Britain, patterns of marital mobility are changing. Evidence from novels etc. again suggests that with the expansion of higher education there is a 'flow' up the ladder of boys from artisan homes who marry middle-class girls as part of their pattern of social mobility. The strains and hostilities involved in such marriages really ram home that 'we marry our enemies', if some authors are to be believed. There must be many examples of such changes in flow over the years. In the future, the relative endogamy of racial groups will provide yet another complication. Thus, while it is hard to compare our society with primitive socie-ties which are composed of extended kin groups as the basic units, we can easily look at it as a variant on the alliance theme and ask how women (and men for that matter) are distributed round the system through marriage, and what the directions and intensities of these flows are. Thus, we can compare ourselves with other stratified societies such as the feudal Kachin, or with the caste systems of India or the estates of medieval Europe. On the basis of alliance theory, we can expect that there will be no free exchange of women between strata: this would make for equality. Thus a higher caste, class or estate, if it wishes to form alliances with a lower, must construe the situation as unequal. It can, in extreme cases (as with some castes) refuse to enter into alliance at all and so preserve its identity. No one is allowed to marry 'below his station'. If marriage is allowed, then it could for example be secondary marriage or concubinage in which lower caste/class/estate women are taken as mistresses or concubines. If real legal marriage is allowed, then the upper strata can either condescendingly 'give' women on the Kachin model, or they can treat women as 'tribute' from the lower classes. As long as peers marry heiresses it is the peers who are condescending (theoretically) and the heiress and her bourgeois family who are buying prestige through the aristocratic 'connexion'. But when the younger sisters of the peers begin to marry merchants and professional men, then there is no hope for the maintenance of an invidious relationship. We have reached the position of balance.

This is pushing alliance theory far beyond what was intended. From a strict theoretical point of view the 'units' in our system are families; classes are not social groups. But if we are looking for the channels along which alliances flow, then we move into this wider sociological perspective which may give us new insights into the dynamics of our own society.

CHAPTER NINE

Kinship Terminology

I

A⊤ least half the anthropological literature on kinship has been largely concerned with the terms various systems employ in addressing and referring to kinsfolk and affines. Morgan saw in the study of terminology the royal road to the understanding of kinship systems. He was the first to see that the terminology was a method of *classification*, and that what it told us was how various systems classified 'kin'. If we could understand this, we could understand the system. 'Understanding' for Morgan, however, meant understanding the *evolution* of kinship systems, and what the terminology held for him was the clue to the *past* state of the system. While not necessarily denying that such clues may exist, anthropologists have been inclined to see the terms as pertaining largely to current realities. They have mainly argued 'monocausally' – that is, they have looked for one good reason that would explain the differing usages. And usages differ enormously. If we just take ego's parental generation for example, we find that in some systems *all* the men of the parental generation on both mother's and father's side are called by the same term. We tend to write this as 'father' but of course this is begging the question of what it really 'means'. All we know is that they are all called by the same term. In some systems, the father and his brothers are called by one term, and the mother's brothers by another. In yet others – such as our own – the father is called by one term and the mother's brothers and father's brothers are lumped together. This seems to us natural and obvious. There are 'fathers' and there are 'uncles', and people who can't see the difference must be lacking in discrimination. But to many peoples our failure to distinguish between mother's and father's brothers would seem not only evidence of stupidity but downright immoral into the bargain. Finally, it is possible that all three of these kin-types could be called by different terms, as with the Romans (*pater, patruus,* and *avunculus*).

We can envisage these four possibilities as follows:

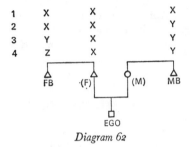

Diagram 62

Usually, anthropologists have approached the problem of terminology by taking a few terminological oddities and asking 'how can these be explained?'. They have fallen back, for example, on marriage customs. Thus, situation 2 above, was derived from the levirate. If one brother can substitute for another, then to Ego they are in a sense 'equivalent'; the FB is a potential father so he is called 'father'. Situation 1, according to Morgan, derived from the practice of incestuous promiscuity in which anyone in the clan or band might be ego's father so he took no chances and called them all dad. Situation 2 was also supposed to derive from matriliny and 'group marriage'. Here all the men of ego's father's clan married all the women of his own (mother's) clan, so he called all the men of his father's clan 'father'.

The more anthropologists looked at the *total* distribution of terms in kinship systems, the less likely this kind of explanation appeared. Radcliffe-Brown proposed that the terms really paralleled the distribution of ego's 'rights and duties'. People who were called by the same term were those to whom he had similar obligations. Thus, with the terms we have been looking at, we can see that in unilineal systems ego would want to distinguish the men of his own lineage from those of either mother's or father's lineage. In a unilineal system, as the reader by now will be well aware, the father and his brothers on the one hand, and the mother's brothers on the other, are quite different kettles of fish. Ego's 'rights and duties' towards his father and father's brothers differ markedly from those towards his mother's brothers, and in consequence he distinguishes them in terminology. Our system does not have this distinction of rights and duties between one 'side' of the family and the other; hence we lump both 'uncles' together because there is no need to discriminate between them. Similarly with 'cousins' – we lump them all together, because our rights and duties towards them are the same.

This kind of explanation, while superficially attractive, again does not seem to account for all the distributions of terms in a system. It is often the case that relatives with markedly different rights and duties towards ego will be called by the same term, and vice versa. There is often a rough correlation between rights and terms but it is indeed very rough and not adequate to account for total distributions.

It is not surprising that descent and alliance theorists have differed in emphasis in their handling of kinship terminology. Thus, Radcliffe-Brown has said that many aspects of terminology are there to emphasize the 'unity of the lineage group' – such as classing together under one term all the men of the father's lineage in a matrilineal society. Lévi-Strauss has argued that what the terminology does is to classify people into 'marriageable' and 'unmarriageable'. Thus, in some complex systems one cannot marry anyone to whom one applies a kinship term, while in elementary systems one can only marry into a category of persons to whom one applies a particular kinship term. Needham – another alliance theorist – has argued that where one gets 'prescriptive' alliance then terms apply to categories of people who are respectively 'marriageable' and 'unmarriageable', but where one does not get this form of alliance the terms refer to specific genealogically-defined kin-types. I do not want to enter too deeply into these controversies, but simply to supply some information that will help the reader to follow them up.

Behind all these controversies, there is the even deeper question of the relevance of terminology. Malinowski despised 'kinship algebra', as he called the study of terms, and many anthropologists follow him in this distaste insisting that what we should study is 'behaviour' or 'rules' and not language. Others – in particular, alliance theorists – feel that to understand the system is to understand the native categories, and these are given in the terminology. The terms are therefore the starting point of analysis.

It may be that there is no absolute correlation between the kinship system and the terminology as long as the system is seen to be made up of isolated marriage practices, or 'rights and duties'. It seems much more adequate to look at kinship terminologies simply as ways in which people classify their kinship universe. This may often be an 'ideal' classification and not correspond very closely to 'real' groups or categories. On the other hand, it may give quite an accurate picture of the significant categories of kin-types in the kinship universe. We must remember, however, that kinship systems are many-sided and that the terminology may not reflect every side of them. What it may tell us is *how the people themselves* see their world of kin. Who do they distinguish from whom and on what basis? It is often the case that they regard a certain distinction as crucial which has no meaning for us in terms of *our* analysis of the system of groups, alliances, etc. But our analysis is not always theirs, and since they after all are working the system, it behoves us to respect the 'analysis' that is latent in their own classification.

II

Classification is a human proclivity as deeply embedded in our natures as the urge to exchange. A whole language can be viewed as an elaborate system of classification, and within it there are sub-languages which classify various aspects of the universe. These classifications change as the aspects change. Thus, we have categories of persons like 'men', 'women', 'boys', 'girls', 'adults', 'juveniles', 'minors' etc. Recently, we have had to invent 'teenagers' to meet the need for a new category. We have classifications of material things, of colours, of psychological states etc. etc. Sometimes, these show the kinds of 'inconsistencies' that often crop up in kinship classifications. For example, in the classification of animals one might expect the same distinctions to be observed as occur in 'man', 'woman', 'boy', 'girl'; that is, 'adult male', 'adult female', 'young male', 'young female'. Now with some animals we do this, with others not. Thus we get 'stallion', 'mare', 'colt', 'filly', but only 'ram', 'ewe' and 'lamb', or 'dog', 'bitch' and 'puppy'. In other words, we sometimes ignore the sex distinction in the young of an animal, even though it might seem 'natural' to make it. Thus 'objectively' these categories of 'young male' and 'young female' exist, and we react quite differently to them in practice, but we do not always make a distinction in terminology. This doesn't mean we can't talk about them, but we have to make up circumlocutions; the distinction is not 'there' in the vocabulary.

Systems of kinship terms are like this. They are ways of classifying kin into categories and sub-categories – 'uncles', 'nephews', 'cousins', etc. in English for example – which sometimes correspond to 'social reality' and sometimes not. I stress this point because so much of the anthropological discussion of terms seems to consist in attempts to 'rationalize' the hiatus between language and 'reality'. But reality changes faster than language, which is very conservative. Sometimes, also, distinctions are *built into the language* which have no bearing on reality. I don't suppose a Frenchman has any more need to distinguish between male and female cousins than we do; but his language has the feminine form of '*cousin*' – '*cousine*' – built into it. I doubt if we will get anywhere if we try to correlate this distinction with 'rights and duties'.

Having accepted, then, that systems of kinship termi-nology must be looked at as implicit classifications of an ideal kinship universe, let us look at some of them. Our view demands that we look at *total* systems, and not just at pieces of them. It would be no use, for example, to try and under-stand the distinctions we are employing in our classification of cows by taking only the terms 'heifer' and 'bullock'. We have to examine the total 'set' of terms.

Perhaps we can approach this logically by imagining a system of great simplicity and asking how many distinctions ego needs to make in order to distinguish all the significant categories of 'kin'. Let us imagine a system which consists simply of two moieties, with a rule of moiety exogamy: a man must marry a woman of the opposite moiety. He would need, then, only a distinction between men of his own moiety and those of the opposite, and women of his own moiety and those of the opposite. As a start, this would do, and four terms would suffice. But few, if any, systems are that simple and as a rule ego would want to sort out several more categories. To take the most elementary of elementary systems, the Kariera type, we can see at once that *generation* is of enormous importance. As ego is supposed to marry into his own generation (the 'sister exchange' rule), then he needs to distinguish his own generation from the two adja-cent generations. He could get by with the following:

1. Men of own generation and own lineage/clan
2. Men of adjacent generations and own lineage/clan
3. Women of own generation and own lineage/clan
4. Women of adjacent generations and own lineage/clan
5. Men of own generation and affinal lineage/clan
6. Men of adjacent generations and affinal lineage/clan
7. Women of own generation and affinal lineage/clan
8. Women of adjacent generations and affinal lineage/ clan

This leaves ego's 'grandparental' and 'grandchild' genera-tions. He could really get by with one term (9) for these meaning 'grandrelative' – he does not really *need* to distin-guish lineage or sex as these people are not involved in alliance relationships with him. But he might do so out of consistency with the pattern of the other terms.

How would this look in a Kariera-type system?

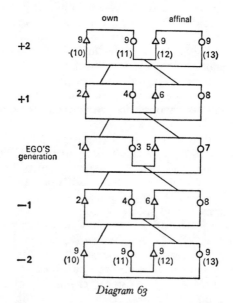

Diagram 63

This would constitute a kind of rock bottom minimum set of distinctions for significant categories of kin in such a system, if the basis of the distinctions is truly the 'alliance' criterion; that is, if the system of terms really does sort out 'marriageable' and 'unmarriageable'. We would not expect in such a system that there would be any terms for 'affines' as opposed to 'kinsmen'. All our 'in-laws' are people to whom we are *already* related – this being the defining characteristic of such a system.

We may have started here at an even more complex level than was necessary. I have assumed a terminology appropriate to a system of bands or unilineal descent groups which exchange women directly. But as we saw with our simple Shoshone, the direct exchange of women can occur in even simpler circumstances. Thus, a 'Kariera' type of terminology can occur in the absence of bands, clans, sections etc., as long as a rule of 'cross-cousin marriage' or 'sister exchange' is *ideally* followed. In the absence of unilineal descent groups or patrilocal bands, there may, as we have seen, still be a tendency for an alliance made in one generation to be perpetuated in the next. Thus, among the Shoshone, if two families intermarried in one generation, then their children were expected to marry each other in the next. The perpetuation of this 'sister' or 'daughter' exchange would mean that ego would classify his kin into 'cross' and 'parallel', 'marriageable' and 'unmarriageable'. The rule basically would be that the children of a brother and sister should marry each other; the 'folding in' tendency – essence of elementary systems. Now, as we saw in Chapter seven, it may be in such a system that ego will not be able to find an 'actual' cross-cousin, and so will have to marry outside his circle of kin. He will then marry someone to whom he does not apply kinship terms. So what happens to the terminology? Usually, it is simply brought into line; ego calls his wife by the 'cross-cousin' term, he calls his wife's father 'mother's brother' and his wife's mother 'father's sister' and so on. In future generations, this new alliance will be perpetuated, and ego's children will marry 'kin'.

When we superimpose unilineal descent groups onto such a system, such problems must arise more rarely. For even if ego does not have close cross-cousins to marry, he can marry any of his classificatory cross-cousins, that is, the women of his own generation in his own mother's clan/ lineage or any of the lineages with which his has alliance relationships. All these women will be called by the 'cross-cousin' term. It might be better translated as 'child of a man who was a potential brother-in-law of my father''.

Most simple direct-exchange systems make some refinements on the basic model. In terms simply of their 'alliance' status, ego has no need to distinguish persons in the 2 category – 'fathers' and 'sons' – but he usually does so. Similarly with category 4. On the other hand, he often does not make a distinction in the 8 category – that is he equates 'mothers' with 'sons' wives' or 'sisters' daughters'. Taken in isolation such an equation seems very odd indeed, but set in the total system it makes sense as an 'alliance' classification. (These women would all be in the same section of course, the one into which ego could *not* marry.)

Now, we have plunged in here and looked at the distinctions in terms of the model of the system as a reciprocal-exogamic direct-exchange system. If we looked at it from the point of view of ego classifying his near 'relatives', it would look most odd. Unless we knew we were dealing with a simple direct-exchange system, it would make no sense. Let us set out the terms as they would appear for ego's generation and the two ascending generations:

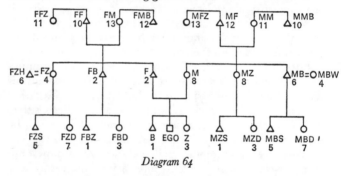

Diagram 64

Now, one can imagine oneself as an anthropologist who has taken down a genealogy from a native and has asked him what he calls all his relatives. The result at first sight must be puzzling. Why does he classify his parallel-cousins with his siblings (1 and 3) and distinguish these from cross-cousins whom he classifies together (5 and 7)? Why does he equate his FF with his MMB? And his MFZ with his FM? When we see that he equates his FZH with his MB, and his MBW with his FZ, we begin to see daylight. Obviously his FZ is supposed to marry his MB; it follows then that in his grandparental generation the same process must have occurred; this would produce the identifications between FF and MMB,

FM and MFZ, etc. In ego's own generation, the division is into 'unmarriageable' – siblings and parallel-cousins (1 and 3), and 'marriageable' – all cross-cousins (5 and 7). If we added the descending generations, we would get such tell-tale equations as SW = ZD = M, and perhaps ZS = MB, D = ZSW. Add to this the 'identity of alternate generations', and the system is complete.

Now, as we have said before, it is no use just taking one area of the terminology – say the terms for cousins – and trying to deduce everything from them. There are other types of system which equate parallel-cousins with siblings and distinguish them from cross-cousins, but the rest of the system can be totally different from the 'Kariera-type' of direct exchange. However, from certain 'giveaway' equations we can usually tell what kind of system we are dealing with. Once we start collecting terms for affines and find the following types of identification are made, we know where we are:

$$WF = MB = FZH$$
$$W = MBD/FZD/MMBDD$$
$$ZH = MBS/FZS$$
$$SW = ZD/MBSD (M)$$
$$DH = ZS/MBSS \quad \text{etc. etc.}$$

We soon discover that there are no 'affinal' terms – that every affine is a kinsman of some kind. By determining what kind of kinsman, we can tell what kind of system.

Again, the reader can work out for himself what will happen under an Aranda-type system. How many distinctions must minimally be made? What relatives will be equated with what other relatives? What affinal status will be equated with kin statuses? What are the 'key' equations? Clearly, as a start, ego will have to distinguish in the terminology between MMBDD on the one hand and MBD/FZD on the other, if the terms are alliance-determined. In a Kariera system, there is no distinction between these three statuses, but in an Aranda system the distinction between first cross-cousins and second cross-cousins is crucial and should be reflected in the terminology. Also, in an Aranda system, the

FF and the MMB must be distinguished, and so on. In fact if we take just cross-cousins and these two members of the grandparental generation, we can distinguish between the four types of elementary system.

'Kariera'   (MBD = FZD = MMBDD) : (FF = MMB)
Aranda   (MBD = FZD) $\neq$ (MMBDD) : (FF) $\neq$ (MMB)
Matrilateral (MBD = MMBDD) $\neq$ (FZD) : (FF) $\neq$ (MMB)
Patrilateral (MBD) $\neq$ (MMBDD = FZD) : (FF = MMB)

The reader can go back over the various diagrams of the systems and verify the equations.

III

While we are with elementary systems, let us look briefly at the classification of kin in the 'matrilateral' system. Here the primary distinctions, as we saw, are between 'us', 'wife-givers', and 'wife-takers'. Wife-givers, remember, are usually senior to us, and wife-takers junior. It might be thought that we should use completely distinctive terms for wife-givers and wife-takers, but some systems achieve considerable economy on this. Take the Purum for example. A skeleton of their terminology is set out opposite. I have not included all the terms as it would be too complicated to discuss some of the seeming inconsistencies in them; here I only want to point out how ego classifies his superior 'wife-givers' and his inferior 'wife-takers'. Look at ego's grandparental generation. His FF is *pu*, as is his MF (FMB). Then look at his grandchild generation. His grandchildren are collectively *tu* irrespective of sex. Now, see what he does to the male members of his wife-giving lineage: he equates them collectively with the members of the *senior* generation; they are all *pu* ('grandparents') to him. Look at the wife-taking lineage: he equates them with the *junior* generation; they are all *tu* ('grandchildren') to him. Thus, the senior-junior affinal relation is expressed in the terminology with brilliant economy by using the senior-junior generation terms. Ego's *pu* will of course call him *tu*, and so the *pu-tu* relationship of the Purum is the same as the *mayu-dama* relationship of the Kachin that we discussed earlier.

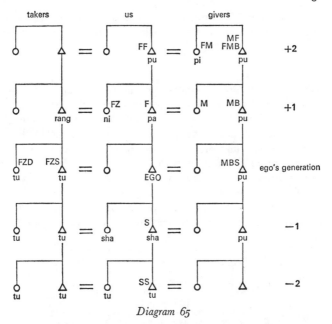

Diagram 65

Within all elementary systems there is room for enormous variation in the manner in which the basic 'equations' are made. What matters though is the equations themselves: who is classified with whom? We have seen how in the 'matrilateral' system the rigid distinction between generations that we found in the direct exchange systems is absent. On the contrary, the distinction between generations is ruthlessly overridden and members of a lineage are classified together regardless of generation. This may emphasize the 'unity of the lineage group' as Radcliffe-Brown said, but this is inadequate as an explanation. It is only when we look at the total alliance framework that we can see why these lineages should be so classified. It is necessary not only to know, for example, that MB = MBS, but that (MBS = WB)/(FZS = ZH). This latter gives the 'alliance chain' in ego's generation, and when this is added to the 'lineal equations' (patrilineal in this instance) we can be sure that we are dealing with a system of asymmetrical alliance – ideally that is.

IV

We saw how Crow-Omaha systems were a kind of halfway house between elementary and complex systems and that they seem to combine, in a complex way, elements of direct and indirect exchange. How is this reflected in their terminological classifications? Let us take Crow systems as our example. Those systems that have been dubbed 'Crow' in fact differ considerably from each other in details; what is similar is an overall framework. Quite early in the analysis of kinship terminologies in societies with matrilineal descent groups, observers noticed distributions like the following:

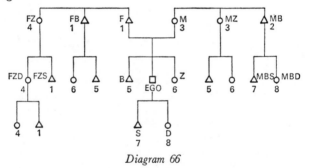

Diagram 66

These particular equations are characteristically Crow:

$F (FB) = FZS = FZDS : FZ = FZD = FZDD$

$B = FBS = MZS : Z = FBD = MZD$ (i.e. parallel-cousins = siblings)

$S = MBS : D = MBD$

We can see at once several features that are reminiscent of direct exchange. (1) F and FB are classed together and distinguished from MB. (2) M and MZ are classed together and distinguished from FZ. (3) Parallel cousins are classed with siblings and distinguished from cross-cousins.

But here the similarity ends, for the classification of cross-cousins clearly does not tally with direct exchange at all. They are classified on the father's side with the father and father's sister, and on the mother's side with the son and daughter. Now if we look at cross-cousins simply as the children of brother and sister this makes more sense:

Diagram 67

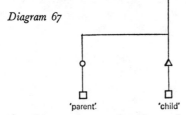

Given that I am going to classify my father's sister's children with the parental generation, they must reciprocate by calling me 'child'. However, this is less important than the fact that the terms emphasize the 'unity of the lineage group' as far as the father's matrilineage is concerned. Terms 1 and 4 could be seen as referring to 'men of my father's matrilineage/clan' and 'women of my father's matrilineage/clan'. This is reinforced when we look at the way ego classifies members of his other 'wife-taking' lineage – his mother's father's lineage:

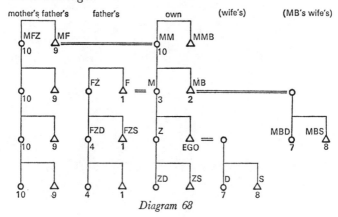

Diagram 68

His MM is 10 and his MF 9, and he classifies all the men and women of his MF's clan as 9 and 10. In a sense he equates them with 'grandparents' in the same way as he equates his father's clan with 'parents'. Now this is much more reminiscent of the Purum. They ignored the generation differences which were so crucial in direct-exchange systems and classified together all the members of wife-giving and wife-taking lineages, irrespective of generation, by means of 'grandparental' and 'grandchild' terms. The Crow systems also ignore generation in the case of lineages related to ego's lineage, and classify all the members together by means of parental and grandparental generation terms. They reverse the 'seniority' rating however, in that the 'wife-taking' lineages are given the 'superior generation' terms.

Some Crow systems only seem to half-ignore the distinction between generations. Compare the following two sets of terms from two Pueblo Indian tribes.

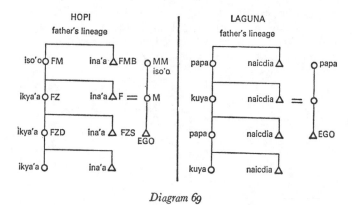

Diagram 69

The Hopi class all the men of the father's lineage together as *ina'a*. The father's mother they class with the mother's

mother as *iso'o*, but all the other women of the father's lineage are classed as *ikya'a*. Now, with the Laguna, all the men of the father's lineage are again classed together (as *naic-dia*). Again the father's mother is classed with the mother's mother (*papa*), and the father's sister is called *kuya*. But then note what happens with the women of the father's lineage: they are classed *alternately* as *papa* and *kuya*, and this alternation continues up and down the line of women of the father's lineage and clan. This type of classification, which affects all aspects of the Laguna system, stresses the 'unity of alternate generations' which we have seen as characteristic of 'elementary' systems and particularly of systems of direct exchange. (Although it does occur with indirect – the Murngin have it.)

The more we look at 'Crow' systems, then, the more does the terminology suggest that they are indeed a curious mixture of 'direct' and 'indirect' exchange – and hence, perhaps, some kind of development from elementary systems. (We find, for example that very often MB = ZS, and ZD = M – see ideal 'Kariera' system, Diagram 63.) Some systems seem to have gone further in a Crow direction than others.

We are only beginning to scratch the surface of this enormously complex problem. Here again, it seems that an alliance approach may help us to put the various systems on the same continuum and that to treat the terminology as basically expressing marriage patterns may be the best approach. The 'unity of the lineage group' and the 'distribution of rights and duties' do *something* to explain some features of Crow systems. But they seem unable to account for the total distribution of terms in the system. They do nothing to account for the fact that parallel cousins are classed with siblings, for example. The very complexity of Crow systems suggests that they are indeed reflections of various stages of transition.

We have taken Crow systems as our example. The Omaha system is the patrilineal opposite. Perhaps the reader might like, as an exercise, to fill in the 'logical' equations following the method of numbers used for the Crow system on Diagram 66. Here ego will be inclined to classify together the members of the *patrilineages* that are linked in marriage to his own, namely, his mother's and his father's mother's. The key equation to start with is obviously MB = MBS = MBSS.

(I have up to this point been deliberately vague about the sex of ego or just assumed him to be male. But it is an important point that particularly with Crow-Omaha systems the classification of kin may be quite different for males and females. This particular aspect of the 'code' has not yet been cracked, but again it may reflect the very different status of men and women in the system of alliances.)

I have not dealt here with the way ego classifies the totality of the members of his *own* lineage in Crow-Omaha systems. This varies enormously but very often it does not differ from the way he might classify them under a system of direct exchange. The problem now is to try to identify the various types of Crow-Omaha system and to correlate them with their nearest equivalents in known and theoretical types of 'elementary' systems. Then we may discover how it is that various types of elementary systems 'change gear' into various versions of Crow-Omaha, and so move off in a complex direction.

v

We must now move on to look at terminology in systems which lack unilineal groups and which are undoubtedly complex in their marriage arrangements. Our own system comes under this heading, but before we get to it let us look at a very common form of terminology which defies all the principles we have discovered so far. It is usually known as 'Hawaiian' after one of its exemplars, but is found on all continents. It is mainly concentrated in areas where the language is Malayo-Polynesian. What it stresses is the separateness of generations, but it makes no concessions to lineality or to systematic exchange.

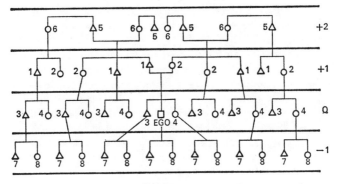

Diagram 70

Here we see the eminent simplicity of the scheme. All the men and women of each generation are called by the same term. Thus:

    1 = males of first ascending generation
    2 = females of first ascending generation
    3 = males of own generation
    4 = females of own generation
                    etc. etc.

It may be even simpler in that sex differences may be ignored in generations +2 and −2, thus reducing it to a scheme of six terms only. Clearly, in terms of correlation with marriage patterns this fits a system in which the exogamous group is not a discrete kin-group such as a lineage but an ego-centred bilateral group of kinsmen. The obvious marriage rule should be that ego should not marry any woman in the categories 6, 2, 4 and 8. He would have to look outside his 'kin' for a marriage partner. This is a ruthlessly 'complex' rule. In societies with this type of kinship terminology, the actual range of 'prohibited degrees' in fact varies a lot, but it is always bilateral – affecting both sides of the kinship network equally. Because this terminology stresses the identity of members of a generation, it is often called *generational*.

This takes us on to our own system which is geared to a similar, but perhaps not quite so ruthless marriage rule. It is one of those precious anthropological jokes that our system is classified as 'Eskimo' after another proponent of the scheme. It is, in fact, quite a common scheme amongst peoples lacking unilineal descent-groups or elementary forms of exchange. What it seems to do is carve out the nuclear family for special emphasis, and then to stress the equal balance between the two kindreds united by marriage – the matrilateral and patrilateral kin of ego. Thus, the terms for members of the nuclear family (father, mother, son, daughter, brother, sister) are *not used for anyone outside the family*. This is very different from all the systems we have been discussing, where the nuclear family receives little or no terminological stress. The Eskimo system can be illustrated roughly by reference to our own version of it in Diagram 71.

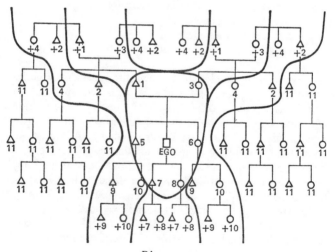

Diagram 71

Where terms are merely compounds of terms with intensifiers (such as 'grand-father', 'great-uncle', 'grand-nephew' etc.), I have simply put a + sign in front of the number for the root term.

While the Hawaiian system is a great respecter of generations, the Eskimo plays havoc with the generation principle. The rogue term 'cousin' (no. 11) is applied promiscuously to relatives outside a narrowly-defined group bounded by 'uncles' and 'aunts', 'nephews' and 'nieces'. It is true we try to accommodate generation by such cumbersome devices as stating 'degrees of removal' ('second cousin twice removed'), but clearly we are not all that interested in the exact status of cousins. I have noticed a certain Hawaiianizing tendency in the habit many people have formed of calling the children of great-aunts and great-uncles ($+2$ and $+4$) 'uncle' and 'aunt'. If followed persistently, this would even-up the first-ascending generation somewhat, but would still leave the father and mother classified by distinctive terms. (Some variants of Hawaiian systems do, in fact, have distinctive terms for F and M, while classing everyone else by generation.)

It is perhaps significant that in most societies having a Hawaiian terminology there is a tendency to some form of *extended* family or cognatic descent group, whereas in societies with Eskimo terms the nuclear family seems more important. If the Hawaiian system can be seen as consisting of *horizontal* layers of kin, our own is much more like the layers of skin round an onion. There is the hard core of nuclear family terms (1, 3, 5, 6, 7, 8), and their compounds ($+1$, $+3$, $+7$, $+8$); then there is a strip of co-laterals – the siblings of the core members, and the children of ego's own siblings (4, 2, 9, 10, $+4$, $+2$, $+9$, $+10$). Outside this there are the ubiquitous 'cousins' (11). Thus, the nuclear families of mother and father are not differentiated ($+1$, $+3$, 4 and 2 in each case); neither are the children of brother differentiated from the children of sister (9 and 10 in each case). Thus, the perfect bilateral symmetry of the system is reflected in the terminology. As the one irreducible feature of these systems is the negative marriage rule applied to the nuclear family, then the core of terminology which sets this unit off from the rest of the system makes sense. Whatever the extent of the negative marriage rule (and it varies enormously), this unit is always exogamous. Very often the next 'layer' is prohibited also (uncles, aunts, nephews, nieces). Prohibitions on cousins vary, but as one might expect, are inevitably bilateral.

I have deliberately left this terminological system until the end so that we may see it in perspective as just one of many ways of classifying kin. It is usual in introductory essays on kinship terminology to start with our system, and then explain the 'odd' ones. But ours is decidedly odd if we simply count heads. Most other peoples classify their kin differently because they have different kinship systems. Taking our own rather peculiar system as the norm leads only to confusion. Thus, for example, we single out the male parent and give him a distinctive term 'father'. Consequently, in our system 'begetter' and 'father' are (ideally!) synonymous. Thus, when Morgan found systems in which the father's brother, and perhaps the father's sister's son, were called by the same term, he translated this as 'father', assumed it was synonymous with 'begetter', and tried to work out tortuous reasons to account for ego's seeming inability to pin down who begat him. Clearly, because we were Christian monogamists we knew who our begetters were, whereas the poor benighted savages living in a state of promiscuity did not. If it does nothing else, I hope this chapter helps to belie the notion that savages do not know who their fathers are. All these systems have either a term for 'begetter' (like the Roman *genitor* – as opposed to *pater*), or a pronominal system which allows ego to state that of the class of male relatives designated x which includes his own male parent, one of them *is* his *own* x. Once we grasp that kinship terms designate *classes* of kinsmen – as 'uncle' designates 'male sibling of parent' in our system – then the difficulty should evaporate. Of course, it is always possible that the class contains only one kin-type – as with the terms 'father', 'mother' etc. in our own system, or as in other systems where the mother's brother is singled out for special terminological distinction (he is the only member of the class).

VI

I have only been able here to touch on a few aspects of kinship terminology. A whole book (or several books) could be written on the subject, so not much can be attempted in one chapter. I have not tried to be exhaustive; there are many more types and combinations other than those I have listed and illustrated. Unilineal systems are by no means all Crow and Omaha, for example; in fact the majority of them are not. I chose the Crow-Omaha systems because of their particular theoretical interest. I have constantly oversimplified in order to get the general frameworks over. What fascinate the professional anthropologist are the difficulties, seeming inconsistencies, and detailed differences between similar systems. What might interest the general reader or the student is the way in which systems of classification which at first sight seem to him bizarre, in fact make very good sense in context. They are perfectly rational ways of emphasizing the distinctions between significant classes of kin. In many cases, the basis on which the distinctions are made is obscure to us, but modern techniques may well provide the means to crack some of the more difficult 'codes'. We may even be able to state simply and accurately the basis on which we classify kin in our own system! So far, this has not been done succesfully. The reader might try writing a simple formula that would explain, to someone who was not a native speaker of English, exactly who to call 'cousin'. I don't mean a rambling description but a *simple* formula of the order of the Hopi 'all men of father's clan = *ina'a*'.

If we wished to understand the legal rules of an African tribe, we would want to know how they classified offences; if we wanted to understand the hunting and gathering behaviour of some Amazonian forest tribes we would want to know how they classified animals and plants; when we want to understand the religious behaviour of a tribe we ask how they classify supernatural forces and beings; when we want to understand the kinship rules and behaviour of any people we must ask how they classify kin and on what basis they make distinctions.

We have seen that the overall distinction explored in Chapters seven and eight between elementary and complex systems is reflected in the overall trend of the system of terminology. In elementary systems, there are no terms for affines. There cannot be because we are marrying people to whom we are already related. According as the rule of marriage with a 'relative' differs, so will the classification of these relatives differ. In complex systems on the other hand, although they vary enormously, there are terms for affines, who should *not*, ideally, be relatives, however these are defined. Many complex systems of terminology, however, show 'elementary' tendencies, which can either be interpreted as 'survivals' or as reflections of an inbuilt tendency for some kinds of complex systems to 'fold in' on themselves in an elementary way. Our own terminological system reflects our ultra-complex tendency to shrink effective 'kinship' to the nuclear family, and constantly to create fresh alliances between unrelated nuclear families, the absolute opposite of the elementary tendency. It is true that this may also reflect an adaptation to large mobile populations (early Indo-European kinship terminologies show a much less nuclear-family oriented bias), but the fact that we are a subtype of the Eskimo type should make us wary of attaching too much causal significance to size and mobility. Complex systems, as we have seen, are found with all types of society, but most elementary systems do seem geared to small populations marrying within themselves.

References and Further Reading

This list includes works of authors cited in the text, sources of ethnographic examples, and other works relevant to the issues dealt with in each chapter. Some books and articles are obviously relevant so more than one chapter. The list is not intended to be comprehensive.

INTRODUCTION AND CHAPTER ONE

E. E. EVANS-PRITCHARD: *The Nuer*, Oxford University Press, 1940.

Kinship and Marriage among the Nuer, Oxford University Press, 1951.

R. FIRTH: *Man and Culture: An Evaluation of the Work of Bronislav Malinowski*, Routledge and Kegan Paul, 1957.

M. FORTES: *The Dynamics of Clanship among the Tallensi*, Oxford University Press, 1945.

The Web of Kinship among the Tallensi, Oxford University Press, 1949.

C. LÉVI-STRAUSS: *Les Structures élémentaires de la parenté*, Presses Universitaires de France, Paris, 1949.

H. S. MAINE: *Ancient Law*, John Murray, 1861.

B. MALINOWSKI: *The Sexual Life of Savages*, Routledge and Kegan Paul, 1929.

J. F. MCLENNAN: *Primitive Marriage*, Black, 1865.

Studies in Ancient History, Macmillan, 1876.

L. H. MORGAN: *Ancient Society*, Holt and Co., New York, 1870.

Systems of Consanguinity and Affinity of the Human Family, Smithsonian Institution, Washington, 1877.

G. P. MURDOCK: *Social Structure*, Macmillan, New York, 1949.

A. R. RADCLIFFE-BROWN: *Structure and Function in Primitive Society*, Cohen and West, 1952.

and D. FORDE (Eds.): *African Systems of Kinship and Marriage*, Oxford University Press, 1950.

W. H. R. RIVERS: *The History of Melanesian Society*, Cambridge University Press, 1914.

N. W. THOMAS: *Kinship Organizations and Group Marriage in Australia*, Cambridge University Press, 1906.

CHAPTER TWO

D. ABERLE *et al.*: 'The Incest Taboo and the Mating Patterns of Animals', *American Anthropologist*, vol. 65, pp. 253–65, 1963.

C. S. FORD and F. A. BEACH: *Patterns of Sexual Behavior*, Harper, New York, 1951.

R. FOX: 'Sibling Incest', *British Journal of Sociology*, vol. 13, pp. 128–50, 1962.

S. FREUD: *Totem and Taboo*, (first published in Vienna in 1913: first English translation by A. A. Brill, New York, 1918).

MARIAM K. SLATER: 'Ecological Factors in the Origin of Incest', *American Anthropologist*, vol. 61, pp. 1042–59, 1959.

E. WESTERMARCK: *The History of Human Marriage*, Macmillan, 1889.

CHAPTER THREE

F. EGGAN: *The Social Organization of the Western Pueblos*, Chicago University Press, Chicago, 1950.

C. R. KAUT: *The Western Apache Clan System: Its Origins and Development*, University of New Mexico, Albuquerque, 1957.

J. STEWARD: *Theory of Culture Change*, University of Illinois Press, Urbana, 1955. (Shoshone: Hopi)

CHAPTER FOUR

M. FORTES: *The Dynamics of Clanship among the Tallensi*, Oxford University Press, 1945.

'Time and Social Structure', *Social Structure: Essays presented to A. R. Radcliffe-Brown*, (M. Fortes, Ed.), Oxford University Press, 1949. (Ashanti)

M. FREEDMAN: *Lineage Organization in Southeastern China*, Athlone Press, 1958.

Chinese Lineage and Society, Athlone Press, 1966.

B. MALINOWSKI: *The Sexual Life of Savages*, Routledge and Kegan Paul, 1929. (Trobriand)

J. C. MITCHELL: *The Yao Village*, Manchester University Press, 1956.

AUDREY RICHARDS: 'Some types of family structure among the Central Bantu', *African Systems of Kinship and Marriage*, (A. R. Radcliffe-Brown and D. Forde, Eds.) Oxford University Press, 1950. (Bemba, Kongo etc.)

D. SCHNEIDER and K. GOUGH (Eds.): *Matrilineal Kinship*, University of California Press, Berkeley and Los Angeles, 1961. (Nayar, etc.)

CHAPTER FIVE

D. FORDE: *Yako Studies*, Oxford University Press, 1964.

M. FORTES: 'The Structure of Unilineal Descent Groups', *American Anthropologist*, vol. 55, pp. 17–41, 1953.

C. LÉVI-STRAUSS: *Structural Anthropology*, Basic Books, New York, 1963.

I. M. LEWIS: 'Problems in the Comparative Study of Unilineal Descent,' *The Relevance of Models for Social Anthropology*, (M. Banton, Ed.), Tavistock Publications, 1965.

MARGARET MEAD: *Sex and Temperament in Three Primitive Societies*, New York, 1935. (Arapesh)

C. NIMUENDAJU: *The Apinayé*, Catholic University of America, Washington, 1939

CHAPTER SIX

D. ABERLE: *The Kinship System of the Kalmuk Mongols*, University of New Mexico, Albuquerque, 1953.

F. EGGAN: 'The Sagada Igorots of Northern Luzon', *Social Structure in Southeast Asia*, (G. P. Murdock, Ed.), Quadrangle Books, Chicago, and Tavistock Publications, 1960.

R. FOX: 'Prolegomena to the Study of British Kinship', *Penguin Survey of the Social Sciences*, (J. Gould, Ed.) Penguin Books, 1965.
'Kinship and Land Tenure on Tory Island', *Ulster Folklife*, vol. 12, 1966.

D. FREEMAN: 'The Concept of the Kindred', *Journal of the Royal Anthropological Institute*, vol. 91, 1961. (Iban)

W. GOODENOUGH: *Property, Kin and Community on Truk*, Yale University, New Haven, 1951.
'A Problem in Malayo-Polynesian Social Organization', *American Anthropologist*, vol. 57, 1955. (Gilbert Islands)

M. MEGGITT: *The Lineage System of the Mae-Enga*, Oliver and Boyd, 1965.

G. P. MURDOCK: 'Cognatic Forms of Social Organization', *Social Structure in Southeast Asia*, (G. P. Murdock, Ed.), Quadrangle Books, Chicago, and Tavistock Publications, 1960.

I. SCHAPERA (Ed.): *Studies in Kinship and Marriage*, Royal Anthropological Institute, 1963.

CHAPTER SEVEN

A. P. ELKIN: *The Australian Aborigines*, Angus and Robertson, Sydney, 1954.

W. E. LAWRENCE: 'Alternating Generations in Australia', *Studies in the Science of Society*, (G. P. Murdock, Ed.), Yale University, New Haven, 1957.

M. MAUSS: *The Gift*, Cohen and West, 1954.

M. MEGGITT: *Desert People*, Angus and Robertson, Sydney, 1962.

A. R. RADCLIFFE-BROWN: 'The Social Organization of Australian Tribes', *Oceania Monograph* I, Sydney, 1930.

A. K. ROMNEY AND P. J. EPLING: 'A simplified model of Kariera Kinship', *American Anthropologist*, vol. 60, 1958.

E. B. TYLOR: 'On a method of investigating the development of institutions', *Journal of the (Royal) Anthropological Institute*, vol. 18, 1888.

CHAPTER EIGHT

M. FORTES: 'Descent, Filiation and Affinity', *Man*, vol. 59, 1959.

E. R. LEACH: *Rethinking Anthropology*, Athlone Press, 1961 (Kachin).

R. NEEDHAM: *Structure and Sentiment*, Chicago University Press, Chicago, 1962. (Purum)

W. L. WARNER: *A Black Civilization*, Harper, New York, 1937. (Murngin)

CHAPTER NINE

F. G. LOUNSBURY: 'The Formal Analysis of Crow- and Omaha-type Kinship Terminologies', *Explorations in Cultural Anthropology*, (W. E. Goodenough, Ed.), McGraw Hill, New York etc., 1964.

L. H. MORGAN: *Systems of Consanguinity and Affinity of the Human Family*, Smithsonian Institution, Washington, 1870.

G. P. MURDOCK: *Social Structure*, Macmillan, New York, 1949.

A. R. RADCLIFFE-BROWN: *Structure and Function in Primitive Society*, Cohen and West, 1952.

W. H. R. RIVERS: *Kinship and Social Organization*, Constable, 1914.

RECENT PUBLICATIONS

GENERAL BOOKS ON KINSHIP PUBLISHED SINCE 1967

M. FORTES: *Kinship and the Social Order*, Aldine Press, Chicago, 1969.

J. BARNES: *Three Styles in the Study of Kinship*, Tavistock Publications, 1971.

J. GOODY (ed.): *The Character of Kinship*, Cambridge University Press, 1973.

R. NEEDHAM: *Remarks and Inventions: Sceptical Essays about Kinship*, Tavistock Publications, 1971.

R. NEEDHAM (ed.): *Rethinking Kinship and Marriage*, Tavistock Publications, 1971.

D. SCHNEIDER: *American Kinship: A Cultural Account,* Prentice-Hall, 1968.

WORKS THAT DEAL WITH KINSHIP AND EVOLUTION

R. FOX: *The Red Lamp of Incest: An Enquiry into the Origins of Mind and Society,* University of Notre Dame Press, 1983.
'Primate Kin and Human Kinship', *Biosocial Anthropology,* (R. Fox, ed.), Malaby Press, 1975.

N. CHAGNON AND W. IRONS (eds.): *Evolutionary Biology and Human Social Behavior: An Anthropological Perspective,* North Scituate, Mass., Duxbury Press, 1979. (This contains the author's 'Kinship Categories as Natural Categories', q.v.).

R. ALEXANDER: *Darwinism and Human Affairs,* University of Washington Press, 1979.
A book due for future publication by Cambridge University Press will contain a number of the author's published and unpublished essays on these and related topics.

ON PATRILATERAL PARALLEL COUSIN MARRIAGE

J. GOODY: *Production and Reproduction,* Cambridge University Press. 1976.

G. TILLION: *Le Harem et Les Cousins,* Paris, 1966.

J. BOONE AND D. SCHNEIDER: 'Kinship vis-à-vis Myth', *American Anthropologist,* 76:4, pp. 799–817, 1974.

J. BOONE: *The Anthropological Romance of Bali,* Cambridge University Press, 1977.

R. MURPHY AND L. KASDAN: 'The Structure of Parallel Cousin Marriage', *American Anthropologist,* 61, pp. 17–29, 1959.

ON 'MURNGIN' TYPE SYSTEMS

W. SHAPIRO: *Miwuyt Marriage: The Cultural Anthropology of Affinity in Northeast Arnhem Land,* Institute for the Study of Human Issues, Philadelphia, 1981.
'The exchange of sisters' daughters' daughters in northeast Arnhem Land', *Southwestern Journal of Anthropology,* 24, pp. 346–53,. 1968.

L. HIATT: *Kinship and Conflict: A Study of an Aboriginal Community in Northern Arnhem Land,* Australian National University Press, 1965.

ON 'COGNATIC' SYSTEMS

H. SCHEFFLER: *Choiseul Island Social Structure,* University of California Press, Berkeley, 1965.

R. FOX: *The Tory Islanders: A People of the Celtic Fringe*, Cambridge University Press, 1978.

TWO EXCELLENT EXAMPLES OF THE FORMAL ANALYSIS OF KINSHIP TERMS

I. BUCHLER AND H. SELBY: *Kinship and Social Organization*, Macmillan, 1968.

H. SCHEFFLER: *Australian Kin Classification*, Cambridge University Press, 1978.

A GOOD 'READER' WITH MANY USEFUL ARTICLES

N. GRABURN: *Readings in Kinship and Social Structure*, Harper and Row, 1971.

AN UP-TO-DATE CRITICAL REVIEW OF LINEAGE THEORY

A. KUPER: 'Lineage Theory: A Critical Retrospect', *Annual Review of Anthropology*, 11, pp. 71–95, 1982

Index

CAMBRIDGE STUDIES IN SOCIAL ANTHROPOLOGY

EDITOR: JACK GOODY

*Also issued as a paperback